Beginning Windows 8 Data Development

Using C# and JavaScript

Vinodh Kumar

apress

Beginning Windows 8 Data Development: Using C# and JavaScript

ISBN-13 (pbk): 978-1-4302-4992-4

ISBN-13 (electronic): 978-1-4302-4993-1

President and Publisher: Paul Manning
Lead Editor: Ewan Buckingham
Technical Reviewer: Fabio Claudio Ferracchiati
Editorial Board: Steve Anglin, Mark Beckner, Ewan Buckingham, Gary Cornell, Louise Corrigan, Morgan Ertel,
    Jonathan Gennick, Jonathan Hassell, Robert Hutchinson, Michelle Lowman, James Markham,
    Matthew Moodie, Jeff Olson, Jeffrey Pepper, Douglas Pundick, Ben Renow-Clarke, Dominic Shakeshaft,
    Gwenan Spearing, Matt Wade, Tom Welsh
Coordinating Editor: Katie Sullivan
Copy Editor: Teresa Horton
Compositor: SPi Global
Indexer: SPi Global
Artist: SPi Global
Cover Designer: Anna Ishchenko

Distributed to the book trade worldwide by Springer Science+Business Media New York, 233 Spring Street, 6th Floor, New York, NY 10013. Phone 1-800-SPRINGER, fax (201) 348-4505, e-mail orders-ny@springer-sbm.com, or visit www.springeronline.com. Apress Media, LLC is a California LLC and the sole member (owner) is Springer Science + Business Media Finance Inc (SSBM Finance Inc). SSBM Finance Inc is a Delaware corporation.

For information on translations, please e-mail rights@apress.com, or visit www.apress.com.

Apress and friends of ED books may be purchased in bulk for academic, corporate, or promotional use. eBook versions and licenses are also available for most titles. For more information, reference our Special Bulk Sales–eBook Licensing web page at www.apress.com/bulk-sales.

Any source code or other supplementary materials referenced by the author in this text is available to readers at www.apress.com. For detailed information about how to locate your book's source code, go to www.apress.com/source-code/.

Contents at a Glance

Contents

About the Author

Vinodh Kumar has been working with .NET technologies since prior to its alpha release. He has been a recipient of multiple Microsoft Most Valuable Professional (MVP) awards. He is also the author of many books and articles, including *Professional .NET Network Programming*. He enjoys working with new technologies, and has been developing mobile apps for Windows Phone, iOS, and Windows 8. In fact, he started developing mobile apps in the iPAQ days using Pocket PC 2000. Follow Vinodh on Twitter using Twitter handle @w3force and on the web at www.dotnetforce.com.

About the Technical Reviewer

Fabio Claudio Ferracchiati is a senior consultant and a senior analyst/developer using Microsoft technologies. He works for Brain Force (http://www.brainforce.com) in its Italian branch (http://www.brainforce.it). He is a Microsoft Certified Solution Developer for .NET, a Microsoft Certified Application Developer for .NET, a Microsoft Certified Professional, and a prolific author and technical reviewer. Over the past ten years, he's written articles for Italian and international magazines and coauthored more than ten books on a variety of computer topics.

Acknowledgments

It has been a long excursion writing this book. I would like to especially thank my loving wife, Sudha, who had immense belief in my writing skills and persuaded me to start authoring. I would also like to thank Ewan Buckingham from Apress, who has made the publication of this book possible. I would like to thank every person at Apress, with a very special thanks to Katie Sullivan and Mark Powers, for their involvement with this book and for their continuous support, without which this milestone wouldn't have happened.

I also would like to give a special thanks to my parents for their support and best wishes, and my daughter, Taniya, for all her support, passion, and understanding while I was missing in action for several months.

CHAPTER 1

■ ■ ■

Introduction to Windows 8 Development

With Windows 8, Microsoft introduced significant changes to the underlying platform and user interface. These new features include a new start screen experience, Windows stores to purchase apps from a single repository, and a new platform known as Windows Runtime (WinRT).

WinRT provides a new set of APIs and tools to create a new style of touch-first apps that are fast and fluid. These apps are generally called Windows Store Apps.

For the purposes of this book, some of the key things to know about WinRT and Windows Store apps include

- Windows 8 Apps runs in Windows X86, x64, and ARM processors.

- Windows 8 Apps can either run in full-screen mode or be docked to the side of the screen.

- WinRT supports programming languages such ac C, C++, VB.NET, and C#, along with HTML5 and JavaScript.

- WinRT APIs are designed to be asynchronous. APIs that take more than 50 ms to run are made asynchronous.

- The WPF/Silverlight XAML UI model is exposed to developers.

- To ensure stability and security, the Windows Store Apps run within a sandboxed environment.

- Finally, the most important thing to know is that there is no direct way to connect to the database servers using data providers in Windows RT.

As this book is more about data access in Windows 8, this chapter provides an overview of the Windows 8 app framework and briefly looks into the development choices, UI data controls, MVVM patterns, and other necessary concepts that will be used in various examples throughout this book. In the later part of this chapter we'll write our first data-driven Windows 8 App that displays the *New York Times* Best Sellers list.

Windows App Framework

In Figure 1-1, we see the Windows 8 modern-style app framework compared to that of desktop applications, where both share the same Windows core OS services. If we look at the desktop application section, JavaScript and HTML are used to target Internet Explorer, C and C++ are used for Win32 apps, and C# and Visual Basic for .NET and Silverlight. Each of these will have a separate set of APIs. But with Windows 8 Apps, we have one set of APIs that for WinRT whether we use XAML, C#, C/C++, Visual Basic, HTML/CSS, or JavaScript.

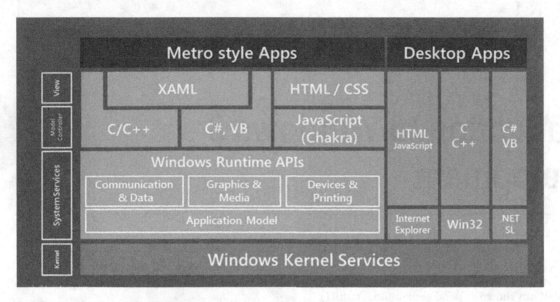

Figure 1-1. *Windows App framework*

Development Choices

For developing Windows 8 Apps, we can choose either of the two development paths shown in Figure 1-2.

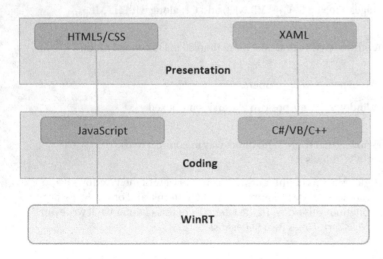

Figure 1-2. *Development choices*

In the HTML path we will be able to use the traditional Web technologies like HTML5, CSS, and JavaScript. For presentation, you use HTML tags such as div, table, spans, and input, and CSS for styling. For coding, JavaScript can be used. Apart from the HTML controls, Windows Library for JavaScript provides a set of new controls designed for Windows Store Apps. This WinJS library is our path for the WinRT.

If you are a WPF, Silverlight, or Windows Phone developer, then designing the UI and presentation layer using XAML is an ideal fit. Here we will be using C#, Visual Basic, or C++ for coding.

Creating the New York Times Best Sellers App

The New York Times Best Sellers app is a simple Windows 8 App that uses the MVVM pattern to display the *New York Times* Best Sellers list. Building this app is a starting point to learn to use Visual Studio 2012, the MVVM framework, data binding, data controls, and other necessary concepts to create a data-driven Windows 8 Modern UI app.

Introducing the MVVM Application Framework

Model-View-ViewModel (MVVM) is the most widely used framework in WPF/Silverlight/Windows Phone XAML-based development. Considering MVVM as the central concept of Windows 8, it supports XAML-based development and is ideologically similar to the technologies that use MVVM as the application framework, so it is an ideal choice. This chapter introduces you to the MVVM framework. In later chapters you will learn about some of the most commonly used MVVM frameworks like MVVM Light and Prism.

What Is MVVM?

The MVVM pattern splits the user interface code into three conceptual parts: Model, View, and ViewModel (see Figure 1-3). The concept of the ViewModel is the new, and it controls the View's interactions with the rest of the app.

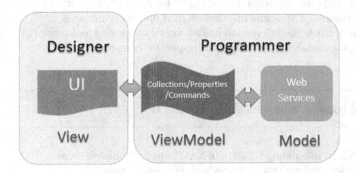

Figure 1-3. *The basic relationships of the MVVM framework*

- **Model** represents actual data or information and holds only the data and not the behavior or service that manipulates the data.

- **View** visually represents the data in the ViewModel by holding a reference to the ViewModel.

- **ViewModel** serves as the glue between the View and the Model by exposing commands, notifiable properties, and observable collections to the View.

Advantages in Using MVVM

These are the some of the advantages of using MVVM over other patterns:

- The MVVM pattern is designed specifically for the data binding capabilities that are available in XAML applications, allowing views to be simple presentations that are abstracted from the business logic process, which should not happen at the user interface layer.

- Another primary benefit of the MVVM pattern is the unit testability of codebase. The lack of connection between the View and ViewModel helps in writing the unit test against the ViewModel.

- MVVM allows developers and UI designers to more easily collaborate when developing their respective parts of the application.

- The MVVM pattern is widely used and there are several mature MVVM frameworks like Caliburn Micro and MVVMLight that provide all the base template code out of the way, of course, but they also can add advanced binding, behaviors, actions, and composition features.

Setting Up the Development Environment

Download the developer tools from `http://dev.windows.com`. The developer tool includes the Windows 8 Software Development Kit, a blend of Visual Studio and project templates. Microsoft Visual Studio for Windows 8 is our integrated development environment (IDE) to build Windows 8 Apps and this version runs only on Windows 8.

Optionally, Microsoft Visual Studio 2012 can also be used. The full version has advanced debugging tool support, multi-unit testing framework and refactoring support, code analysis, profiling, and support for connecting to Team Foundation Server.

■ **Note**   Windows 8 Apps cannot be developed with Windows 7, Windows Vista, or Windows XP.

Visual Studio project templates give a great jump-start to building HTML and XAML applications. We create a new Visual C# Windows Store Blank App (XAML) project and name it NYTimesBestSeller (see Figure 1-4).

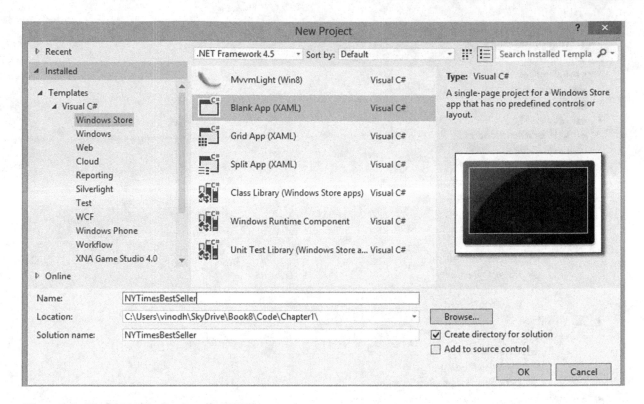

Figure 1-4. Visual Studio templates for XAML

The New York Times Best Sellers app displays the details of the *New York Times* fiction best sellers in a grid view. Before we go further let's see the project structure in Figure 1-5.

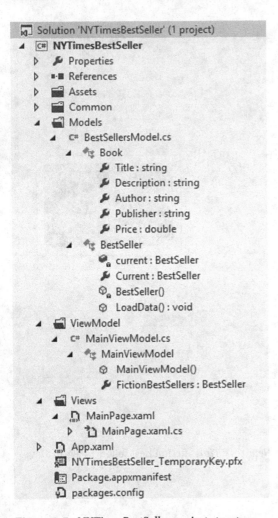

Figure 1-5. *NYTimesBestSeller project structure*

In the default project structure, we have created three new folders via Models, Views, and ViewModel. These folders are used for the Models, Views, and ViewModel. Also we moved the MainPage.xaml to the Views folder.

Creating the Model

Now, we create the application's data model. This class are created in the Model folders in the C# file BookSellersModel.cs.

The BookSellersModel.cs file implements two classes:

- Book

- BestSellersModel

The Book class shown in Listing 1-1 represents details of one of the books on the best sellers list. The details include book title, description, author, and price.

Listing 1-1. Adding Book Class to the Project

```
public class Book
    {
        public string Title { get; set; }
        public string Description { get; set; }
        public string Author { get; set; }
        public string Publisher { get; set; }
        public double Price { get; set; }
    }
```

The BestSellersModel class shown in Listing 1-2 is an ObservableCollection of Book object. This class loads the *New York Times* best seller books into the observable class.

Listing 1-2. BestSeller Class to Store the Best Seller Information

```
public class BestSeller : ObservableCollection<Book>
    {
        private static BestSeller current = null;

        public static BestSeller Current
        {
            get
            {
                if (current == null)
                    current = new BestSeller();

                return current;
            }
        }

        private BestSeller()
        {
            LoadData();
        }

        public async void LoadData()
        {
            //Code here to get New York Times best seller
        }
    }
```

The New York Times best seller API is called by the LoadData method to get the book details (see Listing 1-3). This API returns a JSON object that will be parsed using the WinRT APIs residing in the Windows.Data.Json namespace.

Listing 1-3. LoadData Method Fetch Data Using the New York Times API

```
public async void LoadData()
    {
        string url = "http://api.nytimes.com/svc/books/v2/lists//hardcover-fiction.json?&offset=
&sortby=&sortorder=&api-key=76038659ae9258d87cfb6dc8d6f02d35:11:66739421";
        HttpResponseMessage response = await client.GetAsync(url);
        string jsonData = await response.Content.ReadAsStringAsync();
```

```
        JsonObject jsonObject = JsonObject.Parse(jsonData);
        var resultObject = jsonObject.GetObject();
        var result = resultObject["results"].GetArray();
        foreach (var item in result)
        {
            JsonObject bookdetails =
item.GetObject().GetNamedValue("book_details").GetArray()[0].GetObject();
            Book book = new Book();
            book.Title = bookdetails.GetNamedString("title");
            book.Description = bookdetails.GetNamedString("description");
            book.Author = bookdetails.GetNamedString("author");
            book.Price = bookdetails.GetNamedNumber("price");
            book.Publisher = bookdetails.GetNamedString("publisher");
            Add(book);
        }
    }
```

We have used await and the async keyword that was introduced with .NET 4.5 to asynchronously process the network request to avoid GUI locking and freezing. Here the async keyword flags a method as containing asynchronous components, and the await keyword triggers an asynchronous process and resumes execution when it completes without blocking the main thread. We use await and async a lot throughout this book as the entire WinRT framework is built with performance in mind and in WinRT any potential task that takes longer than 50 ms is defined asynchronously. Responsiveness of the app is one of the minimum requirements of the Windows 8 App certification.

Creating the ViewModel

The ViewModel is designed to list the best sellers, and we use the FictionBestSellers property to hold the list (see Listing 1-4). Here we create the instance of the Model. Apart from this, ViewModel can also be used to expose various commands by implementing ICommand.

Listing 1-4. MainViewModel works a DataContext for view MainPage.xaml

```
public class MainViewModel
    {
        public MainViewModel()
        {
        }

        public BestSeller FictionBestSellers
        {
            get
            {
                return BestSeller.Current;
            }
        }
    }
```

Command objects are derived from the ICommand interface, which has two important methods: The CanExecute method controls whether the corresponding control that is bound to this command is enabled or disabled, and the Execute method specifies the action to be taken once the control is clicked. We see the use of the command object later in this book.

Creating the View

Now that the Model and ViewModel are ready, let's focus on the View. Let's use the default page, which is `MainPage.xaml`. Here we move the page from the root to the Views folder so that we will have a manageable project structure. The page template comes with a `Grid` where `TextBlock` is added to showcase the application title and `GridView` to display data (see Listing 1-5).

Listing 1-5. MainPage.xaml View Defined in the XAML

```xml
<Grid Background="{StaticResource ApplicationPageBackgroundThemeBrush}">
    <Grid.RowDefinitions>
        <RowDefinition Height="9*"/>
        <RowDefinition Height="55*"/>
    </Grid.RowDefinitions>
    <TextBlock
        TextWrapping="Wrap"
        Text="New York Times Best Sellers"
        Margin="60,20,0,20"
        FontSize="64"/>

    <GridView Grid.Row="1"
        Margin="60,0,0,0"
        ItemsSource="{Binding FictionBestSellers}"
        ItemTemplate="{StaticResource BookDataTemplate}"/>

</Grid>
```

Visual Studio generates code for us at the `OnLaunched` event in `app.xaml.cs` so that `MainPage.xaml` will be used as the start page of the app (see Listing 1-6).

Listing 1-6. Configuring Application's Startup Page

```csharp
protected override void OnLaunched(LaunchActivatedEventArgs args)
    {
        Frame rootFrame = Window.Current.Content as Frame;
        if (rootFrame == null)
        {
            /* Create a Frame to act as the navigation context and navigate to the first page*/

            rootFrame = new Frame();
            if (args.PreviousExecutionState == ApplicationExecutionState.Terminated)
            {
                //TODO: Load state from previously suspended application
            }
            // Place the frame in the current Window
            Window.Current.Content = rootFrame;
        }

        if (rootFrame.Content == null)
        {
            // When the navigation stack isn't restored navigate to the first page,
            // configuring the new page by passing required information as a navigation
            // parameter
            if (!rootFrame.Navigate(typeof(MainPage), args.Arguments))
```

```
        {
            throw new Exception("Failed to create initial page");
        }
    }
    // Ensure the current window is active
    Window.Current.Activate();
}
```

The next step is to create the connection between the View and ViewModel, which is done by creating the instance of the ViewModel in the View's constructor and setting it to the data context of the page (see Listing 1-7).

Listing 1-7. Connecting View and ViewModel

```
public MainPage()
    {
        this.InitializeComponent();
        MainViewModel vm = new MainViewModel();
        this.DataContext = vm;
    }
```

Windows 8 Data Binding

Data binding is a useful tool in putting an application together and WinRT relies heavily on the usage of data binding. WPF, Silverlight, or Windows Phone developers are mostly familiar with data binding, but for someone who is new to this, we show an example of data binding in The New York Times Best Sellers app.

A data binding consists of a target and a source. The target is usually a property of a control, and the source is usually a property of a data object. In Listing 1-5 we bound the source BestSeller collection to the target control's ItemsSource property. Also in Listing 1-8 we bind the Book class Title property to the Control Text property.

Before we go further, let's see how the application looks when it runs for the first time.

If we have a close look at Listing 1-5, we'll see that the ViewModel FictionBestSellers property is bound to the GridView. GridView along with ListView are two powerful data controls in WinRT that are designed for touch input. Both these controls are derived from ListViewBase and neither adds any properties, methods, or events other than ListView used for vertical scrolling, and GridView for horizontal scroll.

By seeing the app one would notice that the book title, author, and description are formatted nicely and for that to happen GridView needs to know how to display each object in the list, the properties of the object that need to be displayed, and how they should appear. We do this more often with a DataTemplate. Here we create a DataTemplate named BookDataTemplate, which is assigned to the GridView ItemTemplate property as shown in Listing 1-5. The ItemTemplate gets or sets the template for each item and the DataTemplate customizes the appearance of the data. In this case, we created a layout with Border and StackPanel and three TextBlock instances that we bind to the various Book object properties like Title, Author, and Description (see Listing 1-8). The result is shown in Figure 1-6.

Listing 1-8. The BookDataTemplate Is Defined Inside the MainPage.xaml

```
<DataTemplate x:Key="BookDataTemplate">
    <Grid
        HorizontalAlignment="Left"
        Width="250"
        Height="150">
        <Border
            Background="{StaticResource ListViewItemPlaceholderBackgroundThemeBrush}">
            <TextBlock
                Text="{Binding Description}"
```

```xml
                    Foreground="{StaticResource ListViewItemOverlayForegroundThemeBrush}"
                    Style="{StaticResource TitleTextStyle}"
                    FontWeight="Normal"
                    FontSize="13.333"
                    Margin="10,0"/>
            </Border>
            <StackPanel
                VerticalAlignment="Bottom"
                Background="{StaticResource ListViewItemOverlayBackgroundThemeBrush}">
                <TextBlock
                    Text="{Binding Title}"
                    Foreground="{StaticResource ListViewItemOverlayForegroundThemeBrush}"
                    Style="{StaticResource TitleTextStyle}"
                    Height="20"
                    Margin="15,0,15,0"/>
                <TextBlock
                    Text="{Binding Author}"
                    Foreground="{StaticResource ListViewItemOverlaySecondaryForegroundThemeBrush}"
                    Style="{StaticResource CaptionTextStyle}"
                    TextWrapping="NoWrap"
                    Margin="15,0,15,5"/>
            </StackPanel>
        </Grid>
    </DataTemplate>
```

Figure 1-6. *Windows 8 Application displaying the New York Times Best Sellers List*

Conclusion

This chapter introduced Windows 8 App development and various concepts that are needed to build an XAML-based data-driven Windows 8 App by building our first Windows 8 App. As you can see, this was just a brief introduction to the concepts and frameworks. As you look to move beyond the basics of Windows 8 development, there are many more advanced scenarios that are available, and among them are user-updated data, two-way binding, value converters, and advanced MVVM techniques like passing data between pages, dialog UI, and so forth. In the next chapter we use the MVVM pattern and data binding that we learned in this chapter and will them in building an HTML5 and JavaScript-based Windows 8 application using JavaScript patterns, MVVM, and KnockoutJS.

■ ■ ■

CHAPTER 2

HTML5 and JavaScript Apps with MVVM and Knockout

In Chapter 1 we built an XAML-based app using MVVM and in this chapter we build a JavaScript-based data-driven app using HTML5, CSS, and Knockout JS.

Knockout JS is a popular open source MVVM JavaScript framework. This framework helps us to adpot some of the principles like BaseModel, inheritance, and data binding in a way that helps us write code that remains manageable, testable, and maintainable.

This chapter begins by helping you get started with Knockout, going through the resources and tools needed to start with Knockout and use it with Visual Studio. We then provide a demonstration using MVVM with Knockout, data binding, and jQuery to develop a Pocket (Read it later) client Windows 8 App.

What Is Knockout?

Every web application developer either has used or at least heard of jQuery, which is designed to greatly simplify JavaScript programming. jQuery is not a solution for every problem, as when developing a complex web application it becomes tricky to make the UI and data communicate with each other dynamically. Also jQuery doesn't have a concept of an underlying data model, so for data manipulation jQuery always infers with DOM. Hence there is a need for a library that provides a more sophisticated means of communication between the UI and the underlying data model; that solution is Knockout.

Understanding Knockout

Knockout is a JavaScript library that helps create rich, desktop-like web UIs. It simplifies user interactions and is fully amenable to any data source changes. Using observations, Knockout helps the UI stay in sync with the underlying data model.

- Knockout is a free, open source JavaScript library.

- Knockout implements the MVVM pattern for JavaScript that we discussed in Chapter 1.

- Knockout is a small and lightweight library.

- Knockout is compatible with Internet Explorer 6+, Firefox 2+, and the latest versions of Chrome, Safari, and Opera.

- Knockout provides a complementary, high-level way to link a data model to a UI.

- Knockout itself doesn't depend on jQuery, but can certainly use jQuery at the same time.

Knockout is entirely built on three core concepts (see Figure 2-1):

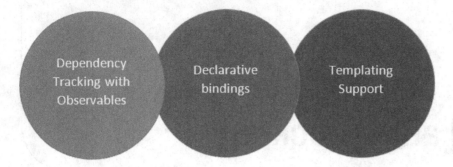

Figure 2-1. *Knockout core concepts*

- **Dependency tracking with observables:** If one is familiar with XAML technologies, then this concept can be related to the INotifyPropertyChanged interface. For instance, if a property is loaded or changed, it will automatically notify the UI to bond to it in one or more places whereas the changes have been made. The UI will reflect the changes and will also have an option for whether the UI can change the value to automatically update the source object again.

- **Declarative bindings:** This concept helps in connecting parts of the UI to the data model in a simple and convenient way. This is where source objects are bonded to the target elements through the HTML itself. Instead of using JavaScript code to find an element by ID, or by some other means embedded in the value by a JavaScript object with JSON data and then pushing it in and pulling it out of the UI, it can be accomplished through declarative bindings. This is done within the HTML binding by setting the element's ID to fetch particular attributes, properties, or values from the source object.

- **Templating:** Repetitive structures in a web page, like rows or list boxes, can created using templates. This is similar to item templates or data templates in WPF/Silverlight and XAML-based Windows 8 Apps. jQuery templates can also be used as a template with Knockout along with the native templates with Knockout or some other templating engine.

Creating the Pocket (Read It Later) App

Pocket is a very popular bookmark service that allows users to catalog articles and create a personal archive of items they are interested in. In this chapter, we create a Windows 8 App for Pocket bookmark services named Read It Later using HTML5, JavaScript, CSS, and Knockout JS.

Read It Later is a very basic app that displays bookmarked articles (see Figure 2-2). In building this app, we will be learning about some of the following Windows 8 concepts and practices.

- Learn to allow apps to use Internet authentication and authorization protocols like OpenID or OAuth to connect to online identity providers like Facebook, Twitter, Google, and Microsoft Account.

- Learn to use the WinJS.xhr JavaScript function to make cross-domain requests and intranet requests. Some of the common scenarios are uploading and downloading files and connecting to a web service to GET and POST to REST API.

- Learn JavaScript data binding by data-binding data from JavaScript objects to HTML elements.

Figure 2-2. *Read It Later Windows 8 App displays articles from Pocket bookmark services*

Tools and Utilities

Using tools and extensions not only makes the developer's life easier; it also increases productivity and reduces startup time for new projects. Let's take a look at some of the tools and extensions that we can use in our Read It Later app.

JsFiddle

JsFiddle is a free online shell editor that eases writing JavaScript code by creating convention environs based on JavaScript frameworks and for snippets built from HTML, CSS, and JavaScript, hosted at http://jsFiddle.net. This free code-sharing tool has an interface that is divided into four sections, as shown in Figure 2-3.

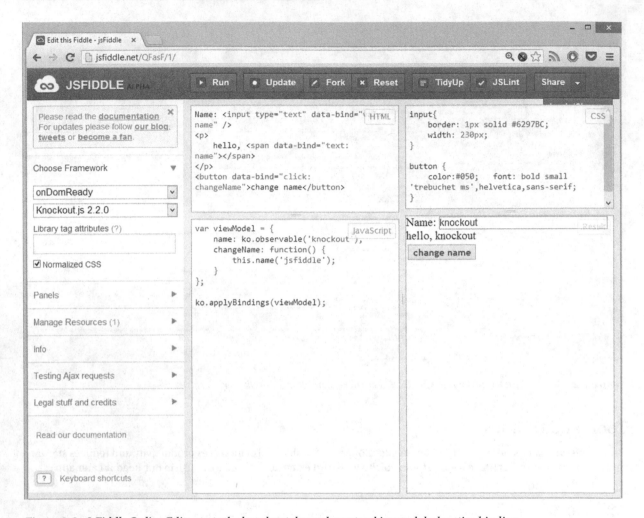

Figure 2-3. *JsFiddle Online Editor tests the knockout dependency tracking and declarative binding*

■ **Note**   Visit `http://jsfiddle.net/QFasF/1/` to experiment with the live sample.

Sometimes when there is a need to build a POC or ideas quickly, that's where JsFiddle comes in handy, as you can quickly set up and run the code without having a full-blown IDE. Out of the box, JsFiddle provides an option to share the work, along with built-in version control, debugging, and code forking.

JsFiddle has the ability to share and save the code with a unique URL generated and one can choose a default JavaScript framework like JQuery, Mootools, Prototype, Vanilla, and so on, and can also add new resources like the Knockout plug-in or a JQuery UI.

Visual Studio Extensions

One of the best things about development with JavaScript inside Visual Studio 2012 is using the various Visual Studio extensions that can enhance the experience. The following are some of the recommended extensions.

- **NuGet:** This free extension is used to manage third-party libraries and references.

- **Web Essentials:** This is used for code collapsing, adding vendor-specific CSS properties and much more.

- **JSLint:** This linting tool for JavaScript helps to spot mistakes in the code.

- **CSSCop:** This makes it easy to perceive the best practices for writing stylesheets and helps users catch common issues that affect browser compatibility.

- **Resharper:** This is one of the best productivity tools for Visual Studio, but it is not free.

Getting Started

To start, let's create a new Windows Store Blank App (JavaScript) project and name it ReadItLater. Blank Application (see Figure 2-4) is a single-page project for Windows 8 App that has no predefined controls or layouts.

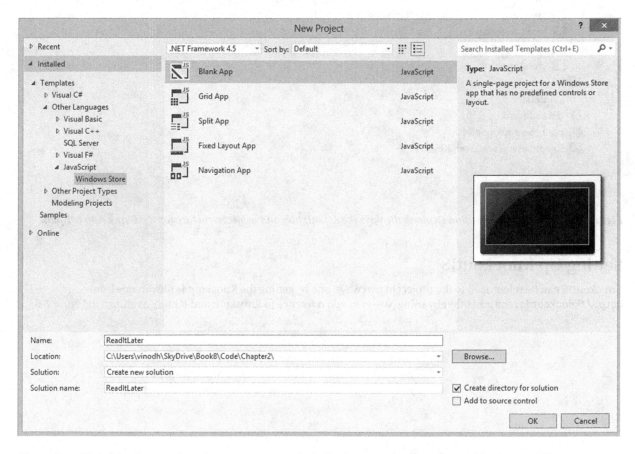

Figure 2-4. *Visual Studio templates for JavaScript creates a Blank App with HTML, CSS, and JavaScript files*

■ **Note**   Like Blank Application, Visual Studio also provides a few more templates, like Split Application, Fixed Layout Application, Navigation Application, and Grid Application.

Blank App incudes files that are essential for the Windows 8 Apps using JavaScript, as shown in Figure 2-5.

Figure 2-5. *Visual Studio Soution Explorer displays the default files and project structure for the Blank App template*

Setting Up KnockoutJS

KnockoutJS can be referenced to the project in two ways: one by getting the Knockout.js file directly from http://knockoutjs.com and other by using NuGet to add reference to Knockout and JQuery as shown in Figure 2-6.

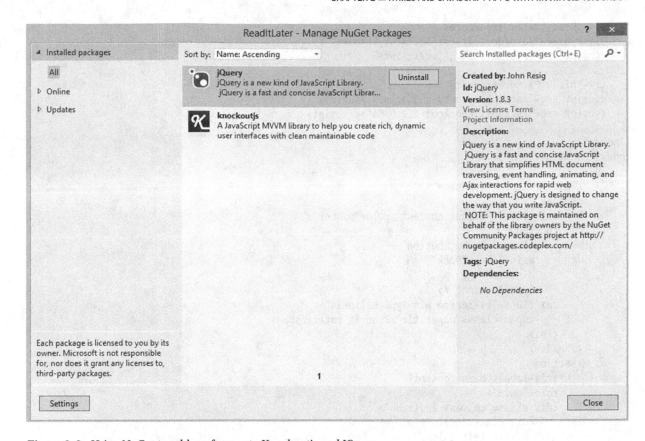

Figure 2-6. *Using NuGet to add a reference to Knockoutjs and JQuery*

Designing the App Start Page

As you saw in Figure 2-4, the Visual Studio Blank App template creates `default.html` as our app start page. This page contains references to the app's code files and style sheets. We update this page layout as shown in Listing 2-1. The layout consists of a header section that displays the app title. The right column has the necessary HTML elements for displaying list of bookmarked articles and the left column shows the content of the selected article.

Listing 2-1. Updated default.html Page with Two-Column Layout

```
<!DOCTYPE html>
<html>
<head>
    <meta charset="utf-8" />
    <title>Read It Later</title>

    <!-- WinJS references -->
    <link href="//Microsoft.WinJS.1.0/css/ui-dark.css" rel="stylesheet" />
    <script src="//Microsoft.WinJS.1.0/js/base.js"></script>
    <script src="//Microsoft.WinJS.1.0/js/ui.js"></script>
```

```html
    <!-- ReadItLater references -->
    <link href="/css/default.css" rel="stylesheet" />
    <script src="/js/default.js"></script>

    <!--Thirdy Party Reference -->
    <script src="/scripts/jquery-1.8.3.js"></script>
    <script src="/scripts/knockout-2.2.0.js"></script>

</head>
<body>
    <div
        class="fragment homepage">
        <header
            aria-label="Header content" role="banner">
            <button
                class="win-backbutton"
                aria-label="Back"
                disabled
                type="button" />
            <h1 class="titlearea win-type-ellipsis">
                <span class="pagetitle">Read It Later</span>
            </h1>
        </header>
        <section
            aria-label="Main content"
            role="main">
            <div class="colmask leftmenu">
                <div class="colleft">
                    <!--left col-->
                    <div class="col1"
                        data-bind="with: selectedItem">
                        <!-- Main Content Start-->
                        <h2>
                            <span data-bind="text: $root.ShowContent(url)"/>
                        </h2>
                            <div id="siteloader"></div>
                        <!-- Main Content end -->
                    </div>
                      <!--right col-->
                    <div class="col2">
                        <!-- Articlet List start -->
                        <div data-bind="foreach: model">
                            <div data-bind="foreach: keys"
                                class="link-container">
                                <h2>
                                    <span  data-bind="click: $root.setItem, text: title" />
                                </h2>
                                <p><span data-bind="text: excerpt"></span></p>
                            </div>
```

```
        </div>
          <!-- Articlet List End -->
        </div>
      </div>
    </div>
  </section>
  </div>
</body>
</html>
```

Enabling Windows 8 Web Authentication

The Pocket service implements oAuth authorization to access the data when the Pocket API is called. The calls to the APIs are signed with encrypted details that include an expiry time. There are many services similar to Pocket, like Facebook, Digg, and Google, that use oAuth and learning oAuth authorization will be a great help in developing Windows 8 Apps that consume web services.

The first step is to register the app with the Pocket service. A consumer key is provided on registration as shown in Figure 2-7.

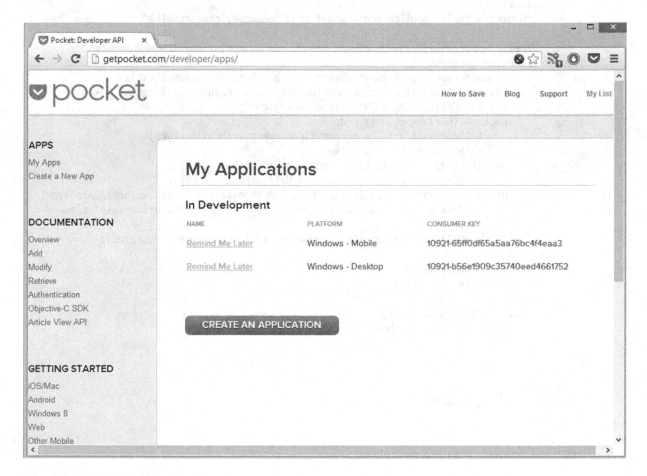

Figure 2-7. *Pocket developer dashboard*

Getting Request Token

To begin the process, one needs to pass the consumer key and redirect URL to the service to acquire a Request Token. WinRT provides the WinJS.xhr function to send cross-domain requests and intranet requests. WinJS.xhr abstracts all the complexity of XMLHttpRequest and provides a simple interface that uses Promises to handle the asynchronous responses, as shown in Listing 2-2.

Listing 2-2. WinJS.xhr Function Used to Consumer Key as HTTP POST to Pocket Service

```
function launchPocketWebAuth() {
var pocketReqUrl = "https://getpocket.com/v3/oauth/request";
var callbackURL = "readitlater123:authorizationFinished";
var dataString = "consumer_key=" + consumer_id
                    + "&redirect_uri=" + callbackURL;
try {
    WinJS.xhr({
        type: "post"
        , data: dataString
        , url: pocketReqUrl
        , headers: {
            "Content-type": "application/x-www-form-urlencoded; charset=UTF8"
        }
        }).done(
            function (request) {
                request_code = getParameterByName("code", request.responseText);
                var pocketAuthUrl = "https://getpocket.com/auth/authorize?request_token=";
                var authCallbackURL = "http://www.myweb.com";
                pocketAuthUrl += request_code
                    + "&redirect_uri=" + encodeURIComponent(authCallbackURL)
                    + "&webauthenticationbroker=1";
                var startURI = new Windows.Foundation.Uri(pocketAuthUrl);
                var endURI = new Windows.Foundation.Uri(authCallbackURL);
                Windows.Security.Authentication.Web.WebAuthenticationBroker.authenticateAsync(
                    Windows.Security.Authentication.Web.WebAuthenticationOptions.useTitle,
                    startURI,
                    endURI).then(callbackPocketWebAuth, callbackPocketWebAuthError);
            },
            function error(error) {
                //handle error here
            },
            function progress(result) {
                //Do somehting to show the progress
            });

}
catch (err) {
    /*Error launching WebAuth"*/
    return;
}
}
```

One of the prerequisites of the Pocket API is that we have to POST the request and set the request header manually to application/x-www-form-urlencoded; charset=UTF8 as shown in Listing 2-2. Different services will have different requirements, and the best way to determine what they are is to look in the developer documentation provided by the service.

Exchanging Request Token for Access Token

The next step is to exchange a request token with an access token. WinRT has a built-in API named Web Authentication Broker that provides the necessary infrastructure for apps to use Internet authentication and authorization protocols such as OAuth and OpenID. When the Web Authentication Broker is invoked using the WebAuthenticationBroker. authenticateAsync function (see Listing 2-3), the user see a dialog box like the one shown in Figure 2-8, which displays the Pocket service authorization page for the user to sign in.

Listing 2-3. Invoking Pocket Login Windows Using Web Authentication Broker

```
var pocketAuthUrl = "https://getpocket.com/auth/authorize?request_token=";
var authCallbackURL = "http://www.myweb.com";
pocketAuthUrl += request_code
    + "&redirect_uri=" + encodeURIComponent(authCallbackURL)
    + "&webauthenticationbroker=1";
var startURI = new Windows.Foundation.Uri(pocketAuthUrl);
var endURI = new Windows.Foundation.Uri(authCallbackURL);
Windows.Security.Authentication.Web.WebAuthenticationBroker.authenticateAsync(
    Windows.Security.Authentication.Web.WebAuthenticationOptions.useTitle
    , startURI
    , endURI).then(callbackPocketWebAuth, callbackPocketWebAuthError);
```

Figure 2-8. *Modal dialog box opens at the start of the app to authorize the user*

Receiving the Access Token

Once logged into the Pocket service, and the Read It Later app has the necessary authorization to use the service, the dialog box closes and the Pocket service will return an access token as shown in Listing 2-4. This access token will be stored locally for future requests.

Listing 2-4. Callback Method That Stores the Access Token

```
function callbackPocketWebAuth(result) {
    var pocketAuthUrl = "https://getpocket.com/v3/oauth/authorize";
    var dataString = "consumer_key=" + consumer_id
        + "&code=" + request_code;

    WinJS.xhr({
        type: "post"
        , data: dataString
        , url: pocketAuthUrl
        , headers: { "Content-type": "application/x-www-form-urlencoded; charset=UTF8" }
    }).done(
            function (request) {
                var access = request.responseText;
                access_token = getParameterByName("access_token", access);
                var username = getParameterByName("username", access);
                var localSettings = applicationData.localSettings;
                localSettings.values["pocket_access_token"] = access_token;
                localSettings.values["pocket_username"] = access_token;
                retriveList(access_token);
            },
            function error(error) {
                //handle error here
            },
            function progress(result) {
                //Do something to show the progress
            });

    if (result.responseStatus == 2) {
        response += "Error returned: " + result.responseErrorDetail + "\r\n";
    }
}
```

■ **Note**   Pocket provides a set of Rest APIs to accomplish various actions like retrieving, adding, modifying, and deleting bookmarks. For more details go to http://getpocket.com/developer/docs/overview.

Retrieving Bookmarks Using oAuth Credentials (Access Token)

For retrieving the bookmarks, we will post the consumer ID along with the access token to the Pocket /v3/get endpoint using WinJS.xhr as shown in Listing 2-5. This request responds with a JSON list object that contains titles and URLs of each item as the detailType specified in the request URL is simple.

Listing 2-5. Retrieving Bookmarks from the Pocket Service

```
function retrieveList(token) {
    var pocketGetUrl = "https://getpocket.com/v3/get";
    var dataString = "detailType=simple&consumer_key=" + consumer_id
        + "&access_token=" + token;
    WinJS.xhr({
        type: "post"
        , data: dataString
        , url: pocketGetUrl
        , headers: { "Content-type": "application/x-www-form-urlencoded; charset=UTF8" }
    })
    .done(
        function (response) {
            var json = JSON.parse(response.responseText);
            ko.applyBindings(new ArticleViewModel(response.responseText));
        },
        function error(error) {
            //handle error here
        },
        function progress(result) {
            //Do something to show the progress
        });
}
```

■ **Note** Visit http://getpocket.com/developer/docs/v3/retrieve to learn more about the various types of information that can be accessed using Pocket API.

Defining the ViewModel and Binding It to the View

Now that we have the data from the Pocket service, the next step is to bind the data to the View using the KnockoutJS framework. For this we create a ViewModel ArticleViewModel (see Listing 2-6). ArticleViewModel will have a selectedItem observable to track the currently selected article and a method ShowContent that will display the article content in the right column.

Listing 2-6. Defining ArticleViewModel with Function and Properties

```
function ArticleViewModel(data) {
    var self = this;
    self.selectedItem = ko.observable();
    self.setItem = function (item) {
        self.selectedItem(item);
    }

    self.ShowContent = function (url) {
        $.get(url, function (data) {
            var szStaticHTML = toStaticHTML(data);
            $('#siteloader').html(szStaticHTML);
        });
```

```
    };
    self.model = ko.utils.arrayMap(data, function (jsonData) {
        return new ListStatus(jsonData.list);
    });
}
```

Also to make the JSONObject useful in Knockout, we need to do some computing. For that we use Knockout's mapping plug-in to map the value of the array of objects by using ko.utils.arrayMap (see Listing 2-6), which executes a function for each item in an array and pushes the result of the function to a new array that is returned, as shown in Listing 2-7.

Listing 2-7. Mapping the JavaScript Object to the ArticleViewModel

```
function Item(item) {
    var self = this;
    self.title = item.given_title;
    self.url = item.given_url;
    self.excerpt = item.excerpt;
}

function ListStatus(list) {
    var self = this;
    self.keys = ko.observableArray(ko.utils.arrayMap(list, function (article) {
        return new Item(article);
    }));
}
```

■ **Note**   The mapping plug-in gives us a straightforward way to map the Pocket bookmark JavaScript object into an ArticleViewModel with the appropriate observables instead of us manually writing our own JavaScript code that creates a view model based on the data.

To tie the view model to the view we simply need to call the KnockoutJS applyBinding function and pass it in a new instance of the ArticleViewModel that takes the JSON object from the Pocket service as a parameter (see Listing 2-8).

Listing 2-8. ArticleViewModel Object Is Used to Bind the Data to the Page

```
ko.applyBindings(new ArticleViewModel(response.responseText));
```

The ko.applyBindings method activates Knockout and wires up the view model to the view.

Rendering Article List Using foreach Binding

Now that we have a ViewModel, we create the bindings as shown in Listing 2-9 to generate the bookmared article list in the left column. In Knockout.js, we do this by adding data-bind attributes to HTML elements. The foreach binding iterates through the array and creates child elements for each object (read article) in the array.

Listing 2-9. Binding the Article List to the HTML Element

```
<!-- Article List start -->
<div data-bind="foreach: model">
    <div data-bind="foreach: keys" class="link-container">
        <h2><span  data-bind="click: $root.setItem, text: title"></span></h2>
        <p><span data-bind="text: excerpt"></span></p>
    </div>
</div>
<!-- Article List End -->
```

Bindings on the child elements can refer to properties on the array objects; for example, the `<div>` element occurs within the scope of the `foreach` binding. That means Knockout.js will render the element once for each article in the articles array. All of the bindings within the `<div>` element refer to that article instance. We use the text binding to set the values for article title and excerpt. The `<span>` element is also bound to the click binding, where the article instance is passed as a parameter to each function.

Now with all the codes in place, when we run the Read It Later app, it shows the Pocket service login page (see Figure 2-8) and after authenticating the user, the bookmarked articles by the logged user will be retrieved from the Pocket service and will be displayed in the app as shown in Figure 2-2.

Conclusion

This chapter introduced us to developing a Windows 8 App using HTML, JavaScript, and CSS, not in a traditional approach of using WinJS UI controls, but instead using a JavaScript MVVM framework, KnockoutJS. In Chapters 5 and 8 we will see the recommended approach for developing a data-driven Windows 8 App using HTML, JavaScript, and CSS. Also in this chapter we learned to implement oAuth authorization, using JsFiddle as an online HTML editor and various Visual Studio extensions to complement our app development experience.

In the next chapter we discuss various data storage options that can be considered while building Windows 8 Apps along with the various WinRT APIs that can be used.

CHAPTER 3

■ ■ ■

Windows 8 Modern App Data Access Options

The Windows 8 platform redefines the way apps access and manipulate data, as there is no direct way to access a local or remote database server as we do with .NET using ADO.NET, Linq2SQL, or the Entity framework. WinRT APIs do not provide any of the following options for security and platform-related reasons.

- Built-in local databases like SQLCE
- Connection to SQL Express Instances
- Accessing databases using ODBC or OLEDB providers
- Direct access to the disk

With these limitations, managing data becomes a critical part in developing a Windows 8 app. In this chapter we take a look at various data storage options that can be considered when building Windows Store apps, along with the various WinRT APIs that can be used.

Data Storage Options

Most of the applications, irrespective of platform, need to store data pertaining to the application in a location within a predefined format. Location and format of the data depend on various factors like platform, application, and pricing. As for Windows 8 Store apps, data can be stored either locally or remotely.

Local storage is where data is stored locally within a device. In Windows 8 Store apps, data stored within an app cannot be shared with another app, as each app is restricted to a sandbox. There are various options for storing data locally and the following are some of the options that are discussed in detail in this chapter.

- Application data
- Using built-in File Picker contracts
- IndexedDB
- JET API
- SQLite

Application Data

Every app installed in Windows 8/RT will be allocated space for storing application data. This application storage can be used to store an app's settings, preferences, context, app status, and files. This storage cannot be accessed by other apps and can be only accessed using the APIs provided in WinRT.

For storing and retrieving application data, use the `ApplicationData` class, which is a part of the `Windows.Store` namespace and this data can be stored in three different ways:

- **Local application data:** Stores the data locally. Use local storage only if you have good reason not to roam the setting to the cloud.

- **Roaming application data:** Data will be synced across all the devices on which the user has installed the app. If we use roaming and there is no Microsoft account, it will be stored locally.

- **Temporary application data:** Data is stored temporarily during an application session and can be removed any time by a system maintenance task.

We learn more about application data in Chapter 5.

File System

Databases based on a file system in Windows 8 using WinRT provide another way to store information. There are many open source options available and WinRT File Based Database is one of the popular file-based databases found in `www.codeplex.com`.

WinRT File Based Database is a file-system-based database written using the WinRT framework. This API allows users to create tables based on classes. Each database consists of many tables and these tables are serialized and stored in Application Data Storage. We learn about this in detail in Chapter 5.

File Picker Contracts

File Picker contracts can be used to store and retrieve the data as files from the device hard disk in a format that is understood by the Windows 8 Store app. File Picker is the only way for an app to gain access to files and folders located in any part of the system. Unlike .NET APIs, WinRT doesn't provide an option to manage files without user intervention. That is, the app cannot gain access to a file in the system without the user explicitly acting on the files or folder using the File Picker contract.

There are three types of File Picker contracts.

- **FileOpenPicker:** After calling this class, the user will be presented with a UI to pick a file.

- **FileSavePicker:** This class helps to save a file.

- **FolderPicker:** This class is used to pick a folder.

To open a file using the `FileOpenPicker` class, we have to add at least one file extension to the `FileTypeFilter` collection, to indicate what file types are supported by the app. The `FileTypeFilter` will throw an Unspecified error exception if it is empty. Apart from `FileTypeFilter`, all other properties are optional, including `ViewMode` and `SuggestedStartLocation`. In Listing 3-1 we use `FileOpenPicker` to open a picture from the Pictures Library as a stream.

Listing 3-1. Using FileOpenPicker to Open a File from the Picture Library

```
string selectedFileName=null;
string photoStream=null;
FileOpenPicker openPicker = new FileOpenPicker();
openPicker.ViewMode = PickerViewMode.Thumbnail;
openPicker.SuggestedStartLocation = PickerLocationId.PicturesLibrary;
openPicker.FileTypeFilter.Add(".jpg");
openPicker.FileTypeFilter.Add(".jpeg");
openPicker.FileTypeFilter.Add(".png");
StorageFile file = await openPicker.PickSingleFileAsync();
if (file != null)
{
        selectedFileName = file.Name;
        photoStream = await file.OpenReadAsync();
}
```

Similar to FileOpenPicker we have to add at least one file type to the FileTypeChoices collection and the rest of the properties are optional. As shown in Listing 3-2, apart from providing the options to save the files in various types by adding to the FileTypeChoices collection we also used the DefaultFileExtension property to define a preferred format in which the file can be stored.

Listing 3-2. Using FileSavePicker to Save a File within a Device File System

```
var fileSavePicker = new FileSavePicker();
fileSavePicker.FileTypeChoices.Add("Raw Images", new List<string> { ".raw", ".dat" });
fileSavePicker.FileTypeChoices.Add(".jpg Image", new List<string> { ".jpg" });
fileSavePicker.DefaultFileExtension = ".jpg";
fileSavePicker.SuggestedFileName = "NewImage1.jpg";
var fileToSave = await fileSavePicker.PickSaveFileAsync();
```

The FolderPicker is very similar to the FileOpenPicker with resembling properties as shown in Listing 3-3.

Listing 3-3. Using FolderPicker to Pick a Folder from the Picture Library

```
var folderPicker = new FolderPicker();
folderPicker.FileTypeFilter.Add(".jpg");
folderPicker.ViewMode = PickerViewMode.Thumbnail;
folderPicker.SuggestedStartLocation = PickerLocationId.PicturesLibrary;
folderPicker.SettingsIdentifier = "FolderPicker";
var folder = await folderPicker.PickSingleFolderAsync();
```

IndexedDB

IndexedDB is a nonrelational data store, designed to store structured objects in collections known as an Object Store. The Object Store holds records as key/value pairs. Each record in the Object Store has a single key, which can be configured to autoincrement or can be provided by the application. This key is like the primary key in a relational database table, where no two records within an Object Store can be identified by the same key.

Internet Explorer 10 and Windows Store apps using JavaScript support the Indexed Database API defined by the World Wide Web Consortium (W3C) Indexed Database API specification, so applications written using HTML5 and JavaScript will be able to use IndexedDB as a local storage option. The following are some of the common IndexedDB contracts.

- **Database:** A database consists of one or more object stores that hold the data stored in the database. It also contains indexes and is used to manage transactions. There can be multiple databases in an application.

- **Object Store:** An object store is a primary storage solution used for storing data in a database. It's a collection of JavaScript objects where attributes have key/value pairs.

- **Key:** A key is used to uniquely identify an object within a database. It has values of type float, date, string, and array. It's very similar to the primary key columns in a relational database table. It also imposes an ascending sort order on the associated objects.

- **Value:** A value is a JavaScript object that associated with a given key. Every record is associated with a value. It can be a complex object that has no schematization requirements.

- **Key Path:** A key path is a string that defines a way to extract a key from a value. A key path is said to be valid when it has either an empty string or a multiple JavaScript separated by periods.

- **Index:** An index is an alternative method to retrieve records in an object store rather than using a key. It's a specialized storage solution that supports searching objects in the store by attribute values.

- **Transaction:** This is used to read or write data into the database. Transactions are always operated in one of three modes: read-only, readwrite, or versionchange.

- **Request:** A request is used to perform a read or write operation on a database. It's analogous to a SQL statement.

- **Key Range:** The key range is used to retrieve records from object stores and indexes.

- **Cursor:** A cursor is a brief mechanism used to iterate over multiple records in a database. They are bidirectional, and can skip duplicate records in a nonunique index.

Even though IndexedDB concepts looks similar to relational database management elements, one key difference is that there is no relational semantics, which mean we will not be able to use joins. In Chapter 4 we will learn in detail about using IndexedDB as a storage option for a Movie Collection and Inventory Windows Store app.

ESENT/JET API

Extensible Storage Engine (ESENT), also known as JET API, is an Indexed Sequential Access Method (ISAM) data storage technology from Microsoft. The ESENT runtime has been a part of Windows since Windows 2000 and has been used in products like Microsoft Exchange, Active Directory, Windows Update, and Desktop Search. This application stores and retrieves data from tables using indexed or sequential cursor navigation.

We can use ESENT for applications that need reliable, high-performance, low-overhead storage of structured or semistructured data. The ESENT engine can help with data needs ranging from something as simple as a hash table that is too large to store in memory to something more complex, such as an application with tables, columns, and indexes.

ESENT incorporates all the benefits of the ISAM data storage technique, including the following.

- ACID transaction

- Snapshot isolation

- Concurrent access storage

- Cursor navigation

- Advanced indexing: Indexing over multivalued columns, sparse, and tuple

- Fixed, variable, and tagged columns

- Data integrity and consistency

- Column size ranging from 1 bit to 2 GB

We will be learning in detail about using JET API in Chapter 5. We will build a Windows Store Password Manager app that stores data using JET API.

SQLite

SQLite is a software library that implements a self-contained, serverless, zero-configuration, transactional SQL database engine. It's a file-based database that can be used without any need for a database engine like SQLServer, Oracle, and so on. SQLite is a relational database management system that is contained in a small C programming library. SQLite is the most widely deployed SQL database engine in the world and its source code exists in the public domain. It is free for use for both private and commercial purposes.

SQLite is very similar to the SQL Server compact in characteristics. It's an embedded database that should be included explicitly with in the app and run in-process within the app unlike SQL Serve Compact, which in most cases will be part of the OS (Windows Phone OS, Windows Mobile OS). We will learn in detail about using SQLite in Windows 8 projects in Chapter 6.

Remote Data

Not all Windows 8 Store apps store data locally. Many line of business (LOB) apps store data in a central repository like Windows Azure, SQL Server, Oracle, and so on. WinRT doesn't provide the necessary APIs to directly access this data, so we have to access it in a way that is similar to accessing data in Silverlight applications; that is, building a service layer that exposes the entities, in a format like XML, JSON, and binary using transfer protocols like HTTP, HTTPS, and TCP.

In the next part of this chapter we look in to some of the data transfer techniques that can be used to access data remotely.

Windows Communication Framework

The Windows Communication Framework (WCF) is widely used as a service layer in enterprise applications. This service can be leveraged with minimum changes when porting an existing application to WinRT or building a companion Windows 8 Store app to an existing LOB application, as WinRT provides the necessary APIs to consume WCF services. WCF provides different options for consuming data.

- **WCF Web Services:** WCF Web Services is based on the Simple Object Access Protocol (SOAP), which returns data in XML format. Consuming WCF Web Services is very similar to how we do that with .NET.

- **WCF Data Services:** WCF Data Services is based on the oData protocol, which returns XML or JSON data, using REST queries. We learn more about this in Chapter 8.

Apart from these two straightforward techniques, we can also use the more complex and powerful WCF HTTP/.NET TCP. Using this technique, we can implement our own protocol, format, and query method that is supported by WinRT, as WinRT support is not as broad as that for .NET.

ASP.NET Web API

The ASP.NET Web API introduced with ASP.NET MVC 4.0 and .NET Framework 4.5 is a new addition to the ASP.NET stack that allows us to create a RESTful and AJAX API that helps to build web or HTTP-based client or server endpoints.Why Should We Use Web API?

ASP.NET Web API is Microsoft's answer to a modern programming landscape for building a service layer that can be easily consumed by most clients. Web API is an ideal platform for building pure HTTP-based services that can be useful when building multiplatform applications like apps for desktop application, HTML5, iOS, Android, Windows 8, and Windows Phone, as all these clients can make GET, PUT, POST, and DELETE requests and get the Web API response.

In Chapter 7 we learn to set up a CRUD ASP.NET Web API Rest service and consume this service from a Windows Store JavaScript app by building a Party Planner app.

Windows Azure Mobile Web Services

WCF and ASP.NET Web APIs are ideal for enterprise apps in which the data are stored in a datacenter of that enterprise. But if you are looking to store the data in a cloud and if you like to use Windows Azure as a scalable cloud back end, then Windows Azure Mobile Web Services is the way to go.

Windows Azure Mobile Services allows users to quickly connect any mobile client like Windows 8, Windows Phone, iOS, Android, or HTML5 apps to a cloud-based back end hosted on Windows Azure. Windows Azure Mobile Services also offer built-in functionality to authenticate users via Microsoft, Google, Facebook, or Twitter credentials, and send push notifications. Windows Azure Mobile Services can be easily integrated into a Windows 8 Store app as Microsoft provides the necessary tools and SDKs to do so. In Chapter 9 we learn to uses Windows Azure Mobile Services as a back-end storage option by building an Instagram-inspired application, Instashot.

Conclusion

This chapter gave a brief introduction to some of the data options that can be used along with Windows 8 Store apps. In the coming chapters we will be learning about some of these in greater detail.

Apart from this, WinRT provides APIs to interact with public data applications like Facebook, Twitter, and LinkedIn. As mentioned in Chapter 2, we can use WebAuthenticationBroker for authenticating the user against user authentication providers like Facebook, Twitter, Google, and Microsoft. The WebAuthenticationBroker class provides the necessary infrastructure for apps to use Internet authentication and authorization protocols such as OAuth and OpenID. Furthermore, WinRT provides built in APIs to query RSS, oData, and more.

■ ■ ■

CHAPTER 4

Local Data Access: I: IndexedDB

WinRT does not have any built-in database capabilities like SQL Server CE. It doesn't provide any APIs to connect directly to a SQL Server; instead we need to use a cloud storage solution or rely on third-party options like SQLite. Cloud storage is not an ideal solution in many cases, as it requires complex data management. Also it might not be an affordable solution, as storing data in the cloud is not free in most cases. In the next three chapters we learn about local storage options like indexedDB, JET API, Application Storage, and SQLite. To start with, in this chapter we learn to use IndexedDB for storing structured data locally and build a Movie collection and Inventory app that use IndexedDB as data storage.

What Is IndexedDB?

IndexedDB or the Indexed Database API is a nonrelational data store, designed to store structured objects in collections known as the object store. The object store holds records as key–value pairs. Each record in the object store has a single key, which can be configured to autoincrement or can be provided by the application. This key is like the primary key in a relational database table, where no two records with in an object store can be identified by the same key.

■ **Note**   IndexedDB is supported by Firefox (since version 4), Internet Explorer 10, and Google Chrome (since version 11). Safari and Opera support an alternate mechanism for client-side database storage called Web SQL Database. As of November 2010, the W3C Web Applications Working Group ceased working on the Web SQL Database specification, citing lack of independent implementations.

Using IndexedDB in Windows 8 Application

Internet Explorer 10 and Windows Store apps using JavaScript support the Indexed Database API defined by the World Wide Web Consortium (W3C) Indexed Database API specification, so applications written using HTML5 and JavaScript will be able to use IndexedDB as a local storage options. The following are some of the common IndexedDB contracts.

- **Database:** A database consists of one or more object stores that hold the data stored in the database. It also contains indexes and is used to manage transactions. There can be multiple databases in an application.

- **Object store:** An object store is the primary storage used for storing data in a database. It's a collection of JavaScript objects where attributes have key–value pairs.

- **Key:** A key is used to uniquely identify an object within a database. It has values of type float, date, string, and array. It's very similar to the primary key columns in a relational database table. It also imposes an ascending sort order on the associated objects.

- **Value:** A value is a JavaScript object that is associated with a given key. Every record is associated with a value. It can be a complex object that has no schematization requirements.

- **Key path:** A key path is a string that defines a way to extract a key from a value. A key path is said to be valid when either it is has an empty string, or multiple JavaScript elements separated by periods.

- **Index:** An index is an alternative method to retrieve records in an object store rather than using a key. It's a specialized form of storage that supports searching objects in the store by attribute values.

- **Transaction:** A transaction is used to read or write data into the database. Transactions are always operated in one of the three modes: read-only, readwrite, or versionchange.

- **Request:** A request is used to perform read or a write operation on a database. It's analogous to a SQL statement.

- **Key range:** The key range is used to retrieve records from object stores and indexes.

- **Cursor:** A cursor is a brief mechanism used to iterate over multiple records in a database. It is bidirectional, and can skip duplicate records in a nonunique index.

Even though IndexedDB concepts looks similar to relational database management elements, one key difference is that there is no relational semantics, which means we cannot use joins. With this introduction we learn how to use IndexedDB as data storage by creating My Collections, a movie collection and inventory Windows Store app using HTML5 and JavaScript.

Creating the My Collections App

Many movie buffs have a huge collection of DVD and Blu-ray movies that they share with their friends and family. Sometimes keeping track of all these movies becomes a tedious process. To manage and keep track of the collection, here we build a simple app that helps to add and track movies within the collection. This app has three HTML pages.

- **Start page:** This page displays the list of movies in the collection.

- **Search page:** The Search page is invoked from the Windows 8 Search charm. This page displays the matching results from the collections and it also searches for matching results on one of the most popular movie review and information sites, www.Rottentomatoes.com, and displays the results.

- **Add/Edit page:** This page can be accessed from the Start page or from the search result page. It displays the movie details and provides an option to add it to one's collection. We can also edit the movie information and its available status (see Figure 4-1).

Figure 4-1. *My Collection Windows 8 app displays the movies in the collection*

Getting Started

To start with, let's create a new Windows Store Blank App (JavaScript) project and name it MyCollections (see Figure 4-2). We add two new pages to the project: `Home.html` and `Details.html`.

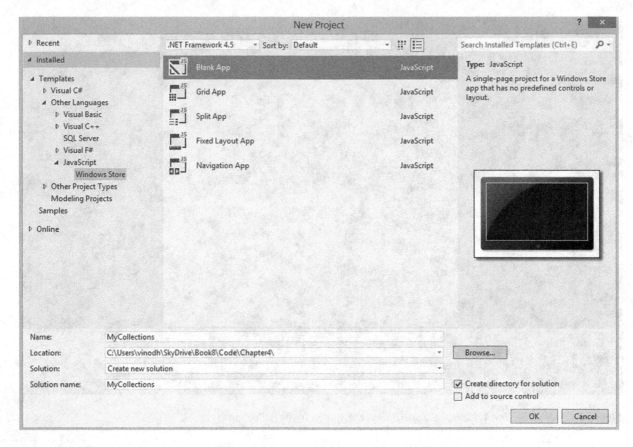

Figure 4-2. *Visual Studio templates for JavaScript creates a Blank application with HTML, CSS, and JavaScript files*

We also add a Search Contract and name it `searchResults.html` as shown in Figure 4-3. As mentioned before, this is the page that will be involved when we search for movies from the Windows 8 Search charm.

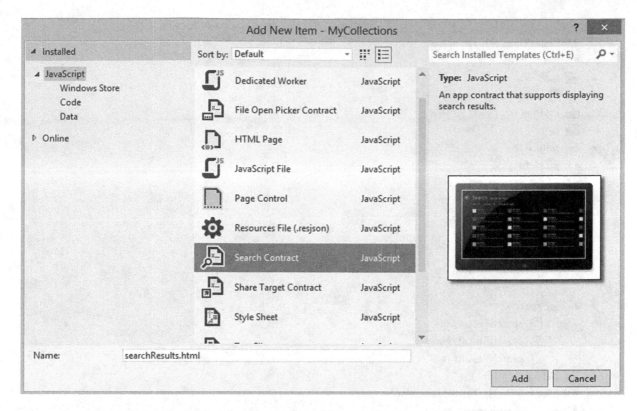

Figure 4-3. *Adding support for the Search contract by using the Visual Studio template*

Finally we add a JavaScript file, `Movie.js`. This is the main file and it contains the functionality that drives the entire application.

With all the files in place and after you move some files to restructure the project for better management, the final MyCollections Windows 8 app project will look like the one shown in Figure 4-4.

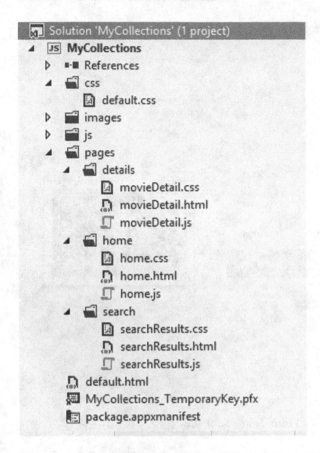

Figure 4-4. *Visual Studio Solution Explorer displaying the MyCollections project structure*

Defining the Schema

The MyCollections IndexedDB database CollectionDB will have only one object store called Movies. The Movies object store will have six key paths, as follows.

- **Id:** Autoincrement acts like a primary key.
- **Title:** Stores the title of the movie.
- **Year:** Stores the release year of the movie.
- **Thumbnail:** Stores the Rotten tomatoes.com thumbnail link.
- **poster:** Stores the Rotten tomatoes.com poster link.
- **Status:** Current status of the movie like Available, Borrowed, Lent Out.

Creating the Database

We start the coding by creating the CollectionDB database as soon as the application starts at the activated event in default.js by calling a function createDB as shown in Listing 4-1.

Listing 4-1. createDB Function Is Called Inside the Activated Event

```
app.addEventListener("activated", function (args) {
    if (args.detail.kind === activation.ActivationKind.launch) {
        if (args.detail.previousExecutionState !== activation.ApplicationExecutionState.terminated) {
            // TODO: This application has been newly launched. Initialize
            // your application here.
        } else {
            // TODO: This application has been reactivated from suspension.
            // Restore application state here.
        }

        if (app.sessionState.history) {
            nav.history = app.sessionState.history;
        }
        args.setPromise(WinJS.UI.processAll().then(function () {
            if (nav.location) {
                nav.history.current.initialPlaceholder = true;
                return nav.navigate(nav.location, nav.state);
            } else {
                return nav.navigate(Application.navigator.home);
            }
        }));
        //creating the indexeddb database
        createDB();
    }
});
```

The CreateDB function creates the request to open the databases. If it doesn't exist, create it and it will immediately upgrade to version 1. At any given time with in the app only a single version of a database can exist. After it's created, a database and its object stores can only be changed through a specialized type of transaction mode known as a *versionchange*. To change a database after its creation, we must open the database with a higher version number, and that is the reason to change it to version 1. This action causes the upgradeneeded event to fire and the code to create the Movies object store in onupgradeneeded.

The Movies object store is created using the IndexedDB `createObjectStore` function. This function gets a name for the object store and sets the key path and key generator. This object store also has indexes that hold additional information. These indexes are created using the `createIndex` function. Success callback is invoked on opening the database. Here we set the database context to an attribute, as shown in Listing 4-2.

Listing 4-2. Database and Table Are Created in the createDB Function

```
function createDB() {
    // Create the request to open the database, named CollectionDB. If it doesn't exist,
create it and immediately
    // upgrade to version 1.
    var dbRequest = window.indexedDB.open("CollectionDB", 1);
    dbRequest.onupgradeneeded = function (e) {
        MyCollection.db = e.target.result;
        var txn = e.target.transaction;
        var movieTable = MyCollection.db.createObjectStore(
```

```
                                        "Movies"
                                        ,{
                                            keyPath: "id"
                                            , autoIncrement: true
                                        });
        movieTable.createIndex("title"
            , "title"
            , { unique: false });
        movieTable.createIndex("year"
            , "year"
            , { unique: false });
        movieTable.createIndex("image"
            , "image"
            , { unique: false });
        movieTable.createIndex("poster"
            , "poster"
            , { unique: false });
        movieTable.createIndex("status"
            , "status"
            , { unique: false });
        txn.onerror = function () {
            WinJS.log && WinJS.log("Database creation failed"
                , "Log"
                , "Status");
        };
        txn.oncomplete = function () {
            WinJS.log && WinJS.log("Database table created"
                , "Log"
                , "Status");
        };
    };
    dbRequest.onsuccess = function (e) {
        MyCollection.db = e.target.result;
    };
}
```

Creating the Movie Object in Windows 8 JavaScript

Movie.js contains a self-executing anonymous function where objects are created inside the MyCollections namespace. This object contains a property, Movie.

The Movie object is defined as a WinJS.Class using the WinJS.Class.define() method. As can be seen in Listing 4-3, this method takes various parameters that are assigned to the corresponding properties of the Movie class. The Movie class has five properties that match the IndexedDB objectstore Movie and one other propety, IsInCollection, that is used to determine whether the object is already in the collection.

Listing 4-3. Defining Movie Object in Movie.js

```
WinJS.Namespace.define("MyCollection", {
        Movie: WinJS.Class.define(
            function () {
                this.title = "";
                this.year = 0;
                this.image = "";
                this.isInCollection = false;
                this.status = "";
                this.poster = "";
                this.id = 0;
            },
            {
                getTitle: function () { return this.title; },
                setTitle: function (newValue) { this.title = newValue; },

                getImage: function () { return this.image; },
                setImage: function (newValue) { this.image = newValue; },

                getIsInCollection: function () { return this.isInCollection; },
                setIsInCollection: function (newValue) { this.isInCollection = newValue; },

                getYear: function () { return this.year; },
                setYear: function (newValue) {
                    this.year = newValue;
                },

                getPoster: function () { return this.poster; },
                setPoster: function (newValue) { this.poster = newValue; },

                getStatus: function () { return this.status; },
                setStatus: function (newValue) { this.status = newValue; },

                getID: function () { return this.id; },
                setID: function (newValue) {
                    this.id = newValue;
                },
            },
        },
```

The Movie object also has CRUD functions that we use to add, delete, and update data to IndexedDB. Let's look at each one of them in detail.

Saving the Movie Object

To add a movie to the movie collection, we call the saveMovie function. This function first checks to see if the movie details already exist in the IndexedDB Movie objectStore. If this information is already present, it will update the existing row; otherwise, it will add a new row to the IndexedDB Movie objectStore. To do this, first create a new transaction involving the Movie objectStore as shown in the Listing 4-4 and set the mode to readWrite and will get a handle of the Movie object store. Now that we have access to the objectstore, we can just pass a **JSON** object to either add or put command depending on the value of the ID parameter.

Listing 4-4. Saving Movie Object to IndexedDB Using the saveMovie Function

```
saveMovie: function (id, title, year, image, poster, status ) {
                var txn = MyCollection.db.transaction(["Movies"], "readwrite");
                var movieTable = txn.objectStore("Movies");
                var saveRequest;
                if (id > 0)
                    saveRequest = movieTable.put(
                    {
                        id: id,
                        title: title,
                        year: year,
                        image: image,
                        poster: poster,
                        status: status
                    });
                else {
                    saveRequest = movieTable.add(
                    {
                        title: title,
                        year: year,
                        image: image,
                        poster: poster,
                        status: status
                    });

                }

                saveRequest.onsuccess = function () {
                    WinJS.log && WinJS.log("Movie Updated: " + this + ".", "Log", "Status");
                };
                saveRequest.onerror = function () {
                    WinJS && WinJS.log("Failed to update Movie: " + this + ".", "Log", "error");
                };
            }
```

■ **Note**   In IndexedDB, `objectStore.add()` is used to add an object to the store and `objectStore.put()` is used to update an object.

Deleting the Movie Object

The `deleteMovie` function deletes a row from the Movie `objectStore`. Just like `saveMovie`, we start a transaction, reference the object store that contains the Movie object, and issue a delete command with the unique ID of our object (see Listing 4-5).

Listing 4-5. Deleting Movie Object From IndexedDB Using the deleteMovie Function

```
deleteMovie: function ( id ) {
                var txn = MyCollection.db.transaction(["Movies"], "readwrite");
                var movieTable = txn.objectStore("Movies");
                var deleteRequest = movieTable.delete(id)
                deleteRequest.onsuccess = function () {
                    WinJS.log && WinJS.log("Movie Deleted: " + this + ".", "Log", "Status");
                };
                deleteRequest.onerror = function () {
                    WinJS && WinJS.log("Failed to delete Movie: " + this + ".", "Log", "error");
                };
        }
```

Retrieving Movie Details

Movie details are retrieved either from the database that is part of the user's collection or from the Rotten Tomatoes database using the REST API. These two actions are perfomaed within the JavaScript functions loadFromDB and loadSearchResult. These functions in turn call the buildMovie function to build a Movie object. The buildMovie function checks the model passed in as a parameter, creates a new Movie object, tries to set its values from the model passed, and returns a bondable object with the help of the WinJS.Binding.as() method (see Listing 4-6).

Listing 4-6. buildMovie Function Creates a Movie Object From the Model

```
buildMovie: function (model) {
                var newMovie = new MyCollection.Movie();
                if (model.hasOwnProperty("title")) {
                    newMovie.setTitle(model.title);
                }
                if (model.hasOwnProperty("year")) {
                    newMovie.setYear(model.year);
                }
                if (model.hasOwnProperty("movieId")) {
                    newMovie.setID(model.id);
                    newMovie.setIsInCollection(true);
                }
                if (model.hasOwnProperty("status")) {
                    newMovie.setStatus(model.status);
                }
                if (model.hasOwnProperty("thumbnail")) {
                    newMovie.setImage(model.thumbnail);
                }
                if (model.hasOwnProperty("poster")) {
                    newMovie.setPoster(model.poster);
                }
                //only if the request from rottentomatoes
                if (model.hasOwnProperty("posters")) {
                    newMovie.setImage(model.posters.thumbnail);
                    newMovie.setPoster(model.posters.detailed);
                }
                return new WinJS.Binding.as(newMovie);
        }
```

The loadFromDB function, shown in Listing 4-7, takes string as a parameter and returns an array of Movie objects that matches with the title of the movie stores in the IndexedDB Movie objectStore. Like the saveMovie and deleteMovie methods, we first create a new transaction involving the Movie objectStore and set the mode to read-only, as only the data is retrieved here. Then we open a cursor to iterate over records in the Movie object store. The results are passed through to the success callback on the cursor, where we render the result. The callback is fired only once per result, and will call continue to keep iterating across the data on the result object. A JSON object is constructed out of the result and is passed to the buildMovie function to return a WinJS.Binding object that is finally added to the array.

Listing 4-7. Searches the indexedDB and fill the results to an array

```
loadFromDB: function (searchText) {
                var collection = new Array();
                var txn = MyCollection.db.transaction(["Movies"], "readonly");
                var movieCursorRequest = txn.objectStore("Movies").openCursor();
                movieCursorRequest.onsuccess = function (e) {
                    var cursor = e.target.result;
                    if (cursor) {
                        var data = cursor.value;
                        if (data.title.indexOf(searchText) > -1) {

                            var movieData = {
                                movieId: data.id
                                            , title: data.title
                                            , year: data.year
                                            , thumbnail: data.image
                                            , poster: data.poster
                                            , status: data.status
                            };

                            var newMovie = MyCollection.Movie.buildMovie(movieData);
                            collection.push(newMovie);
                        }
                        cursor.continue();
                    }
                };
                return collection;
        }
```

Like loadFromDB, the loadSearchResult function shown in Listing 4-8 takes search text as a parameter and returns an array of Movie objects. This function performs two actions. First it queries the Rotten Tomatoes movie database using a public API and loads the result to an array. Next it calls loadFromDB and adds the matching movie object to the existing array. Now the array has objects that match the search result from the IndexedDB Movie object store and also from the Rotten Tomatoes search results.

Listing 4-8. Search the Rotten Tomatoes Database and Add the Results to an Array

```
loadSearchResult: function (searchText) {
                var searchUrl =
"http://api.rottentomatoes.com/api/public/v1.0/movies.json?apikey=XXXXXXXXXXXXf8&page_limit=10&q="
+ searchText;
```

```
            return WinJS.xhr({ url: searchUrl }).then(
                function (result) {
                    var result = window.JSON.parse(result.responseText).movies;
                    var collection = new Array();
                    if (result) {
                        result.forEach(function (newObject) {
                            var newMovie =
MyCollection.Movie.buildMovieFromRottentomatoes(newObject);
                            collection.push(newMovie);
                        });
                        var txn = MyCollection.db.transaction(["Movies"], "readonly");
                        var movieCursorRequest = txn.objectStore("Movies").openCursor();
                        movieCursorRequest.onsuccess = function (e) {
                            var cursor = e.target.result;
                            if (cursor) {
                                var data = cursor.value;
                                if (data.title.indexOf(searchText) > -1) {

                                    var movieData = {
                                        movieId: data.id
                                      , title: data.title
                                      , year: data.year
                                      , thumbnail: data.image
                                      , poster: data.poster
                                      , status: data.status
                                    };
                                    var newMovie =
MyCollection.Movie.buildMovie(movieData);
                                    collection.push(newMovie);
                                }
                                cursor.continue();
                            }
                        };
                    }
                    return collection;
                });
        }
```

Designing the App Start Page

Home.html is the start page of this app (see Figure 4-1). It displays the Movies in our IndexedDB collection in a grid layout using the WinJS.UI.ListView element by binding to a Movies Collection in Home.js. We also define an item template that contains the markup to display the details of each movie (see Listing 4-9).

Listing 4-9. Home.html Page Includes a ListView With Item Template to Display Movie Details

```
<!DOCTYPE html>
<html>
<head>
    <meta charset="utf-8" />
    <title>homePage</title>
    <!-- WinJS references -->
```

```html
    <link href="//Microsoft.WinJS.1.0/css/ui-dark.css" rel="stylesheet" />
    <script src="//Microsoft.WinJS.1.0/js/base.js"></script>
    <script src="//Microsoft.WinJS.1.0/js/ui.js"></script>

    <link href="/css/default.css" rel="stylesheet" />
    <link href="/pages/home/home.css" rel="stylesheet" />
    <script src="/pages/home/home.js"></script>
</head>
<body>
    <!-- The content that will be loaded and displayed. -->
    <div id="dbItemtemplate"
        class="itemtemplate"
        data-win-control="WinJS.Binding.Template">
      <div class="item">
          <img
              class="item-image"
              src="#"
              data-win-bind="src: image; alt: title" />
          <div class="item-content">
              <h3
                  class="item-title win-type-x-small win-type-ellipsis"
                  data-win-bind="innerHTML: title"></h3>
              <h4
                  class="item-subtitle win-type-x-small win-type-ellipsis"
                  data-win-bind="innerHTML: year"></h4>
              <h4
                  class="item-subtitle win-type-x-small win-type-ellipsis"
                  data-win-bind="innerHTML: status"></h4>
          </div>
      </div>
    </div>

    <div class="fragment homepage">
        <header
            aria-label="Header content"
            role="banner">
            <button
                class="win-backbutton"
                aria-label="Back"
                disabled type="button"></button>
            <h1 class="titlearea win-type-ellipsis">
                <span class="pagetitle">My Collections!</span>
            </h1>
        </header>

        <section aria-label="Main content" role="main">
            <div
                id="listView"
                class="resultslist win-selectionstylefilled"
                aria-label="Movies in my collection"
```

```
                data-win-control="WinJS.UI.ListView"
                data-win-options="{
                itemTemplate: select('#dbItemtemplate'),
                }">

            }"></div>
        </section>
    </div>
</body>
</html>
```

Home.js

Home.js is where we write additional code that provides interactivity for our home.html page. This script file only implements the ready function. This function is called at the time of the page load. Inside this function we iterate through the IndexedDB Movies object store and store it into an array and will bind that array to the ListView, as shown in Listing 4-10. This page also has an itemInvoked function that is attached to the ListView and is called when an item is selected from the ListView. Once called, this function navigates the user to the MovieDetail.html (see Listing 4-11) using the WinJS.Navigation.navigate function. This function takes the detail page location and selected movie object as parameters.

Listing 4-10. Movies in the Collection Are Bound to the ListView Element

```
(function () {
    "use strict";

    WinJS.UI.Pages.define("/pages/home/home.html", {
        // This function is called whenever a user navigates to this page. It
        // populates the page elements with the app's data.
        ready: function (element, options) {
            var listView = element.querySelector(".resultslist").winControl;
            var tapBehavior = listView.tapBehavior;
            listView.tapBehavior = tapBehavior;
            listView.oniteminvoked = this._itemInvoked;
            var collection = new Array();
            var txn = MyCollection.db.transaction(["Movies"], "readonly");
            var movieCursorRequest = txn.objectStore("Movies").openCursor();
            movieCursorRequest.onsuccess = function (e) {
                var cursor = e.target.result;
                if (cursor) {
                    var data = cursor.value;
                    var movieData = {
                                    movieId: data.id
                                    , title: data.title
                                    , year: data.year
                                    , thumbnail: data.image
                                    , poster: data.poster
                                    , status: data.status
                    };
```

```
                var newMovie = MyCollection.Movie.buildMovie(movieData);
                collection.push(newMovie);
                cursor.continue();

            }
            else {
                listView.itemDataSource = new WinJS.Binding.List(collection).dataSource;

            }
        }
    },
    _itemInvoked: function (args) {
        args.detail.itemPromise.done(function itemInvoked(item) {
            WinJS.Navigation.navigate("/pages/details/movieDetail.html"
            , { movieDetail: item.data });
        });
    },

});

})();
```

Designing the Movie Detail Page

The MovieDetail.html page is redirected either from the home or search result page and displays the details of the selected movies from its previous page. MovieDetail.html also provides an option to add or edit the movie object. The markup of this page contains an HTML element that is bound to the properties of the Movie object using the WinJS data-win-bind property. This page also has two app bar buttons that allow us to save or delete the Movie object, as shown in Figure 4-5.

Listing 4-11. MovieDetail.html With HTML Elements to Display Selected Movie Details

```
<!DOCTYPE html>
<html>
<head>
    <meta charset="utf-8" />
    <title>movieDetail</title>

    <!-- WinJS references -->
    <link href="//Microsoft.WinJS.1.0/css/ui-dark.css" rel="stylesheet" />
    <script src="//Microsoft.WinJS.1.0/js/base.js"></script>
    <script src="//Microsoft.WinJS.1.0/js/ui.js"></script>
    <link href="/pages/details/movieDetail.css" rel="stylesheet" />
    <script src="/pages/details/movieDetail.js"></script>
</head>
<body>
    <div class="movieDetail fragment">
        <header
            aria-label="Header content"
            role="banner">
```

```
    <button
        class="win-backbutton"
        aria-label="Back"
        disabled
        type="button" />
    <h1
        class="titlearea win-type-ellipsis">
        <span class="pagetitle">My Collection</span>
    </h1>
</header>
<section
    aria-label="Main content"
    role="main">
    <div
        id="divDetail"
        class="detailView">
        <h3 id="title">Edit Movie</h3>
        <br />
        <!--Movie Image-->
        <img
            src="#"
            data-win-bind="src: poster; alt: title" />
        <!--Movie Title-->
        <label>Title</label>
        <input
            id="txtTitle"
            type="text"
            data-win-bind="value: title Binding.Mode.twoway" />
        <br>
        <!--Movie Release Year-->
        <label>Year</label>
        <input
            id="txtYear"
            type="text"
            data-win-bind="value: year Binding.Mode.twoway" />
        <br>
        <!--Movie Status-->
        <label>Status</label>
        <select
            id="status"
            data-win-bind="selected: status; value: status Binding.Mode.twoway">
            <option value="Avaliable">Avaliable</option>
            <option value="Lend Out">Lend Out</option>
            <option value="Rented">Borrowed</option>
        </select>
        <br />
    </div>
</section>
</div>
```

```
<!--App bar-->
<div
    data-win-control="WinJS.UI.AppBar"
    class="appBar"
    id="appBar">
    <!--Save Movie Button-->
    <button
        data-win-control="WinJS.UI.AppBarCommand"
        data-win-options="{id:'saveButton', label:'Save', icon:'save',section:'global'}"/>
    <!--Delete Movie Button-->
    <button
        data-win-control="WinJS.UI.AppBarCommand"
        data-win-options="{id:'deleteButton', label:'Delete', icon:'delete',section:'global'}"/>
</div>
</body>
</html>
```

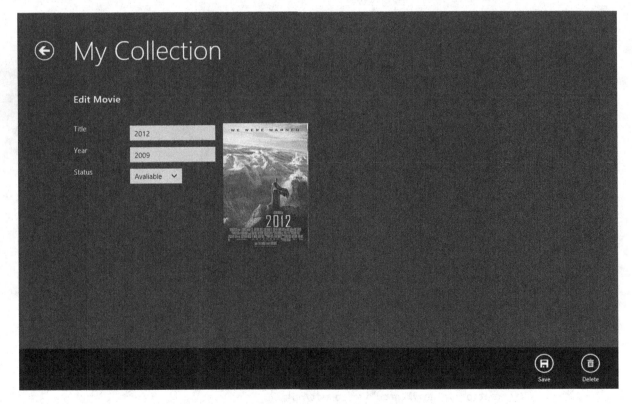

Figure 4-5. *The My Collections app displaying movie details along with the app bar for saving and deleting*

MovieDetail.js

Here we bind the Movie object that is passed on to this page to the div element inside the page ready function. This function, shown in Listing 4-12, also sets the event handler for the save and delete button which in turn calls the saveMovie (see Listing 4-4) and deleteMovie (see Listing 4-5) functions in Movie.js.

Listing 4-12. Binds the Movie Object to the div Element for Adding or Deleting

```
WinJS.UI.Pages.define("/pages/details/movieDetail.html", {
    // This function is called whenever a user navigates to this page. It
    // populates the page elements with the app's data.

    ready: function (element, options) {
        // TODO: Initialize the page here.
        movieDetail = options.movieDetail;
        var src = WinJS.Binding.as(movieDetail);
        var form = document.getElementById("divDetail");
        WinJS.Binding.processAll(form, src);
        document.getElementById("saveButton")
            .addEventListener("click", doClickSave, false);
        document.getElementById("deleteButton")
            .addEventListener("click", doClickDelete, false);

        if (movieDetail.fromSearch == true) {
            document.getElementById("deleteButton").disabled = true;
            document.getElementById("title").innerText = "Add to collection";
        }
    }
});

function doClickSave() {
    MyCollection.Movie.saveMovie(movieDetail.id, movieDetail.title, movieDetail.year,
movieDetail.image, movieDetail.poster, movieDetail.status);
    WinJS.Navigation.back();
}

function doClickDelete() {
    MyCollection.Movie.deleteMovie(movieDetail.id);
    WinJS.Navigation.back();
}
```

Even though we bound the elements to the Movie object properties, the changes we make to the element are not reflected in the Movie object as WinJS doesn't support two-way binding, but adding this functionality is quite easy thanks to the WinJS.Binding.initializer function. This function gets involved when binding is created. WinJS.Binding.initializer give access to both source and target objects and their properties, which allows them to subscribe to the target element's events and push data to the source object, as shown in Listing 4-13.

Listing 4-13. Defining Two-Way Binding Using WinJS.Binding.initializer

```
WinJS.Namespace.define("Binding.Mode", {
    twoway: WinJS.Binding.initializer(function (source, sourceProps, dest, destProps) {
        WinJS.Binding.defaultBind(source, sourceProps, dest, destProps);
        dest.onchange = function () {
```

```
            var d = dest[destProps[0]];
            var s = source[sourceProps[0]];
            if (s !== d) source[sourceProps[0]] = d;
        }
    })
});
```

Once defined, we just need to apply the initializer to binding like the one shown in Listing 4-14.

Listing 4-14. Enabling Two-Way Binding in the HTML Element

```
<input type="text" data-win-bind="value: title Binding.Mode.twoway" />
```

Searching for Movies

The searchResults.html page is invoked when we do the app-level search using the Search charm. This page displays the matching results in a ListView element (see Listing 4-15). The result is shown in Figure 4-6. Displaying movie information in ListView is very similar to Home.html with one exception: Here we use two item templates, one for displaying movie details from the Rotten Tomatoes database and another from the IndexedDB that is dynamically switched using the JavaScript code in searchResult.js as shown in Listing 4-16.

Listing 4-15. Search Page Displays Results in a ListView When Invoked From Search Charm

```
<!DOCTYPE html>
<html>
<head>
    <meta charset="utf-8" />
    <meta name="ms-design-extensionType" content="Search" />
    <title>Search Contract</title>

    <!-- WinJS references -->
    <link href="//Microsoft.WinJS.1.0/css/ui-dark.css" rel="stylesheet" />
    <script src="//Microsoft.WinJS.1.0/js/base.js"></script>
    <script src="//Microsoft.WinJS.1.0/js/ui.js"></script>

    <link href="/css/default.css" rel="stylesheet" />
    <link href="/pages/search/searchResults.css" rel="stylesheet" />
    <script src="/js/data.js"></script>
</head>
<body>
    <!-- This template is used to display each item in the ListView declared
         below. -->
    <!--ItemTemplate to display search from Rotten Tomatoes database -->
    <div
        id="onlineItemtemplate"
        class="itemtemplate"
        data-win-control="WinJS.Binding.Template">
        <div class="item">
            <img
                class="item-image"
                src="#" data-win-bind="src: image; alt: title" />
```

```
            <div class="item-content">
                <h3
                    class="item-title win-type-x-small win-type-ellipsis"
                    data-win-bind="innerHTML: title searchResults.title" />
                <h4
                    class="item-subtitle win-type-x-small win-type-ellipsis"
                    data-win-bind="innerHTML: year searchResults.text" />
            </div>
        </div>
    </div>
    <!--ItemTemplate to display search from IndexedDB -->
    <div id="dbItemtemplate"
        class="itemtemplate"
        data-win-control="WinJS.Binding.Template">
        <div class="item">
            <img
                class="item-image"
                src="#" data-win-bind="src: poster; alt: title" />
            <div class="item-content">
                <h3
                    class="item-title win-type-x-small win-type-ellipsis"
                    data-win-bind="innerHTML: title searchResults.title" />
                <h4
                    class="item-subtitle win-type-x-small win-type-ellipsis"
                    data-win-bind="innerHTML: year searchResults.text" />
                <h4
                    class="item-subtitle win-type-x-small win-type-ellipsis"
                    data-win-bind="innerHTML: status searchResults.text" />
            </div>
        </div>
    </div>

    <!-- The content that will be loaded and displayed. -->
    <div class="searchResults fragment">
        <!--Page Header-->
        <header
            aria-label="Header content"
            role="banner">
            <button
                class="win-backbutton"
                aria-label="Back"
                disabled
                type="button" />
            <div class="titlearea">
                <h1 class="pagetitle win-type-ellipsis" />
                <h2 class="pagesubtitle win-type-ellipsis" />
            </div>
        </header>
        <section
            aria-label="Main content"
            role="main">
```

```
        <div
            class="resultsmessage win-type-x-large">
            No results match your search.
        </div>
        <!--Filter section-->
        <div class="filterarea">
            <ul class="filterbar"></ul>
            <select class="filterselect" />
        </div>
        <!--ListView-->
        <div
            id="searchListView"
            class="resultslist win-selectionstylefilled"
            aria-label="Search results"
            data-win-control="WinJS.UI.ListView" />
    </section>
  </div>
</body>
</html>
```

Figure 4-6. *My Collections app displaying search results*

searchResult.js

The `searchResult.js` page does basically three things: gets the result data and binds it to the `ListView`, dynamically switches the template, and finally generates filters to the page so the user can filter the result by online and in collection.

Dynamic Template Change

Dynamic template change (see Listing 4-16) can be achieved by assigning the function `itemTemplateFunction` to the `ListLiew` `itemTemplate` property. This function returns a DOM element depending on the value of the `Movie` object `isInCollection` property.

Listing 4-16. Dynamically Switching the Template

```
ready: function (element, options) {

        var listView = element.querySelector(".resultslist").winControl;
        // listView.itemTemplate = element.querySelector(".itemtemplate");
        listView.oniteminvoked = this._itemInvoked;
        listView.itemTemplate = itemTemplateFunction;
        this._handleQuery(element, options);
        listView.element.focus();
    }

  function itemTemplateFunction(itemPromise) {
        return itemPromise.then(function (item) {
            var itemTemplate = document.getElementById("onlineItemtemplate");
            if (item.data.isInCollection) {
                itemTemplate = document.getElementById("dbItemtemplate");
            };

            var container = document.createElement("div");
            itemTemplate.winControl.render(item.data, container);
            return container;
        });
    }
```

Getting the Data

When we add the search contract page, Visual Studio includes the necessary code to fulfill the minimum requirements of the Search contract automatically. There are two functions in `searchResults.js` that are of interest to us, `_handleQuery` and `_searchData` (see Listing 4-17). The `_handleQuery` in turn calls the function `_searchData`. In the `_searchData` function we populate a `WinJS.Binding.List` with the search data by calling the methods `loadFromDB` and `loadSearchResult`. Apart from these two functions, we also call `_generateFilters` and the `_populateFilterBar` functions.

Listing 4-17. Handling Search Query and Loading the Result in an Array

```
_handleQuery: function (element, args) {
  var originalResults;
  this._lastSearch = args.queryText;
  WinJS.Namespace.define("searchResults"
  , {
      markText: WinJS.Binding.converter(this._markText.bind(this))
    });
  this._initializeLayout(element.querySelector(".resultslist").winControl
    , Windows.UI.ViewManagement.ApplicationView.value);
  this._generateFilters();
  this._searchData(args.queryText, element, this);
},
// This function populates a WinJS.Binding.List with search results for the
// provided query.
_searchData: function (queryText, element, object) {
  var originalResults;
  originalResults = MyCollection.Movie.loadFromDB(queryText);
  MyCollection.Movie.loadSearchResult(queryText).done(
  function (result) {
    for (var i = 0; i < result.length; i++)
    {
        originalResults.push(result[i]);
    }
    originalResults = new WinJS.Binding.List(originalResults);
        if (originalResults.length === 0) {
            document.querySelector('.filterarea').style.display = "none";
        } else {
            document.querySelector('.resultsmessage').style.display = "none";
        }

        object._populateFilterBar(element, originalResults);
        object._applyFilter(object._filters[0], originalResults);
        return originalResults;
    });
  }
});
```

Generating Filters

The filters are created in the _generateFilters function. Depending on the value of the isInCollection property, we add two filters for the search result, as shown in Listing 4-18: one to showcase the Rotten Tomatoes matches and the other to show the matches from the Indexed database.

Listing 4-18. Creating Filters for the Search Result

```
generateFilters: function () {
  this._filters = [];
  this._filters.push(
```

```
    {
        results: null
      , text: "All"
      , predicate: function (item) {
          return true;
      }
});
this._filters.push(
    {
        results: null
      , text: "Online"
      , predicate: function (item) {
          return item.isInCollection === true;
      }
});
this._filters.push(
    {
        results: null
      , text: "In My Collection"
      , predicate: function (item) {
          return item.isInCollection !== true;
      }
});
}
```

Now with all the codes in place, when we run the My Collections app, at first it shows an empty Start screen, but we can search for movies using the Search charm and add them to our movie collection. Once they are added, the Start screen will look like the one shown in Figure 4-1.

Ideas for Improvement

The My Collections app can be worked on and improved to make it a fully functional inventory app. Here are some of the features that can be added:

- You could add an option to search for books or games using third-party APIs like `http://www.thegamesdb.net/` and Google Books.

- Right now we can only add a movie to the collection by searching the Rotten Tomatoes database. You could provide and option to add ad hoc entries.

- A barcode scan option would allow users to enter movies by quickly scanning the barcodes on the movie cases.

- Back up your movie collection in SkyDrive or Dropbox.

- Add the capability for advanced search features and filters.

- You could categorize the items into books, movies, games, and so on.

Conclusion

In this chapter we learned to use IndexedDB as a local storage option by creating a Windows 8 JavaScript app. As we saw, the IndexedDB API is a simple but powerful option for storing data locally, even though it is a little bit different from the relational database.

There are also some IndexedDB wrappers like IDBWrapper (`https://github.com/jensarps/IDBWrapper`) that can be used to ease the use of IndexedDB. In the next chapter, we continue to explore local storage options by learning to use Jet API and Application Storage.

CHAPTER 5

Local Data Access I: JET API and Application Data

In the last chapter we learned to use IndexedDB as one of the local storage options. Continuing in this chapter, we learn few more local storage options, namely JET API and application storage by creating a Windows 8 Password Manager app using XAML/C#.

What Is ESENT/Jet API?

ESENT/JET API is an Indexed Sequential Access Method (ISAM) data storage technology from Microsoft. ESENT runtime has been a part of Windows since Windows 2000 and has been used in products like Microsoft Exchange, Active Directory, Windows Update, and Desktop Search. This application stores and retrieves data from tables using indexed or sequential cursor navigation.

Why to Use ESENT/Jet API

We can use ESENT for applications that need reliable, high-performance, low-overhead storage of structured or semistructured data. The ESENT engine can help with data needs ranging from something as simple as a hash table that is too large to store in memory to something more complex, such as an application with tables, columns, and indexes.

ESENT incorporates all the benefit on the ISAM data storage technique like the following:

- ACID transaction
- Snapshot isolation
- Concurrent access storage
- Cursor navigation
- Advanced indexing: Indexing over multivalued columns, sparse, and tuple
- Fixed, variable, and tagged columns
- Data integrity and consistency
- Column size ranging from 1 bit to 2 GB

Building Password Manager App

Password Manager App helps to store bank information, financial information, health information, website logins, online subscriptions, credit cards, insurance, and everything else one needs to keep private in a single location for easy access.

Setting Up the Development Environment

To start, we first create a new Windows Store Blank App (XAML) project and name it *PasswordManager*. This app will have two XAML pages. MainPage.xaml is the start page and will list all the stored password information in the database. PasswordDetail.xaml is used for either adding, deleting, or updating passwords.

Creating a Database

We will create a database, _PasswordDB that contains two tables via Categories and Passwords. We will add two POCO classes, Category (see Listing 5-1) and Password, to the project's Models folder that will represent the table and the structure of these two classes will mimic the columns of the tables.

Category is a lookup table that we use to categorize the passwords into Bank, Insurance, Website, Subscription, and other categories.

Listing 5-1. Category POCO Class Representing Category Table

```
public class Category
{
    public int CategoryId { get; set; }
    public string CategoryName { get; set; }
}
```

The Password table holds the password information (see Listing 5-2).

Listing 5-2. Password Class Stores the Password Details

```
public class Password
{
    public Guid PasswordId { get; set; }
    public string Title { get; set; }
    public string UserName { get; set; }
    public string Passcode { get; set; }
    public string WebSite { get; set; }
    public string Key { get; set; }
    public int CategoryId { get; set; }
    public string Note { get; set; }
}
```

To make things interesting we will use both the ESENT database and application data storage as storage options for this app. Application data storage is place where Windows 8 apps can store data into local, temp, and roaming folders using classes under the Windows.Storage namespace.We learn more about Windows 8 application data storage later in this chapter.

For using two different storage options within a single app we create an interface IDataRespository (see Listing 5-1) and two separate classes, JetDataRepository and ApplicationDataRepository, that explicitly implement the methods of the IDataRespository interface. The IDataRespository interface has various methods that allow us to create, instantiate a database, and put, get and delete data, as shown in Listing 5-3.

Listing 5-3. Defining the Interface to Create, Modify, Read, Get, and Delete Data

```
public interface IDataRepository
{
    void CreateInstance();
    void AddCategory(Category cat);
    void DeletePassword(Guid id);
    void SavePassword(Password pwd, bool isnew);
    List<Category> GetCategories();
    List<Password> GetAllPasswords();
}
```

To create, add, modify, and delete data with in ESENT and application data, we add the references of the following DLLs to the project under references.

- ManagedEsent

- WinRT Filebased Database

The ESENT database engine is native to Windows, so to use that within the managed enviroment we need to create a managed ESENT interop layer. Instead of writing one, we will be using an exisitng one, ManagedEsent. ManagedEsent provides managed access to ESENT, the embeddable database engine native to Windows. ManagedEsent uses the esent.dll that is part of Microsoft Windows so there are no extra unmanaged binaries to download and install.

Similarly, instead of building a database from scratch that serializes objects and stores them in application storage, we will use an existing one called WinRT File Based Database available in NuGet by referencing it within our project. WinRT File Based Database includes a simple, yet effective API that allows to create tables based on classes. Each database consists of any number of tables. All operations are asynchronous to support Windows 8 style operations on the file system. It also supports horizontal partitioning of tables to provide for smaller files and faster operations.

The references of these two DLLs are added from NuGet packages as shown in Figure 5-1.

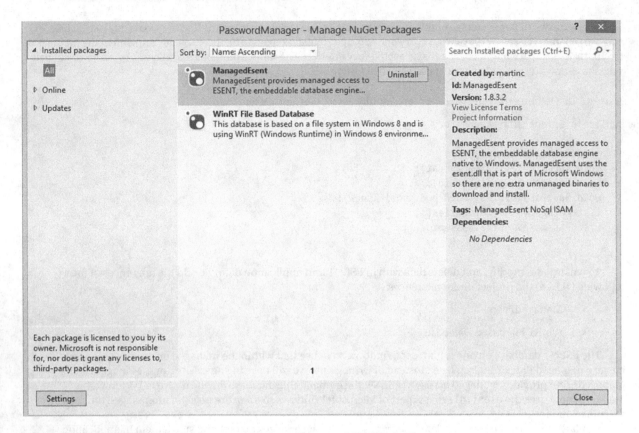

Figure 5-1. Using NuGet to add references to ManagedEsent and WinRT database

With all the files in place, our Password Manager App solution explorer will look like the one shown in Figure 5-2. Now we will look into the classes JetDataRepository and ApplicationDataRepository that implement the IDataRepository interface.

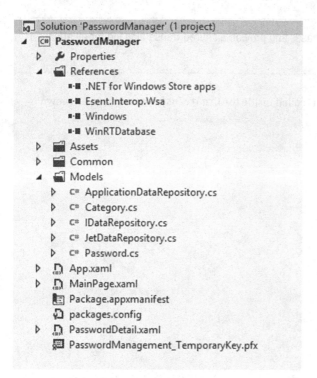

Figure 5-2. *Password Manager Windows 8 App project structure*

Creating ESENT Data Repository

JetDataRepository implements IDataRepository and is used to store data into the ESENT database. The CreateInstance method is used to create an instance of the ESENT database (see Listing 5-4). In this method we build the database file path and then pass the path to the Instance class which is part of the ManagedEsent API. The Instance class wraps a JET_INSTANCE along with JetInit and JetTerm. This class inherits from SafeHandle to make sure that ESENT instances are always terminated.

Listing 5-4. Using CreateInstance to Create an ESENT Instance

```
public void CreateInstance()
{
    _instancePath = Path.Combine(ApplicationData.Current.LocalFolder.Path, DatabaseName);
    _databasePath = Path.Combine(_instancePath, "_Password.edb");
    _instance = new Instance(_databasePath);
    _instance.Parameters.CreatePathIfNotExist = true;
    _instance.Parameters.TempDirectory = Path.Combine(_instancePath, "temp");
    _instance.Parameters.SystemDirectory = Path.Combine(_instancePath, "system");
    _instance.Parameters.LogFileDirectory = Path.Combine(_instancePath, "logs");
    _instance.Parameters.Recovery = true;
    _instance.Parameters.CircularLog = true;
    _instance.Init();
    CreateDatabase();
}
```

■ **Note**   A single ESENT instance can include up to six databases and provide a shared transaction log for all attached databases.

Next we add another method, CreateDatabase, which is called inside the CreateInstance method, as shown in Listing 5-5.

Listing 5-5. Creating the ESENT Database and Tables

```
private  async void CreateDatabase()
{
    if (await IsFileExist(_databasePath))
        return;
    using (var session = new Session(_instance))
    {

        JET_DBID database;
        Api.JetCreateDatabase(session
            , _databasePath
            , null
            , out database
            , CreateDatabaseGrbit.None);

        // create database schema
        using (var transaction = new Transaction(session))
        {

            //Schema for Category Table
            JET_TABLEID categoryTableId;
            Api.JetCreateTable(session
                , database
                , "Categories" //table name
                , 1
                , 100
                , out categoryTableId);
            JET_COLUMNID categoryColumnid;

            //CategoryId column
            Api.JetAddColumn(session
                , categoryTableId
                , "CategoryId" //column name
                , new JET_COLUMNDEF
                {
                    cbMax = 16,
                    coltyp = JET_coltyp.IEEESingle,
                    grbit = ColumndefGrbit.ColumnFixed | ColumndefGrbit.ColumnNotNULL
                }
                , null
                , 0
                , out categoryColumnid);
```

```
//CategoryName column
Api.JetAddColumn(session
    , categoryTableId
    , "CategoryName" //column name
    ,  new JET_COLUMNDEF
    {
        coltyp = JET_coltyp.LongText,
        cp = JET_CP.Unicode,
        grbit = ColumndefGrbit.None
    }, null, 0, out categoryColumnid);

//Creating Index
var categoryindexDef = "+CategoryId\0\0";
Api.JetCreateIndex(session
    , categoryTableId
    , "CategoryId_index" //index name
    , CreateIndexGrbit.IndexPrimary
    , categoryindexDef
    , categoryindexDef.Length
    , 100);

//Schema for Password table
JET_TABLEID passwordTableid;
Api.JetCreateTable(session
    , database
    , "Passwords" //table name
    , 1
    , 100
    , out passwordTableid);

//creating columns for Password tables
JET_COLUMNID passwordColumnid;
Api.JetAddColumn(session
    , passwordTableid
    , "PasswordId" //column name
    , new JET_COLUMNDEF
    {
        cbMax = 16,
        coltyp = JET_coltyp.Binary,
        grbit = ColumndefGrbit.ColumnFixed | ColumndefGrbit.ColumnNotNULL
    }
    , null
    , 0
    , out passwordColumnid);

Api.JetAddColumn(session
    , passwordTableid
    , "Title" //column name
    , new JET_COLUMNDEF
```

```
            {
                coltyp = JET_coltyp.LongText,
                cp = JET_CP.Unicode,
                grbit = ColumndefGrbit.None
            }
            , null
            , 0
            , out passwordColumnid);

        Api.JetAddColumn(session
            , passwordTableid
            , "UserName" //column name
            , new JET_COLUMNDEF
            {
                coltyp = JET_coltyp.LongText,
                cp = JET_CP.Unicode,
                grbit = ColumndefGrbit.None
            }
            , null
            , 0
            , out passwordColumnid);

        Api.JetAddColumn(session
            , passwordTableid
            , "Passcode" //column name
            , new JET_COLUMNDEF
            {
                coltyp = JET_coltyp.LongText,
                cp = JET_CP.Unicode,
                grbit = ColumndefGrbit.None
            }
            , null
            , 0
            , out passwordColumnid);

        Api.JetAddColumn(session
            , passwordTableid
            , "WebSite" //column name
            ,  new JET_COLUMNDEF
            {
                coltyp = JET_coltyp.LongText,
                cp = JET_CP.Unicode,
                grbit = ColumndefGrbit.None
            }
            , null
            , 0
            , out passwordColumnid);

        Api.JetAddColumn(session
            , passwordTableid
            , "Key" //column name
            , new JET_COLUMNDEF
```

```
            {
                coltyp = JET_coltyp.LongText,
                cp = JET_CP.Unicode,
                grbit = ColumndefGrbit.None
            }
            , null
            , 0
            , out passwordColumnid);

        Api.JetAddColumn(session
            , passwordTableid
            , "CategoryId" //column name
            , new JET_COLUMNDEF
            {
                coltyp = JET_coltyp.IEEESingle,
                cp = JET_CP.Unicode,
                grbit = ColumndefGrbit.None
            }
            , null
            , 0
            , out passwordColumnid);

        Api.JetAddColumn(session
            , passwordTableid
            , "Note" //column name
            , new JET_COLUMNDEF
            {
                coltyp = JET_coltyp.LongText,
                cp = JET_CP.Unicode,
                grbit = ColumndefGrbit.None
            }
            , null
            , 0
            , out passwordColumnid);

        //creating index for Passwords table
        var indexDef = "+PasswordId\0\0";
        Api.JetCreateIndex(session
            , passwordTableid
            , "PasswordId_index" //index name
            , CreateIndexGrbit.IndexPrimary
            , indexDef
            , indexDef.Length
            , 100);

        transaction.Commit(CommitTransactionGrbit.None);
    }
    Api.JetCloseDatabase(session, database, CloseDatabaseGrbit.None);
    Api.JetDetachDatabase(session, _databasePath);
}
```

```
    //Add defult values to the database table
    CreateDefaultData();
}
```

Once the database and the tables are created we can populate the tables with default categories and some test password data, after which we call the CreateDefaultData method within CreateDatabase as shown in Listing 5-6.

Listing 5-6. Inserting Default Values to the Categories and Passwords Table

```
private void CreateDefaultData()
{
    //Adding categories
    AddCategory(new Category {
        CategoryId = 1
        , CategoryName = "Bank"
    });
    AddCategory(new Category {
        CategoryId = 2
        , CategoryName = "Web Site"
    });

    //Adding password
    SavePassword(new Password {
        PasswordId = Guid.NewGuid()
        , Title = "Capital One"
        , UserName = "vinodh-kumar"
        , WebSite = "www.capitalone.com"
        , Passcode = "book8data"
        , CategoryId = 1
    }
    , true);
    SavePassword(new Password {
        PasswordId = Guid.NewGuid()
        , Title = "Bank of America"
        , UserName = "vinodh-kumar"
        , Passcode = "boa8data"
        , CategoryId = 1
        , Key = "3121"
        , WebSite = "www.bankofamerica.com"
    }
    , true);
}
```

CreateDefaultData calls the AddCategory and SavePassword methods to add new rows to the Categories and Passwords tables. We have to carry out the following activities to interact with ESENT data (see Listing 5-7).

- Create a new session using the Instance object.
- Attach the database to the session and open it.
- Start a new transaction for this session.

- Within the transaction, select the active table that we want to work with.

- Data manipulations like updating or deleting rows in the table can be carried out.

Listing 5-7. Adding Data to the Categories Table

```
public void AddCategory(Category ev)
{
    using (var session = new Session(_instance))
    {
        JET_DBID dbid;
        Api.JetAttachDatabase(session
            , _databasePath
            , AttachDatabaseGrbit.None);
        //Opening database
        Api.JetOpenDatabase(session
            , _databasePath
            , String.Empty
            , out dbid
            , OpenDatabaseGrbit.None);
        //within a transaction
        using (var transaction = new Transaction(session))
        {
            //opening the table
            using (var table = new Table(session
                , dbid
                , "Categories"
                , OpenTableGrbit.None))
            {
                //inserting row
                using (var updater = new Update(session, table, JET_prep.Insert))
                {
                    var columnId = Api.GetTableColumnid(session
                        , table
                        , "CategoryId"); //to CategoryId column
                    Api.SetColumn(session
                        , table
                        , columnId
                        , ev.CategoryId);

                    var columnDesc = Api.GetTableColumnid(session
                        , table
                        , "CategoryName"); //to CategoryName column
                    Api.SetColumn(session
                        , table
                        , columnDesc
                        , ev.CategoryName
                        , Encoding.Unicode);
```

```
                    updater.Save();
                }
            }
            transaction.Commit(CommitTransactionGrbit.LazyFlush);
        }
    }
}
```

As mentioned earlier, whenever we interact with ESENT data, we have to create a session, attach and open the database, and start a transaction. Going forward, we encapsulate all the previously mentioned activities for the Passwords table within the ExecuteInTransaction method and will use this method for interaction (CRUD) with the Passwords table, as shown in Listing 5-8.

Listing 5-8. ExecuteInTransaction Encapsulates ESENT Activities

```
private IList<Password> ExecuteInTransaction(Func<Session, Table, IList<Password>> dataFunc)
{
    IList<Password> results;
    using (var session = new Session(_instance))
    {
        JET_DBID dbid;
        Api.JetAttachDatabase(session, _databasePath, AttachDatabaseGrbit.None);
        Api.JetOpenDatabase(session, _databasePath, String.Empty, out dbid, OpenDatabaseGrbit.None);
        using (var transaction = new Transaction(session))
        {
            using (var table = new Table(session, dbid, "Passwords", OpenTableGrbit.None))
            {
                results = dataFunc(session, table);
            }

            transaction.Commit(CommitTransactionGrbit.None);
        }
    }

    return results;
}
```

Adding a Password

Next, we'll add a method, SavePassword, that uses the ExecuteInTransaction (see Listing 5-8) method. This method takes the Password object as one of the parameters and sets the values to the corresponding columns in the Passwords table. When the Save method within the ESENT's Update object is called, as shown in Listing 5-9, it will insert or update a row to the Passwords table.

Listing 5-9. Add or Update a Password to the Passwords Table

```
public void SavePassword(Password pwd, bool isnew)
{
    ExecuteInTransaction((session, table) =>
        {
            using (var updater = new Update(session, table, isnew ? JET_prep.Insert : JET_prep.Replace))
```

```
            {
                //set the password id depending on the isnew parameter
                if (isnew)
                {
                    var columnId = Api.GetTableColumnid(session, table, "PasswordId");
                    Api.SetColumn(session, table, columnId, pwd.PasswordId);
                }
                //Title
                var columnTitle = Api.GetTableColumnid(session, table, "Title");
                Api.SetColumn(session, table, columnTitle, pwd.Title, Encoding.Unicode);
                //UserName
                var columnUserName = Api.GetTableColumnid(session, table, "UserName");
                Api.SetColumn(session, table, columnUserName, pwd.UserName, Encoding.Unicode);
                //Passcode
                var columnPasscode = Api.GetTableColumnid(session, table, "Passcode");
                Api.SetColumn(session, table, columnPasscode, pwd.Passcode, Encoding.Unicode);
                //WebSite
                var columnWebSite = Api.GetTableColumnid(session, table, "WebSite");
                Api.SetColumn(session, table, columnWebSite, pwd.WebSite, Encoding.Unicode);
                //Key
                var columnKey = Api.GetTableColumnid(session, table, "Key");
                Api.SetColumn(session, table, columnKey, pwd.Key, Encoding.Unicode);
                //CategoryId
                var columnCategoryId = Api.GetTableColumnid(session, table, "CategoryId");
                Api.SetColumn(session, table, columnCategoryId, pwd.CategoryId);
                //Note
                var columnNote = Api.GetTableColumnid(session, table, "Note");
                Api.SetColumn(session, table, columnNote, pwd.Note, Encoding.Unicode);

                updater.Save();
            }
            return null;
        });
}
```

Deleting a Password

Similar to the SavePassword (see Listing 5-9) method, DeletePassword also calls the ExecuteInTransaction method (see Listing 5-8) to set up the ESENT for deleting a row from the Passwords table. In this method we take password ID as the parameter and seek a key that matches our password ID using JET API's MakeKey method and then use JetDelete to delete the selected record, as shown in Listing 5-10.

Listing 5-10. Using DeletePassword to Delete Rows from Passwords Table

```
public void DeletePassword(Guid id)
{
    ExecuteInTransaction((session, table) =>
    {
        Api.JetSetCurrentIndex(session, table, null);
        Api.MakeKey(session, table, id, MakeKeyGrbit.NewKey);
```

```
            if (Api.TrySeek(session, table, SeekGrbit.SeekEQ))
            {
                Api.JetDelete(session, table);
            }
            return null;
    });
}
```

Retrieving Passwords

Similar to the previous two methods, first we'll call ExecuteInTransaction and then will use JET API's TryMoveFirst
and TryMoveNext methods to loop through all the records with in the Passwords table and pass the record currently
under construction to the GetPassword method. GetPassword uses JetRetrieveColumn to get the values for all the
columns and assigns them to the corressponding Property of the Password object. Once retrieved, the Password object
is added to the collections (see Listing 5-11).

Listing 5-11. Retrieving Passwords from Passwords Table

```
public List<Password> GetAllPasswords()
{
    List<Password> results = null;
    ExecuteInTransaction((session, table) =>
    {
        results = new List<Password>();
        if (Api.TryMoveFirst(session, table))
        {
            do
            {
                //Call GetPassword method to create password object
                //from the table row
                results.Add(GetPassword(session, table));
            }
            while (Api.TryMoveNext(session, table));
        }
        return results;
    });
    return results;
}

private Password GetPassword(Session session, Table table)
{
    var password = new Password();
    //retrieving PasswordId column
    var columnId = Api.GetTableColumnid(session, table, "PasswordId");
    //assigning it to the PasswordId property
    password.PasswordId = Api.RetrieveColumnAsGuid(session, table, columnId) ?? Guid.Empty;
    //retrieving Title
    var columnTitle = Api.GetTableColumnid(session, table, "Title");
    password.Title = Api.RetrieveColumnAsString(session, table, columnTitle, Encoding.Unicode);
```

```
    //retrieving UserName
    var columnUsername = Api.GetTableColumnid(session, table, "UserName");
    password.UserName = Api.RetrieveColumnAsString(session, table, columnUsername, Encoding.Unicode);
    //retrieving Passcode
    var columnPasscode = Api.GetTableColumnid(session, table, "Passcode");
    password.Passcode = Api.RetrieveColumnAsString(session, table, columnPasscode, Encoding.Unicode);
    //retrieving WebSite
    var columnWebSite = Api.GetTableColumnid(session, table, "WebSite");
    password.WebSite = Api.RetrieveColumnAsString(session, table, columnWebSite, Encoding.Unicode);
    //retrieving Key
    var columnKey = Api.GetTableColumnid(session, table, "Key");
    password.Key = Api.RetrieveColumnAsString(session, table, columnKey, Encoding.Unicode);
    //retrieving Note
    var columnNote = Api.GetTableColumnid(session, table, "Note");
    password.Note = Api.RetrieveColumnAsString(session, table, columnNote, Encoding.Unicode);
    //retrieving CategoryId
    var columnCategoryId = Api.GetTableColumnid(session, table, "CategoryId");
    password.CategoryId = Api.RetrieveColumnAsInt32(session, table, columnCategoryId) ?? -1;
    return password;
}
```

As all of the IDataRepository methods are implemented in JetDataRepository, we will do the same for ApplicationDataRepository, which is used for storing data in application storage. Before going further, a brief introduction to application data storage is in order.

Using Application Data Storage

Every app installed in Windows 8/RT will be allocated space for storing application data. This application storage can be used to store an app's settings, preferences, context, app status, and files. It cannot be accessed by the other apps and will be accessed only using the APIs provided in WinRT.

For storing and retrieving application data we should use the ApplicationData class, which is a part of the Windows.Store namespace. This data can be stored in three different ways.

- **Local application data:** Stores the data locally. Use local storage only if you have good reason not to roam the setting to the cloud.

- **Roaming application data:** Data will be synced across all the devices on which the user has installed the app. If we use roaming and the user doesn't have a Microsoft account, then it will be stored locally.

- **Temporary application data:** Data is stored temporarily during an application session and can be removed any time by a system maintenance task.

With this very brief introduction to application data storage, we now implement the IDataRepository methods in the ApplicationDataRepository class. All the methods in the ApplicationDataRepository class are straight forward and we briefly look at each one of them.

WinRT File Based Database

WinRT File Based Database is a file-system-based database written using the WinRT framework. This API allows us to create tables based on classes. Each database consists of many tables and these tables are serialized and stored in application data storage.

Like the ESANT database, the first thing we do within the CreateInstance method, shown in Listing 5-12, is to create the database and the tables if it doesn't already exist. If it already exists, we open the database and retrieve and assign the table objects to the corresponding properties in the ApplicationDataRepository class.

Listing 5-12. Creating the Application Storage Database and Tables

```
public async void CreateInstance()
{
    var exists = await Database.DoesDatabaseExistsAsync(DatabaseName
        , StorageLocation.Local);
    if (!exists)
    {
        _database = await Database.CreateDatabaseAsync(DatabaseName
            , StorageLocation.Local);
        _database.CreateTable<Category>();
        _database.CreateTable<Password>();

        var categoriesTable = await _database.Table<Category>();
        var passwordsTable  = await _database.Table<Password>();

        Categories = categoriesTable;
        Passwords = passwordsTable;
        CreateDefaultData();

        SaveResult result = await _database.SaveAsync();
        if (result.Error == null)
        {
            Debug.WriteLine(result.Error == null ?
                "Database created with Defult data"
                : result.Error.Message);
        }
    }
    else
    {
        _database = await Database.OpenDatabaseAsync(DatabaseName
            , true
            , StorageLocation.Local);
        Categories = await _database.Table<Category>();
        Passwords = await _database.Table<Password>();
    }
}

public Table<Category> Categories
{ get; set; }

public Table<Password> Passwords
{ get; set; }
```

Next, we insert default values into the Categories tables and test data in the Passwords table using the CreateDefaultData method, shown in Listing 5-13, which is called inside the CreateInstance method in a way that is very similar to the one we had in JetDataRepository.

Listing 5-13. Using `CreateDefaultData` to Insert Default Values into the Table

```
private void CreateDefaultData()
{
    //Adding categories
    Categories.Add(new Category
    {
        CategoryId = 1
        , CategoryName = "Bank"
    });
    Categories.Add(new Category
    {
        CategoryId = 2
        , CategoryName = "Web Site"
    });

    //Adding password
    Passwords.Add(new Password
    {
        PasswordId = Guid.NewGuid()
        , Title = "Capital One"
        , UserName = "vinodh-kumar"
        , WebSite = "www.capitalone.com"
        , Passcode = "book8data"
        , CategoryId = 1
    });
    Passwords.Add(new Password
    {
        PasswordId = Guid.NewGuid()
        , Title = "Bank of America"
        , UserName = "vinodh-kumar"
        , Passcode = "boa8data"
        , CategoryId = 1
        , Key = "3121"
        , WebSite = "www.bankofamerica.com"
    });
}
```

The AddCategory method takes a Category object as a parameter and adds it to the Categories collection. It then makes an async call to the Save method of the database instance of the WinRT File Based Database as shown in Listing 5-14. This Save method serializes the Categories object and stores it in the application data storage.

Listing 5-14. Using AddCategory to Add a Row to the Category Table

```
public async void AddCategory(Category category)
{
    Categories.Add(category);
    SaveResult result = await _database.SaveAsync();
```

```
    if (result.Error == null)
    {
        Debug.WriteLine(result.Error == null
            ? "Saved Category"
            : result.Error.Message);
    }
}
```

Similar to the AddCategory method, the SavePassword method takes the Password object as a parameter and adds it to the Passwords collection if it is new, and then calls the database object Save method, as shown in Listing 5-15.

Listing 5-15. Using SavePassword to Add or Update Rows in the Password Table

```
public async void SavePassword(Password password, bool isnew=true)
{
    if (isnew)
    {
        Passwords.Add(password);
    }
    SaveResult result = await _database.SaveAsync();
    if (result.Error == null)
    {
        Debug.WriteLine(result.Error == null
            ? "Saved Password"
            : result.Error.Message);
    }
}
```

The DeletePassword method deletes the Password row from the Passwords table, as shown in Listing 5-16. This method takes the password ID as a parameter and uses it to get the Password object corresponding to that password ID. This Password object is then removed from the Passwords collection before calling the database object Save method to remove the row permanently from the Passwords table.

Listing 5-16. Using DeletePassword to Delete a Row from Passwords Table

```
public async void DeletePassword(Guid id)
{
    var password = Passwords.Where(p => p.PasswordId == id).FirstOrDefault();
    Passwords.Remove(password);
    SaveResult result = await _database.SaveAsync();
    if (result.Error == null)
    {
        Debug.WriteLine(result.Error == null
            ? "Delete Password"
            : result.Error.Message);
    }
}
```

The GetCategories and GetAllPasswords methods will list the Categories and Password data, as shown in Listing 5-17.

Listing 5-17. GetCategories and GetAllPasswords Are Used to Retrieve Data from Tables

```
public List<Category> GetCategories()
{
    if (Categories == null) return null;
    return Categories.ToList();
}

public List<Password> GetAllPasswords()
{
    if (Passwords == null) return null;
    return Passwords.ToList();
}
```

Now with all the CRUD methods in place we will integrate the database into our Password Manager app. The first thing we do is to create an instance of both of the Repository classes in the App.xaml Launch event and call the CreateInstance method. We also assign the instances to the PasswordDB property so that it can be used across the app. Even though we will be integrating two different storage methods, we will be able to use only one database at a time for the Password Manager app. The ideal place to add this database switch is in the app setting page, but for brevity, here we instead create a Boolean property that can be changed manually before running the application. See Listing 5-19.

Listing 5-19. OnLaunched Will Create an Instance of DataRepository Class

```
protected override void OnLaunched(LaunchActivatedEventArgs args)
{
    Frame rootFrame = Window.Current.Content as Frame;
    //app defualts to application data storage
    //change the  UseApplicationStorage = false for Jet Datastorage
    UseApplicationStorage = true;
    IDataRepository dr = null;
    if (UseApplicationStorage)
    {
        dr = new ApplicationDataRepository();
    }
    else
    {
        dr = new JetDataRepository();
    }
    dr.CreateInstance();
    App.PasswordDB = dr;
    // omitted for brevity
}

public static IDataRepository PasswordDB
{
    get;
    set;
}

public static bool  UseApplicationStorage
{
    get;
    set;
}
```

Designing App Start Page

MainPage.xaml is the start page of this app (see Figure 5-3). This page contains a GridView control that lists all the passwords stored in the Passwords table. The layout out of each item in the GridView is driven by a PasswordDataTemplate. This template is very similar to the BookDataTemplate that we used to display the *New York Times* Best Sellers list in Chapter 1. MainPage.xaml also has three App Bar buttons (see Listing 5-20) and the functionality of each of these buttons is listed here.

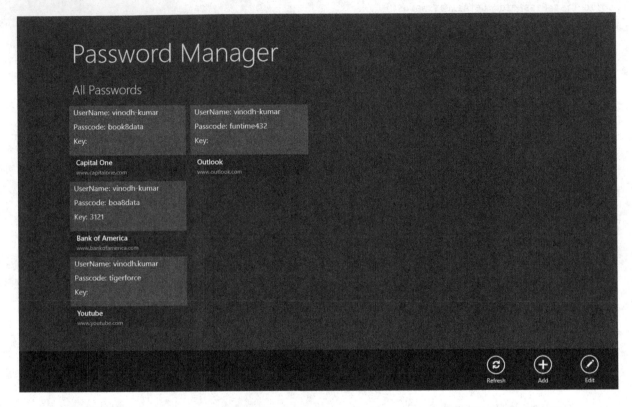

Figure 5-3. *Password Manager app displaying the stored passwords*

- **Refresh:** Used to refresh the items displayed in the grid.
- **Add:** Navigate to PasswordDetail.xaml (see Figure 5-3).
- **Edit:** Navigate to PasswordDetail.xaml along with the selected password from the GridView as a page parameter.

Listing 5-20. MainPage.xaml Includes a GridView with Item Template to Display Password Details

```
<common:LayoutAwarePage
    x:Name="pageRoot"
    x:Class="PasswordManager.MainPage"
    DataContext="{Binding DefaultViewModel, RelativeSource={RelativeSource Self}}"
    xmlns="http://schemas.microsoft.com/winfx/2006/xaml/presentation"
    xmlns:x="http://schemas.microsoft.com/winfx/2006/xaml"
```

```xml
xmlns:local="using:PasswordManager"
xmlns:common="using:PasswordManager.Common"
xmlns:d="http://schemas.microsoft.com/expression/blend/2008"
xmlns:mc="http://schemas.openxmlformats.org/markup-compatibility/2006"
mc:Ignorable="d">
<!--Reduced Markup for better readability-->
<Page.Resources>
    <!--DataTemplae-->
    <DataTemplate x:Key="PasswordDataTemplate">
        <Grid Width="250" Height="150">
            <StackPanel>
                <!--UserName-->
                <StackPanel Orientation="Horizontal">
                    <TextBlock Text="UserName:"/>
                    <TextBlock Text="{Binding UserName}"/>
                </StackPanel>
                <!--Password-->
                <StackPanel Orientation="Horizontal">
                    <TextBlock Text="Passcode:"/>
                    <TextBlock Text="{Binding Passcode}"/>
                </StackPanel>
                <!--Key-->
                <StackPanel Orientation="Horizontal">
                    <TextBlock Text="Key:"/>
                    <TextBlock Text="{Binding Key}"/>
                </StackPanel>
            </StackPanel>

            <StackPanel VerticalAlignment="Bottom">
                <!--Title-->
                <TextBlock Text="{Binding Title}"/>
                <!--WebSite-->
                <TextBlock Text="{Binding WebSite}"/>
            </StackPanel>
        </Grid>
    </DataTemplate>
</Page.Resources>
<!--AppBar-->
<common:LayoutAwarePage.BottomAppBar>
<AppBar IsOpen="True">
  <Grid>
    <Grid.ColumnDefinitions>
      <ColumnDefinition/>
      <ColumnDefinition/>
    </Grid.ColumnDefinitions>
    <StackPanel
                Orientation="Horizontal"/>
    <StackPanel
                Grid.Column="1"
                Orientation="Horizontal">
                <!-- Refresh Button-->
```

```xml
        <Button
                    Style="{StaticResource RefreshAppBarButtonStyle}"
                    Click="Refresh_Click" />
                    <!--New Password Button-->
        <Button
                    Style="{StaticResource AddAppBarButtonStyle}"
                    Click="Add_Click" />
                    <!-- Edit Password Button-->
        <Button
                    Style="{StaticResource EditAppBarButtonStyle}"
                    Click="Edit_Click"/>
        </StackPanel>
    </Grid>
  </AppBar>
</common:LayoutAwarePage.BottomAppBar>

    <!--Page Layout-->
    <Grid Style="{StaticResource LayoutRootStyle}" Margin="0">
        <Grid.RowDefinitions>
            <RowDefinition Height="140"/>
            <RowDefinition Height="48"/>
            <RowDefinition Height="275*"/>
        </Grid.RowDefinitions>

        <!-- GridView to display Password details -->
        <GridView
            Grid.Row="2"
            Name="gvPasswords"
            ItemTemplate="{StaticResource PasswordDataTemplate}"
            Grid.RowSpan="2"/>

        <!-- Back button and page title -->
        <Grid>
            <Grid.ColumnDefinitions>
                <ColumnDefinition Width="Auto"/>
                <ColumnDefinition Width="*"/>
            </Grid.ColumnDefinitions>
            <Button
                x:Name="backButton"
                Click="GoBack"
                IsEnabled="{Binding Frame.CanGoBack, ElementName=pageRoot}"
                Style="{StaticResource BackButtonStyle}"/>
            <TextBlock
                x:Name="pageTitle"
                Text="{StaticResource AppName}"
                Grid.Column="1"
                IsHitTestVisible="false"
                Style="{StaticResource PageHeaderTextStyle}"/>
        </Grid>
```

```xaml
        <TextBlock
            x:Name="pageSubTitle"
            Text="All Passwords"
            IsHitTestVisible="false"
            Style="{StaticResource PageSubheaderTextStyle}"
            Margin="120,0,30,20"
            Grid.Row="1"/>
    </Grid>
</common:LayoutAwarePage>
```

The MainPage.xaml code behind the page has one method, LoadAllPasswords, and three click events for each of the App Bar buttons. LoadAllPasswords is called at the start of the page and also when the Refresh button is clicked. This method gets the Passwords collection object using the method GetAllPasswords (see Listing 5-17) from the DataRepository class and binds it to the GridView's ItemsSource property. Add_Click and Edit_Click events navigate the users to the PasswordDetail.xaml page (see Listing 5.21).

Listing 5-21. MainPage.xaml Code Behind Binds Passwords Collection to GridView

```csharp
public sealed partial class MainPage : PasswordManager.Common.LayoutAwarePage
{
    public MainPage()
    {
        this.InitializeComponent();
    }

    protected override void OnNavigatedTo(NavigationEventArgs e)
    {
        LoadAllPasswords();
    }

    private void Refresh_Click(object sender, Windows.UI.Xaml.RoutedEventArgs e)
    {
        LoadAllPasswords();
    }

    private void LoadAllPasswords()
    {
        gvPasswords.ItemsSource = App.PasswordDB.GetAllPasswords();
    }

    private void Add_Click(object sender, Windows.UI.Xaml.RoutedEventArgs e)
    {
        var rootFrame = new Frame();
        rootFrame.Navigate(typeof(PasswordDetail));
        Window.Current.Content = rootFrame;
        Window.Current.Activate();
    }

    private void Edit_Click(object sender, Windows.UI.Xaml.RoutedEventArgs e)
    {
        var rootFrame = new Frame();
        rootFrame.Navigate(typeof(PasswordDetail), gvPasswords.SelectedValue);
```

```
            Window.Current.Content = rootFrame;
            Window.Current.Activate();
    }
}
```

Adding and Updating a Password

PasswordDetail.xaml is a very simple page (see Figure 5-3) that is used to add a new password or update or delete an existing password (see Listing 5-22). This page has the necessary controls to input password information. Also on this page we have two App Bar buttons for saving and deleting the password.

Listing 5-22. PasswordDetail.xaml Has Controls to Input Password Information

```
<common:LayoutAwarePage
    x:Name="pageRoot"
    x:Class="PasswordManager.PasswordDetail"
    DataContext="{Binding DefaultViewModel, RelativeSource={RelativeSource Self}}"
    xmlns="http://schemas.microsoft.com/winfx/2006/xaml/presentation"
    xmlns:x="http://schemas.microsoft.com/winfx/2006/xaml"
    xmlns:local="using:PasswordManager"
    xmlns:common="using:PasswordManager.Common"
    xmlns:d="http://schemas.microsoft.com/expression/blend/2008"
    xmlns:mc="http://schemas.openxmlformats.org/markup-compatibility/2006"
    mc:Ignorable="d">
    <!--Reduced Markup for better readability-->
    <!--App Bar buttons-->
  <common:LayoutAwarePage.BottomAppBar>
    <AppBar IsOpen="True">
      <Grid>
        <Grid.ColumnDefinitions>
          <ColumnDefinition/>
          <ColumnDefinition/>
        </Grid.ColumnDefinitions>
        <StackPanel
                    Orientation="Horizontal"
                    Grid.Column="1" HorizontalAlignment="Right">
                    <!--Save button-->
          <Button
                    Style="{StaticResource SaveAppBarButtonStyle}"
                    Click="Save_Click"/>
                    <!--Delete button-->
          <Button
                    x:Name="btnDelete"
                    Style="{StaticResource DeleteAppBarButtonStyle}"
                    Click="Delete_Click"
                    IsEnabled="False"/>

        </StackPanel>

      </Grid>
    </AppBar>
  </common:LayoutAwarePage.BottomAppBar>
```

```xml
<!--Page Layout-->
    <Grid Style="{StaticResource LayoutRootStyle}">
        <Grid.RowDefinitions>
            <RowDefinition Height="140"/>
            <RowDefinition Height="*"/>
        </Grid.RowDefinitions>

        <!-- Back button and page title -->
        <Grid>
            <Grid.ColumnDefinitions>
                <ColumnDefinition Width="Auto"/>
                <ColumnDefinition Width="*"/>
            </Grid.ColumnDefinitions>
            <Button
                x:Name="backButton"
                Click="GoBack"
                IsEnabled="{Binding Frame.CanGoBack, ElementName=pageRoot}"
                Style="{StaticResource BackButtonStyle}"/>
            <TextBlock
                x:Name="pageTitle"
                Grid.Column="1"
                Text="{StaticResource AppName}"
                Style="{StaticResource PageHeaderTextStyle}"/>
        </Grid>
        <!--Password Details-->
        <StackPanel Grid.Row="1">
          <TextBlock Text="Add Password"/>
            <!--Title-->
          <StackPanel>
            <TextBlock Text="Title"/>
            <TextBox x:Name="txtTitle"/>
          </StackPanel>
            <!--User Name-->
          <StackPanel>
            <TextBlock Text="User Name"/>
            <TextBox x:Name="txtUserName"/>
          </StackPanel>
            <!--Password-->
          <StackPanel>
            <TextBlock Text="Password"/>
                <TextBox x:Name="txtPassword"/>
          </StackPanel>
            <!--Category-->
          <StackPanel>
            <TextBlock Text="Category"/>
            <ComboBox x:Name="cboCategory"/>
          </StackPanel>
            <!--Web Site-->
          <StackPanel>
            <TextBlock Text="Web Site"/>
            <TextBox x:Name="txtWebSite"/>
          </StackPanel>
```

```
            <!--Key-->
        <StackPanel>
          <TextBlock Text="Key"/>
          <TextBox x:Name="txtKey"/>
        </StackPanel>
          <!--Note-->
        <StackPanel>
          <TextBlock Text="Note"/>
          <TextBox x:Name="txtNote"/>
        </StackPanel>
      </StackPanel>
    </Grid>
</common:LayoutAwarePage>
```

The `PasswordDetail.xaml` code behind the page has the necessary code to save and delete a password. First, when the page is invoked for editing an existing password object, the values will be assigned to the corresponding controls for editing as shown in Listing 5-23.

Listing 5-23. Assigning the Password Values to the Controls

```
protected override void OnNavigatedTo(NavigationEventArgs e)
{
    cboCategory.DisplayMemberPath = "CategoryName";
    List<Category> categories = null;
    categories = App.PasswordDB.GetCategories();
    cboCategory.ItemsSource = categories;
    if (e.Parameter != null)
    {
        _password = (Password)e.Parameter;
        if (_password != null)
        {
            txtTitle.Text = _password.Title ?? "";
            txtUserName.Text = _password.UserName ?? "";
            txtPassword.Text = _password.Passcode ?? "";
            txtKey.Text = _password.Key ?? "";
            txtNote.Text = _password.Note??"";
            txtWebSite.Text = _password.WebSite ?? "";
            cboCategory.SelectedValue= categories.Where(c=>c.CategoryId ==
                                                    _password.CategoryId).First();

            btnDelete.IsEnabled = true;
        }
    }
}
```

The `Save_Click` event is called when the Save button is clicked. Within this event we create a `Password` object and pass it as a parameter to the `SavePassword` method in the `DataRepository` instance for saving the object to the database (see Listing 5-24).

Listing 5-24. Creating a Password Object for Saving

```
private void Save_Click(object sender, Windows.UI.Xaml.RoutedEventArgs e)
{
    Password pwd;
    pwd = _password == null ? new Password() : _password;
    pwd.PasswordId = _password == null ? Guid.NewGuid() : _password.PasswordId;
    pwd.Title = txtTitle.Text;
    pwd.UserName = txtUserName.Text;
    pwd.Passcode = txtPassword.Text;
    pwd.Key = txtKey.Text;
    pwd.WebSite = txtWebSite.Text;
    pwd.Note = txtNote.Text;
    Category category = (Category)cboCategory.SelectedValue;
    pwd.CategoryId = category.CategoryId;
    App.PasswordDB.SavePassword(pwd, _password == null ? true : false);
    NagivateToMainPage();
}
```

The DeletePassword method in the DataRepository class is called on a Delete button click event. This deletes the corresponding row in the Password table and navigates back to the MainPage.xaml, as shown in Listing 5-25.

Listing 5-25. Deleting the Password Using the DataRepository DeletePassword Method

```
private void Delete_Click(object sender, Windows.UI.Xaml.RoutedEventArgs e)
{
    App.PasswordDB.DeletePassword(_password.PasswordId);
    NagivateToMainPage();
}
```

Now with all the code in place, when we run the Password Manager app, it will display the default passwords that we added to the Passwords table as shown in Figure 5-4. From here on we will be able to add new password and update and delete existing passwords.

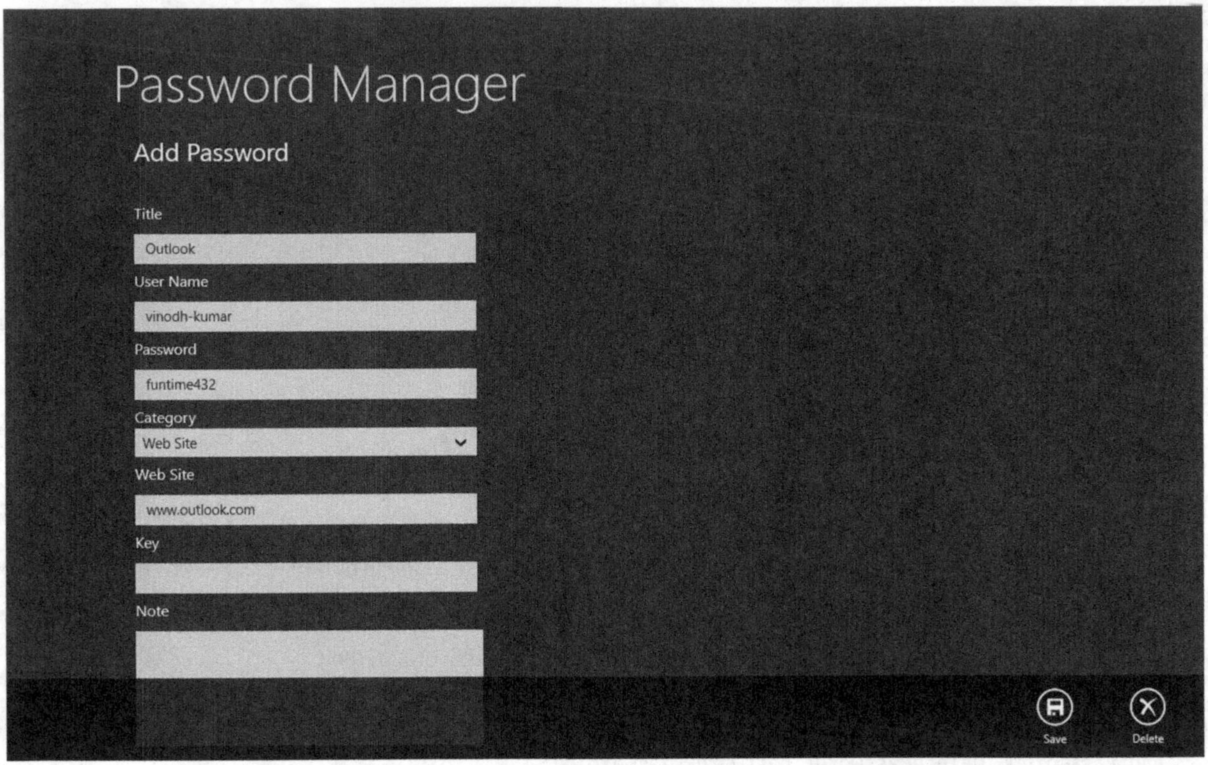

Figure 5-4. Password details page for adding or editing passwords

Ideas for Improvement

The Password Manager app can be worked on and improved to make it a fully functional password management application. The following are some of the features that can be added.

- As you can see, the intention of developing this app is to showcase the use of the ESENT database and application data storage, so we have not gone into writing code to encrypt the data. That should be the first improvement that we make.

- We store the password by categories but considering the length of this chapter we have not implemented it. This could be one enhancement we can make, along with the option to search using the Windows Search function.

- Backup and export capabilites would be helpful.

- Right now we store the app in application local storage. Instead, we can use roaming storage so that the data will syn across all the user's computers and devices.

Conclusion

In this chapter we learned to use the ESENT database and application data storage as a local storage option by building a Password Manager app. The goal here was to provide an intermediate introduction to ESENT and application storage using existing libraries so that decisions in selecting a local data storage option can be made with ease.

In the next chapter we learn about yet another but more widely used local storage option, Sqlite. As always, we will be building an app that uses Sqlite as a local storage database.

■ ■ ■

CHAPTER 6

Local Data Access III: SQLite

In the last two chapters we looked at how to read and write data locally using the Jet API, application storage, and IndexedDB. In this chapter, we discuss yet another local storage option for Windows 8 apps, SQLite. This chapter starts with an introduction to SQLite, and then we will look into various setup procedures needed to include SQLite in a project. We also learn to use sqlite-net, a SQLite wrapper. As always, we end this chapter by developing a Windows 8 app using SQLite as the data storage option. We use MVVM Light as our MVVM framework for this Bill Reminder app, and by doing so we learn to integrate and use MVVM Light, one of the most popular MVVM frameworks, in the project.

Introduction to SQLite

SQLite is a software library that implements a self-contained, serverless, zero-configuration, transactional SQL database engine. It's a file-based database that can be used without any need for a database engine like SQLServer, Oracle, and so on. SQLite is a relational database management system that is contained in a small C programing library. SQLite is the most widely deployed SQL database engine in the world and its source code exists in the public domain. It is free for use for both private and commercial purposes.

SQLite is very similar to SQL Server Compact in its characteristics, but unlike SQL Server Compact, which in most cases is part of the operating system (Windows Phone OS, Windows Mobile OS), SQLite is an embedded database that should be included explicitly within the app and run in-process within the app. Any SQLite database file can be copied from one platform to another regardless of the CPU's byte-ordering.

Integrating SQLite

Now we will see how to integrate SQLite. The SQLite Development Team made intergrating SQLite within a Windows 8 app simple and straightforward by packaging the binaries in such a way that it pulls the right DLLs, depending on the CPU architecture. To install SQLite from the Visual Studio Tools menu, select the Extensions and Updates menu. This opens an Extension and Update dialog window. Search for **sqlite** in the search term. This displays the SQLite for Windows Runtime package as shown in Figure 6-1.

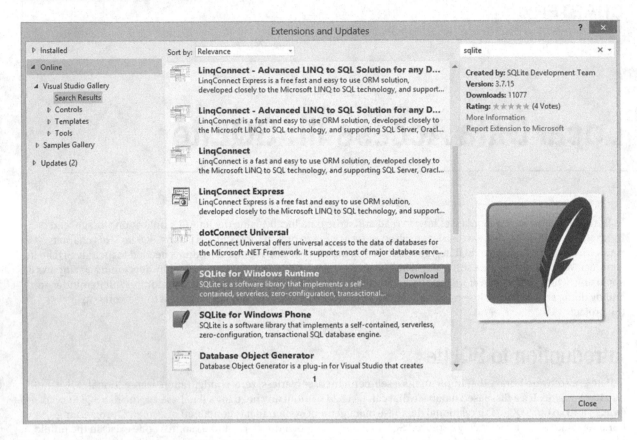

Figure 6-1. *Search result shows SQLite for Windows Runtime package*

Clicking the Download button installs the SQLite runtime and restarts Visual Studio. Once it is installed, you can reference SQLite in the project using the Reference Manager. SQLite will show up in Extensions under the Windows section as shown in Figure 6-2.

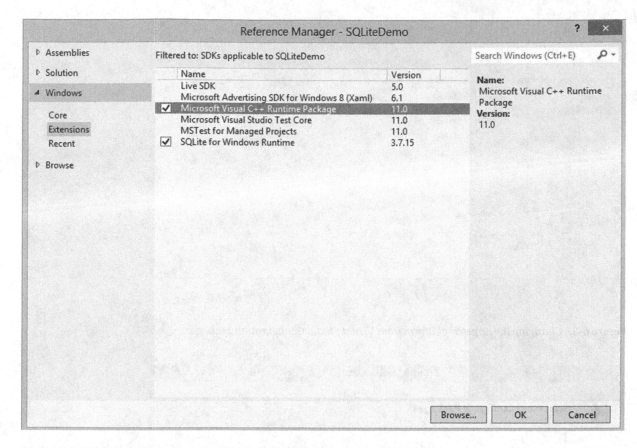

Figure 6-2. *Adding project reference to SQLite for Windows Runtime*

We should also reference the Microsoft Visual C++ Runtime Package because SQLite for Windows Runtime depends on this. In fact, all native libraries require the Visual C++ Runtime package.

Now when you compile the project there will be a compile time error as we can't build the project to target Any CPU; hence we need to go to Project's Configuration Manager Dialog box to change the targeted platform to X86 as shown in Figure 6-3. To target multiple architectures like X86, x64, and ARM we need to create three separate packages—one targeting each architecture—and then upload the packages to the Windows Stores, as shown in Figures 6-4 and 6-5.

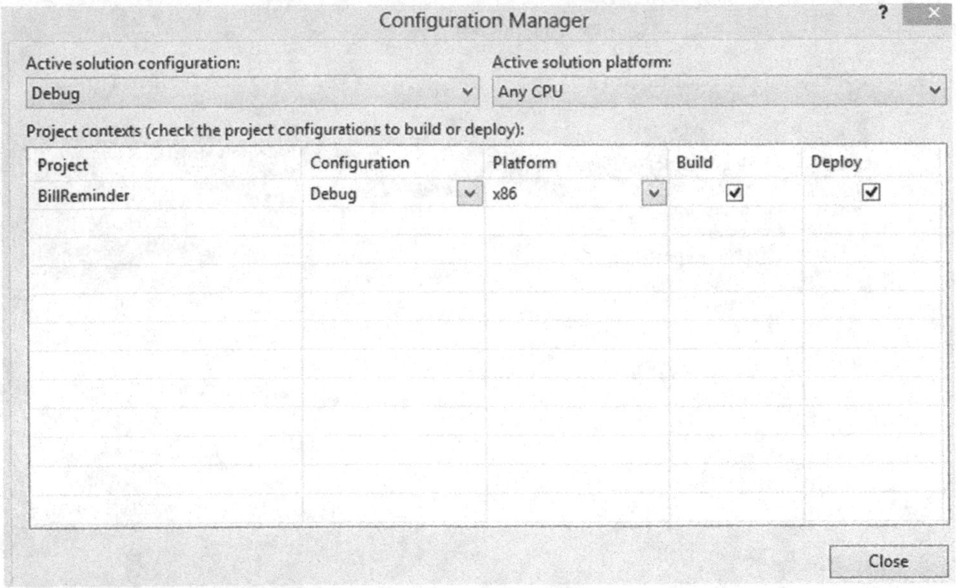

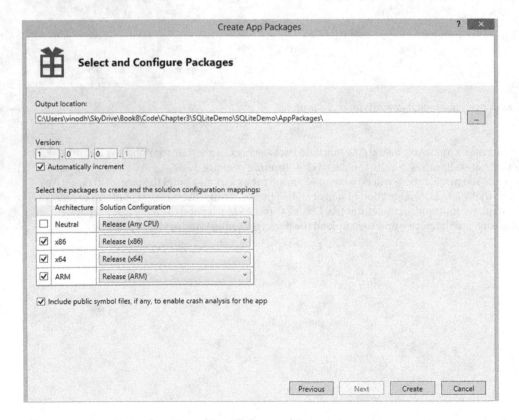

Figure 6-3. *Changing the targeted platform from Visual Studio Configuration Manager*

Figure 6-4. *Creating packages targeting all three architectures*

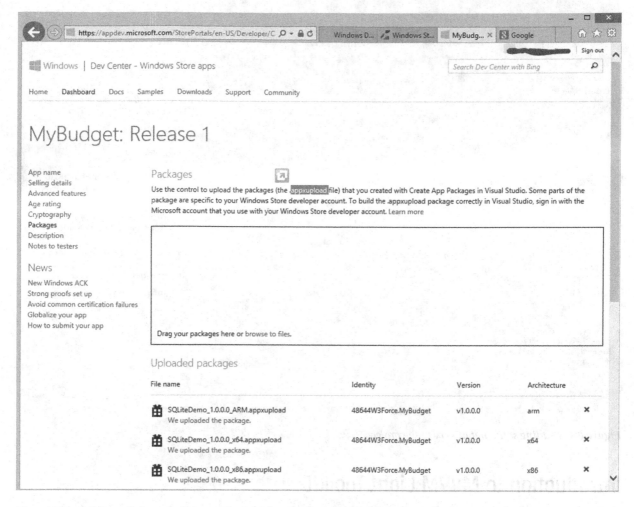

Figure 6-5. *Adding all three packages to the Windows Store App Submission Wizard*

At this point the SQLite library becomes a part of the project but we need a managed wrapper in C# for interacting with the C++ library. Because writing something similar is not within the scope of this book, we use an open source LINQ-based wrapper, sqlite-net, that we will be able to get from NuGet (see Figure 6-6).

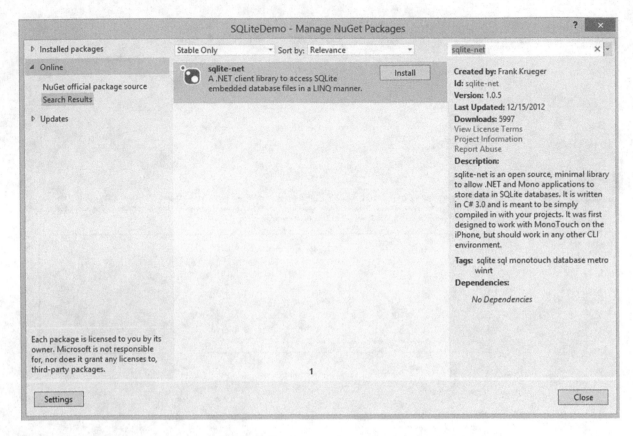

Figure 6-6. *Adding sqlite-net library to the project*

Introduction to MVVM Light Toolkit

One of the most popular MVVM frameworks is MVVM Light Toolkit, which is a versatile framework that allows you to construct customized applications. It provides help getting around some of the main points in building MVVM applications. MVVM Light was developed by Laurent Bugnion initially for Silverlight and Windows Phone, and later was ported to Windows 8 apps. MVVM Light Toolkit consists of several components that make writing MVVM applications easier, including the following.

- `ObservableObject`: This class basically implements `INotifyPropertyChanged` and can be used in the places where `ViewModelBase` is not necessary but the `INotifyPropertyChanged` functionality is still required.

- `ViewModelBase`: This class can be used as the base class for ViewModels and it implements `INotifyPropertyChanged`.

- `Messenger`: This class is used to communicate within the application.

- `RelayCommand`: This implements the `ICommand` interface that a button control needs to pass the calls on to a function in the ViewModel.

- Visual Studio Project Templates.

MVVM Light Toolkit for Visual Studio 2012 can be downloaded from http://mvvmlight.codeplex.com/.

After installing the toolkit you will see that there is a new project template available in the Visual Studio 2012 New Project dialog box, as shown in Figure 6-7.

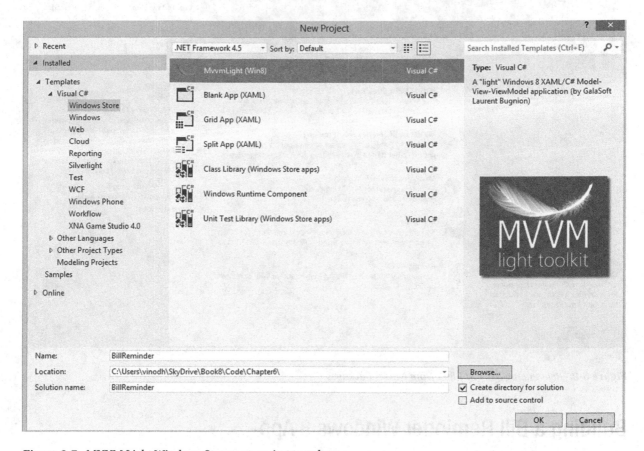

Figure 6-7. *MVVM Light Windows Store app project template*

We can also include the MVVM Light in an existing project by getting it from NuGet as shown in Figure 6-8.

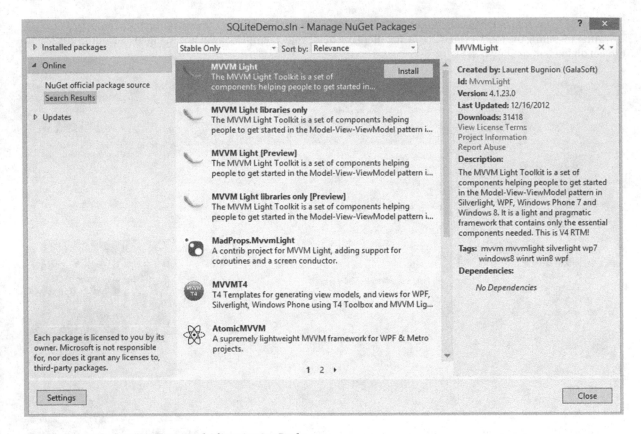

Figure 6-8. *Referencing MVVM Light from NuGet Packages*

Building a Bill Reminder Windows 8 App

Now that we understand the fundementals of SQLite and MVVM Light, we will use these skills in building a simple Bill
Reminder Windows 8 app. By building this app, you will learn to integrate SQLite and use it as a local database within
a Windows 8 app. You will also learn to apply some of the MVVM and XAML techniques like ViewModelLocator, IOC,
EventAggregator, RelayCommand, and ValueConverters. Knowing these techiniques will help you understand some
of the common MVVM implementation practices that can also be applied when using the other MVVM Frameworks
like Caliburn.Micro and Prism.

Our Bill Reminder app is a personal finance application that helps to keep track of one's bills. Using this app,
the user can create a bill reminder. As shown in Figure 6-9, this app displays the recent bills on the start page with an
option to mark a bill as paid.

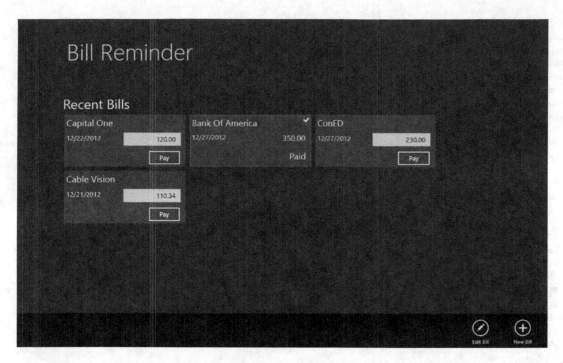

Figure 6-9. *The Bill Reminder app start page lists the recent bills*

Project Structure

The project has three main folders corresponding to Model, ViewModel, and View. The project structure shown in Figure 6-10 is very similar to the *New York Times* Best Seller MVVM sample that we created in Chapter 1.

Figure 6-10. Bil lReminder app project structure

Creating Database Tables

The main functionality of our Bill Reminder app is to help keep track of the bills. In this app we can create a new bill, edit a bill, and mark a bill paid. We create three SQLite database tables for this purpose.

- **Category:** This is a lookup table for grouping bills into various categories, such as credit card, loan, and so on.

- **Bill:** This table stores the bill details.

- **Paid Bill:** This table is used to track the paid bill details.

The sqlite-net approach is similar to other ORM-based databases like SQLCE for Windows Phone. Hence we will create a class for every table that we need to create and will augment the properties with attributes (see Figure 6-11). That will let sqlite-net assign matching column properties when generating the table in SQLite.

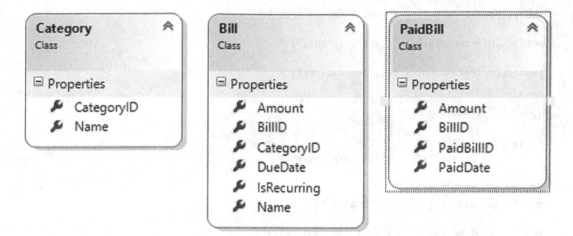

Figure 6-11. *Class diagram of the Bill Reminder SQLite tables*

These classes, shown in Listing 6-1, are enhanced with attributes that are supported by the sqlite-net library. Let's briefly look into the funtionality of each one of these attributes.

- **PrimaryKey:** Used to uniquely identify each record in a table.

- **AutoIncrement:** Used in conjection with the PrimaryKey column to create a value automatically every time a new row is inserted.

- **MaxLength:** Used to specify the maximum number of characters that can be stored in the column.

- **Indexed:** Used in a column that will most likely be the *WHERE* clause, *ORDER BY,* or *JOIN* in the queries. An index on the appropriate columns can improve performance.

Listing 6-1. Category, Bill, and PaidBill Classes

```
public class Category
{
    [PrimaryKey, AutoIncrement]
    public int CategoryID { get; internal set; }

    [MaxLength(50)]
    public string Name { get; internal set; }
}

public class Bill
{
    [PrimaryKey, AutoIncrement]
    public int BillID { get; internal set; }

    [MaxLength(150)]
    public string Name { get; internal set; }

    public DateTime DueDate { get; internal set; }
```

```
            public bool IsRecurring { get; internal set; }

            public int CategoryID{get; internal set; }

            public Decimal Amount { get; internal set; }
        }

        public class PaidBill
        {
            [PrimaryKey]
            public int PaidBillID { get; internal set; }

            [Indexed]
            public int BillID { get; internal set; }

            public DateTime PaidDate { get; internal set; }

            public Decimal Amount { get; internal set; }


        }
```

■ **Note** We intentionally left out some of the code like Value Converters in this chapter to simplify the explanations improve readability. The source code that you can download from the APress web site has the complete implementation.

As mentioned earlier, the SQLite database is a single file database. Let's name it **billreminder.sqlite** and store the file in the app's local folder. To create the database, add the code shown in Listing 6-2 to the APP.xaml OnLaunched method.

Listing 6-2. Creating SQLite Database with Three Tables

```
private string dBPath = string.Empty;

public string DBPath
{
    get
    {
        return dBPath;
    }
    set
    {
        if (dBPath == value)
        {
            return;
        }
        dBPath = value;
    }
}
```

```
protected override void OnLaunched(LaunchActivatedEventArgs args)
{
    Frame rootFrame = Window.Current.Content as Frame;
    // Do not repeat app initialization when the window already has content,
    // just ensure that the window is active
    if (rootFrame == null)
    {
        // Create a frame to act as the navigation context and navigate to the first page
        rootFrame = new Frame();
        dBPath = Path.Combine(
            Windows.Storage.ApplicationData.Current.LocalFolder.Path,
            "billreminder.sqlite");
        // Initialize the database
        using (var db = new SQLite.SQLiteConnection(dBPath))
        {
            // Create the tables if they don't exist
            db.CreateTable<Category>();
            db.CreateTable<Bill>();
            db.CreateTable<PaidBill>();
            LoadDefaultData();
        }
        // Place the frame in the current window
        Window.Current.Content = rootFrame;
    }

    if (rootFrame.Content == null)
    {
        if (!rootFrame.Navigate(typeof(MainPage), args.Arguments))
        {
            throw new Exception("Failed to create initial page");
        }
    }
    // Ensure the current window is active
    Window.Current.Activate();
    DispatcherHelper.Initialize();
}
```

The code in Listing 6-2 creates the database and tables if they are not yet created and will call the LoadDefaultData method to insert default values in to the Category table. We have used the sqlite-net SQLLiteConnection class to create the table. The CreateTable method of the SQLLiteConnection class that takes a class as a parameter is used to create a table in the database based on the properties and attributes of the class (see Listing 6-3).

Listing 6-3. Loading Default Data into the Category Table

```
private void LoadDefaultData()
{
    using (var db = new SQLite.SQLiteConnection(dBPath))
    {
        if (!db.Table<Category>().Any())
        {
            db.Insert(new Category()
```

```
            {
                Name = "Credit Card"
            });
            db.Insert(new Category()
            {
                Name = "Loan"
            });
            db.Insert(new Category()
            {
                Name = "Utilities"
            });
        }
    }
}
```

Model

Apart from the ORM class files (Category, Bill, and PaidBill) that we already discussed, the Model folder also includes the IDataService interface and DataService class. The DataService class is the central repository for all the database interactions, like methods for Create, Read, Update, and Delete (CRUD) actions. Listing 6-4 shows three methods that are in the DataService class to insert, update, and read bills. In each of these methods, after establishing a connection using SQLiteConnection, we use the Insert, Update, or Get method to add, update, or read bill data.

Listing 6-4. Methods for Adding, Updating, and Retrieving Bills

```
public void AddBill(Bill bill)
{
    using (var db = new SQLite.SQLiteConnection(DBPath))
    {
        db.Insert(bill);
    }
}

public void UpdateBill(Bill bill)
{
    using (var db = new SQLite.SQLiteConnection(DBPath))
    {
        db.Update(bill);
    }
}

public Bill GetBillByID(int billID)
{
    using (var db = new SQLite.SQLiteConnection(DBPath))
    {
        return db.Get<Bill>(billID);
    }
}
```

The DataService class also includes a GetBills method that takes date as a parameter. This method gets all the bills for a given month by executing a SQL query using the SQLiteConnection object's Query method (see Listing 6-5). The generic parameter to the Query method specifies the type of object to create for each row. It can be one of your table classes, or any other class with public properties that match the column returned by the query.

Listing 6-5. The GetBills Method Gets All the Bills for a Given Month

```
public ObservableCollection<BillItem> GetBills(DateTime month)
{
    DateTime fromDate = new DateTime(month.Year, month.Month, 1);//first day of the month
    DateTime toDate = fromDate.AddMonths(1).AddDays(-1);// last day of the month
    string sql = string.Format("SELECT b.BillID,b.Name, c.Name as Category, b.DueDate, p.PaidDate,
b.Amount, p.Amount as PaidAmount FROM Bill b Join Category c on b.CategoryID= c.CategoryID LEFT
JOIN PaidBill p on (p.BillID = b.BillID ) WHERE (b.IsRecurring = 1 or b.DueDate BETWEEN  '{0}' AND
'{1}')", fromDate.ToString("MM/dd/yyy"), toDate.ToString("MM/dd/yyy"));
    var bills = new ObservableCollection<BillItem>();
    using (var db = new SQLite.SQLiteConnection(DBPath))
    {
        var query = db.Query<BillItem>(sql);
        foreach (var item in query)
        {
            BillItem bi = new BillItem(this);
            bi.BillID = item.BillID;
            bi.Name = item.Name;
            bi.Category = item.Category;
            bi.DueDate = item.DueDate;
            bi.Amount = item.Amount;
            bi.PaidAmount = item.PaidAmount;
            bi.PaidDate = item.PaidDate;
            if (bi.PaidAmount > 0 && bi.PaidDate > DateTime.MinValue)
            {
                bi.IsPaid = true;
            }
            bills.Add(bi);
        }
    }
    return bills;
}
```

To match the query public property, we create a new class, BillItem, as shown in Listing 6-6. This class inherits MVVM Light ObservableObject, which in turn implements INotifyPropertyChanged.

Listing 6-6. Properties of the BillItem Class That Holds the Bill Information

```
public class BillItem : ObservableObject
{

    private readonly IDataService _dataService;

    public BillItem() { }
```

```csharp
public BillItem(IDataService dataService)
{
    _dataService = dataService;
}

public int BillID { get;  set; }

private string _name = string.Empty;

public string Name
{
    get
    {
        return _name;
    }

    set
    {
        if (_name == value)
        {
            return;
        }

        _name = value;
        RaisePropertyChanged("Name");
    }
}

private string _category = string.Empty;

public string Category
{
    get
    {
        return _category;
    }

    set
    {
        if (_category == value)
        {
            return;
        }

        _category = value;
        RaisePropertyChanged("Category");
    }
}

private DateTime _dueDate = System.DateTime.Today;
```

```csharp
public DateTime DueDate
{
    get
    {
        return _dueDate;
    }

    set
    {
        if (_dueDate == value)
        { return; }
        _dueDate = value;
        RaisePropertyChanged("DueDate");
    }
}

private DateTime _paidDate = System.DateTime.Today;

public DateTime PaidDate
{
    get
    {
        return _paidDate;
    }

    set
    {
        if (_paidDate == value)
        { return; }
        _paidDate = value;
        RaisePropertyChanged("PaidDate");
    }
}

private Decimal _amount = 0;

public Decimal Amount
{
    get
    {
        return _amount;
    }

    set
    {
        if (_amount == value)
        { return; }
        _amount = value;
        RaisePropertyChanged("Amount");
    }
}

private Decimal _paidAmount = 0;
```

```
public Decimal PaidAmount
{
    get
    {
        return _paidAmount;
    }

    set
    {
        if (_paidAmount == value)
        { return; }
        _paidAmount = value;
        RaisePropertyChanged("PaidAmount");
    }
}


private bool _isPaid ;

public bool IsPaid
{
    get
    {
        return _isPaid;
    }

    set
    {
        if (_isPaid == value)
        { return; }
        _isPaid = value;
        RaisePropertyChanged("IsPaid");
    }
}
}
```

The BillItem class also includes a RelayCommand that gets invoked when a bill is marked as paid by pressing the Pay button as shown in Figure 6-9. RelayCommand passes the call to the ExecutePayCommand method, which in turn calls the MarkPaid method in the DataService class, as shown in Listing 6-7.

Listing 6-7. RelayCommand Within the BillItem Class Calls the ExecutePayCommand Method

```
private RelayCommand _payCommand;

public RelayCommand PayCommand
{
    get
    {
        return _payCommand
            ?? (_payCommand = new RelayCommand(ExecutePayCommand));
    }
}
```

```
private void ExecutePayCommand()
{
    PaidAmount = Amount;
    _dataService.MarkPaid(BillID, PaidAmount);
    IsPaid = true;
}
```

The `MarkPaid` method then inserts a row in the `PaidBill` table by using the `SQLiteConnection` object's `Execute` method, as shown in Listing 6-8.

Listing 6-8. MarkPaid Method Inserts a Row in the PaidBill Table

```
public void MarkPaid(int billID, decimal amount)
{
    using (var db = new SQLite.SQLiteConnection(DBPath))
    {
        db.Execute("INSERT INTO PaidBill (BillID, PaidDate, Amount) values (?,?,?)"
            , billID
            , DateTime.Today.ToString("MM/dd/yyyy")
            , amount);
    }
}
```

ViewModel

The ViewModel folder consists of `ViewModelLocator` and two ViewModels: `MainViewModel` and `BillViewModel`. `ViewModelLocator` is a repository of ViewModels enabled by MVVM Light that locates the ViewModel from inside XAML and connects it to the View `DataContent`.

The `App.xaml` defines a global instance of the locator as shown in Listing 6-9, and individual views can bind their `DataContent` to properties of the locator that serve up the individual ViewModels.

Listing 6-9. Global Instance of the ViewModelLocator in App.xaml

```
<Application.Resources>
    <vm:ViewModelLocator x:Key="Locator"
                                  d:IsDataSource="True" />
</Application.Resources>
```

MVVM Light also made it simple to register Services and ViewModels by including a simple IOC container along with the framework, as shown in Listing 6-10.

Listing 6-10. SimpleIOC Container Registers DataService, NavigationService, MainViewModel, and BillViewModel

```
public class ViewModelLocator
{
    static ViewModelLocator()
    {
        ServiceLocator.SetLocatorProvider(() => SimpleIoc.Default);
        SimpleIoc.Default.Register<IDataService, DataService>();
        SimpleIoc.Default.Register<INavigationService>(() => new NavigationService());
```

```
        SimpleIoc.Default.Register<MainViewModel>();
        SimpleIoc.Default.Register<BillViewModel>();
    }

    [System.Diagnostics.CodeAnalysis.SuppressMessage("Microsoft.Performance",
        "CA1822:MarkMembersAsStatic",
        Justification = "This non-static member is needed for data binding purposes.")]
    public MainViewModel Main
    {
        get
        {
            return ServiceLocator.Current.GetInstance<MainViewModel>();
        }
    }

    [System.Diagnostics.CodeAnalysis.SuppressMessage("Microsoft.Performance",
        "CA1822:MarkMembersAsStatic",
        Justification = "This non-static member is needed for data binding purposes.")]
    public BillViewModel Bill
    {
        get
        {
            return ServiceLocator.Current.GetInstance<BillViewModel>();
        }
    }
}
```

As shown in Listing 6-11, the ViewModels are exposed as properties of the ViewModelLocator and can be databound in XAML to the View DataContext.

Listing 6-11. MainViewModel Databound to the MainPage.xaml Datacontext

```
<Page x:Class="BillReminder.MainPage"
    xmlns="http://schemas.microsoft.com/winfx/2006/xaml/presentation"
    xmlns:x="http://schemas.microsoft.com/winfx/2006/xaml"
    xmlns:d="http://schemas.microsoft.com/expression/blend/2008"
    xmlns:mc="http://schemas.openxmlformats.org/markup-compatibility/2006"
    xmlns:ignore="http://www.ignore.com"
    mc:Ignorable="d ignore"
    d:DesignHeight="768"
    d:DesignWidth="1366"
    DataContext="{Binding Main, Source={StaticResource Locator}}">
```

MainViewModel

The MainViewModel constructor takes an IDataService and an INavigationService as parameters, as the SimpleIoc container creates all the objects automatically. This ViewModel containes BillItem ObservableCollection as one of the property named Bills. This property retrieves recent bills using the DataService GetBills method and it will be bound to the GridView control in the MainPage.xaml. MainViewModel also has two additional properties.

- **SelectedBill:** This property is to see if any bill is selected in the MainPage.xaml GridView control and it is bound to the GridView SelectedItem element property.

- **ShowAppBar:** The purpose of this property is to open the MainPage.xaml app bar when we select a Bill from the GridView. The AppBar contains a Button control to edit the selected Bill. ShowAppBar is bound to the AppBar IsOpen element property (see Listing 6-12).

Listing 6-12. ShowAppBar Property Is Bound to the MainPage.xaml AppBar IsOpen Property

```
<AppBar  IsOpen="{Binding ShowAppBar, Mode=TwoWay}">
  <Grid>
    <Grid.ColumnDefinitions>
      <ColumnDefinition/>
      <ColumnDefinition/>
    </Grid.ColumnDefinitions>
    <StackPanel Orientation="Horizontal"/>
    <StackPanel Grid.Column="1" HorizontalAlignment="Right" Orientation="Horizontal">
    <Button x:Name="EditButton"
          Style="{StaticResource EditAppBarButtonStyle}"
           Command="{Binding EditCommand, Mode=OneWay}"
           />
        <Button x:Name="AddButton"
            Style="{StaticResource AddAppBarButtonStyle}"
             Command="{Binding AddCommand, Mode=OneWay}"
             />
      </StackPanel>
    </Grid>
  </AppBar>
```

MainViewModel also implements two RelayCommands that can be invoked by the user for adding new bill or editing a selected bill, as shown in Listing 6-13. AddCommand passes the call to the ExecuteAddCommand method, which in turn navigates to the Bill.xaml page. EditCommand is also used for navigating to Bill.xaml, but it also sends the selected Bill object using the MVVM Light Messaging event aggregator.

Listing 6-13. The MainViewModel Class

```
public class MainViewModel : ViewModelBase
{
  private readonly IDataService _dataService;
  private readonly INavigationService _navigationService;

  public MainViewModel(IDataService dataService, INavigationService navigationService)
  {
    _dataService = dataService;
    _navigationService = navigationService;
  }
```

```csharp
public ObservableCollection<BillItem> Bills
{
  get
  {
    return _dataService.GetBills(DateTime.Now);
  }
}

private BillItem _selectedBill = null;

public BillItem SelectedBill
{
  get
  {
    return _selectedBill;
  }

  set
  {
    _selectedBill = value;
    ShowAppBar = true;
    RaisePropertyChanged("SelectedBill");
  }
}

private bool _showAppBar;

public bool ShowAppBar
{
  get
  {
    return _showAppBar;
  }

  set
  {
    _showAppBar = value;
    RaisePropertyChanged("ShowAppBar");
  }
}

private RelayCommand _addCommand;

public RelayCommand AddCommand
{
  get
  {
    return _addCommand
      ?? (_addCommand = new RelayCommand(ExecuteAddCommand));
  }
}
```

```
private RelayCommand _editCommand;

public RelayCommand EditCommand
{
  get
  {
    return _editCommand
      ?? (_editCommand = new RelayCommand(ExecuteEditCommand));
  }
}

private void ExecuteAddCommand()
{
    _navigationService.Navigate(typeof(BillView));
}

private void ExecuteEditCommand()
{
  _navigationService.Navigate(typeof(BillView));
  Messenger.Default.Send<BillItem>(SelectedBill);
}
}
```

BillViewModel

BillViewModel (see Listing 6-14) is the ViewModel for Bill.xaml. BillViewModel has properties that are bound to the controls in Bill.xaml, which is then used to add or edit a bill.

Listing 6-14. Properties in the BillViewModel Class

```
public class BillViewModel : ViewModelBase
{

  public int BillID { get; set; }

  private string _title = string.Empty;

  public string Title
  {
    get
    {
      return _title;
    }

    set
    {
      if (_title == value)
      {
        return;
      }
```

```csharp
      _title = value;
      RaisePropertyChanged("Title");
    }
  }
}

private string _name = string.Empty;

public string Name
{
  get
  {
    return _name;
  }

  set
  {
    if (_name == value)
    {
      return;
    }

    _name = value;
    RaisePropertyChanged("Name");
  }
}

private Category _selectedCategory = null;

public Category SelectedCategory
{
  get
  {
    return _selectedCategory;
  }

  set
  {
    _selectedCategory = value;
    RaisePropertyChanged("SelectedCategory");
  }
}

private DateTime _dueDate = System.DateTime.Today;

public DateTime DueDate
{
  get
  {
    return _dueDate;
  }
```

```csharp
  set
  {
    if (_dueDate == value)
    { return; }
    _dueDate = value;
    RaisePropertyChanged("DueDate");
  }
}

private Decimal _amount = 0;

public Decimal Amount
{
  get
  {
    return _amount;
  }

  set
  {
    if (_amount == value)
    { return; }
    _amount = value;
    RaisePropertyChanged("Amount");
  }
}

private bool _isrecurring = true;

public bool Isrecurring
{
  get
  {
    return _isrecurring;
  }

  set
  {

    _isrecurring = value;
    RaisePropertyChanged("Isrecurring");
  }
}

public IList<Category> Categories
{
  get
  {
    return _dataService.GetCategories();
  }
}

}
```

In the BillViewModel Constructor we register the MVVM Light Messenger event aggregator so that the Bill object sent from the MainViewModel EditCommand (see Listing 6-15) can be received here.

Listing 6-15. The Private Fields and the Constructor of BillViewModel

```
    private readonly IDataService _dataService;
private readonly INavigationService _navigationService;

public BillViewModel(IDataService dataService, INavigationService navigationService)
{
  _dataService = dataService;
  _navigationService = navigationService;
  Title = "Bill Reminder";
  Messenger.Default.Register<Billtem>(this, message =>
  {
    Bill bill = _dataService.GetBillByID(message.BillID);
    BillID = bill.BillID;
    Name = bill.Name;
    Amount = bill.Amount;
    DueDate = bill.DueDate;
    Isrecurring = bill.IsRecurring;
    SelectedCategory = _dataService.GetCategoryByID(bill.CategoryID);
  });
}
```

Also we have two RelayCommands, shown in Listing 6-16. One is SaveCommand that is used to save the bill by calling AddBill or UpdateBill from the DataService class depending on the action. BackCommand helps to navigate back to MainPage.xaml.

Listing 6-16. The RelayCommands of the BillViewModel

```
private RelayCommand _saveCommand;

public RelayCommand SaveCommand
{
  get
  {
    return _saveCommand
      ?? (_saveCommand = new RelayCommand(ExecuteSaveCommand));
  }
}

private void ExecuteSaveCommand()
{
  if (BillID > 0)
  {
    _dataService.UpdateBill(new Bill()
    {
      BillID = BillID,
      Name = _name,
      Amount = _amount,
      IsRecurring = _isrecurring,
```

```
        CategoryID = _selectedCategory.CategoryID,
        DueDate = _dueDate
      });
    }
    else
    {
      _dataService.AddBill(new Bill()
      {
        Name = _name,
        Amount = _amount,
        IsRecurring = _isrecurring,
        CategoryID = _selectedCategory.CategoryID,
        DueDate = _dueDate
      });
    }
    _navigationService.Navigate(typeof(MainPage));
}


private RelayCommand _backCommand;

public RelayCommand BackCommand
{
  get
  {
    return _backCommand
      ?? (_backCommand = new RelayCommand(ExecuteBackCommand));
  }
}

private void ExecuteBackCommand()
{
  _navigationService.GoBack();
}
```

Views

MainPage.xaml is the starting page of the Bill Reminder Windows 8 app. Its code is shown in Listing 6-17. This view has a GridView control and two app bar buttons for navigating to the Bill.xaml page. The GridView control binds to the Bill property in the MainViewControl and displays the recent bills. We use a data template to customize the way we showcase our bill information in the GridView. The displayed bill information has two modes, depending on the status of the Bill object's IsPaid property. If the IsPaid property is false then we display a Textbox for entering the bill amount and a Button to mark the bill as paid. This button command is bound to the PaidCommand in the MainViewModel. But if the bill is paid instead then this control's Visibility property is set to Collapsed using a ValueConverter BoolToValueConverter.

Listing 6-17. The MainPage.Xaml

```
<Page x:Class="BillReminder.MainPage"
    mc:Ignorable="d ignore"
    d:DesignHeight="768"
    d:DesignWidth="1366"
    xmlns:converters="using:BillReminder.Converters"
```

```xml
        DataContext="{Binding Main, Source={StaticResource Locator}}">
    <Page.Resources>
        <ResourceDictionary>
        <!--Converters declaration-->
            <converters:DateTimeToStringConverter
    x:Key="DateTimeToStringConverter"/>
            <converters:DecimalToStringConverter
    x:Key="DecimalToStringConverter"/>
            <converters:VisibilityConverter
    x:Key="VisibilityConverter"
    TrueValue="Collapsed"
    FalseValue="Visible"/>
            <converters:VisibilityConverter
    x:Key="InverseVisibilityConverter"
    TrueValue="Visible" FalseValue="Collapsed"/>
        <!--Data Template to display bill info-->
            <DataTemplate x:Key="BillDataTemplate">
                <Grid
    Background="{StaticResource ListViewItemPlaceholderBackgroundThemeBrush}">
                    <Grid.ColumnDefinitions>
                        <ColumnDefinition Width="195*"/>
                        <ColumnDefinition Width="97*"/>
                    </Grid.ColumnDefinitions>
                    <Grid.RowDefinitions>
                        <RowDefinition Height="34*"/>
                        <RowDefinition Height="42*"/>
                        <RowDefinition Height="51*"/>
                    </Grid.RowDefinitions>
                    <TextBlock
    Text="{Binding Name}"
    Grid.ColumnSpan="2"/>
                    <StackPanel Grid.Row="1" Grid.ColumnSpan="2">
                        <TextBlock
    Text="{Binding DueDate, Mode= TwoWay, Converter={StaticResource DateTimeToStringConverter}}"/>
                        <TextBox
    Visibility="{Binding IsPaid,Converter={StaticResource VisibilityConverter}}"
    Text="{Binding Amount, Mode=TwoWay, Converter={StaticResource DecimalToStringConverter}}" />
                        <TextBlock
    Visibility="{Binding IsPaid,Converter={StaticResource InverseVisibilityConverter}}"
    Text="{Binding PaidAmount, Mode=TwoWay, Converter={StaticResource DecimalToStringConverter}}"/>
                    </StackPanel>
                    <StackPanel Grid.Row="2" Grid.Column="1">
                        <TextBlock
    Visibility="{Binding IsPaid,Converter={StaticResource InverseVisibilityConverter}}"
    Text="Paid" />
                        <Button
    Content="Pay"
    Visibility="{Binding IsPaid,Converter={StaticResource VisibilityConverter}}"
    Command="{Binding PayCommand, Mode=OneWay}"/>
                    </StackPanel>
                </Grid>
            </DataTemplate>
```

```xml
            <ResourceDictionary.MergedDictionaries>
                <ResourceDictionary Source="../Skins/MainSkin.xaml" />
            </ResourceDictionary.MergedDictionaries>
        </ResourceDictionary>
    </Page.Resources>
<Page.BottomAppBar>
        <AppBar
IsOpen="{Binding ShowAppBar, Mode=TwoWay}">
<Grid>
            <Grid.ColumnDefinitions>
                <ColumnDefinition/>
    <ColumnDefinition/>
    </Grid.ColumnDefinitions>
    <StackPanel Grid.Column="1">
     <!--Edit Appbar Button-->
     <Button x:Name="EditButton"
                                Style="{StaticResource EditAppBarButtonStyle}"
                                Command="{Binding EditCommand, Mode=OneWay}" />
      <!--Add Appbar Button-->
      <Button x:Name="AddButton"
                                Style="{StaticResource AddAppBarButtonStyle}"
                                Command="{Binding AddCommand, Mode=OneWay}"/>
    </StackPanel>
    </Grid>
</AppBar>
</Page.BottomAppBar>

    <Grid
        Background="{StaticResource ApplicationPageBackgroundThemeBrush}">
        <Grid.RowDefinitions>
            <RowDefinition Height="140"/>
            <RowDefinition Height="*"/>
        </Grid.RowDefinitions>
        <Grid>
            <Grid.ColumnDefinitions>
                <ColumnDefinition Width="Auto"/>
                <ColumnDefinition Width="*"/>
            </Grid.ColumnDefinitions>
            <TextBlock x:Name="PageTitle"
                    Text="Bill Reminder"
                    Grid.Column="1"
                    Style="{StaticResource PageHeaderTextStyle}"/>
        </Grid>
        <!--GridView to display the recent bills-->
        <GridView x:Name="BillGridView"
                Grid.Row="1"
                Margin="110,50,0,0"
                Foreground="White"
                SelectionMode="Single"
                IsSwipeEnabled="True"
                IsItemClickEnabled="True"
```

```
    ItemsSource="{Binding Bills}"
    Header="Recent Bills"
    FontSize="32"
    ItemTemplate="{StaticResource BillDataTemplate}"
                SelectedItem ="{Binding SelectedBill, Mode=TwoWay}" >
        <GridView.ItemsPanel>
            <ItemsPanelTemplate>
                <WrapGrid
    Orientation="Horizontal" />
            </ItemsPanelTemplate>
        </GridView.ItemsPanel>
    </GridView>
  </Grid>
</Page>
```

■ **Note**   We intentionally left out the most of the XAML code related to styling and positioning of the controls in this chapter to simplify the explanations and for easier rediability. The source code that you can download from the APress web site has the complete implementation.

BillView.xaml is used to create and edit a bill. This page, shown in Figure 6-12, has controls like TextBox, ComboBox, and CheckBox that binds to the properties of the BillViewModel .

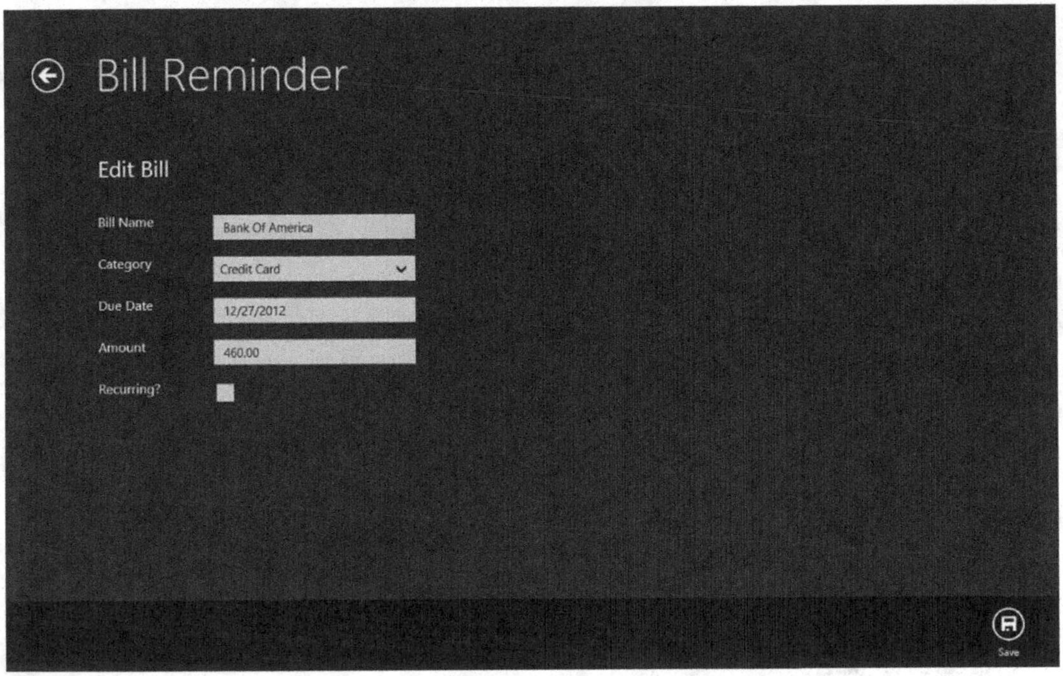

Figure 6-12. *BillView.xaml displays a bill's details*

Also on the page we have two buttons. The Save button is used to save the Bill object to the database and this button command property is bound to the BillViewModel's SaveCommand. The BackButton is used to navigate back to MainPage.xaml. This page has a ComboBox that allows the user to pick a bill category. This ComboBox is bound to the Categories property of the ViewModel, and the SelectedItem is bound two-way to the SelectedCategory property (see Listing 6-18).

Listing 6-18. The Bill.xaml

```xml
<Page x:Class="BillReminder.Views.BillView"
    x:Name="pageRoot"
      xmlns:converters="using:BillReminder.Converters"
      mc:Ignorable="d ignore"
      d:DesignHeight="768"
      d:DesignWidth="1366"
      DataContext="{Binding Bill, Source={StaticResource Locator}}">
  <Page.Resources>
        <ResourceDictionary>
            <converters:DateTimeToStringConverter
  x:Key="DateTimeToStringConverter"/>
            <converters:DecimalToStringConverter
  x:Key="DecimalToStringConverter"/>
        </ResourceDictionary>
    </Page.Resources>
<Page.BottomAppBar>
<AppBar IsOpen="True">
<Grid>
  <Grid.ColumnDefinitions>
    <ColumnDefinition/>
    <ColumnDefinition/>
  </Grid.ColumnDefinitions>
  <StackPanel Orientation="Horizontal"/>
  <StackPanel Grid.Column="1">
  <!--Bill Edit button-->
  <Button x:Name="EditButton"
                    Style="{StaticResource SaveAppBarButtonStyle}"
                    Command="{Binding SaveCommand, Mode=OneWay}" />
      </StackPanel>
</Grid>
</AppBar>
</Page.BottomAppBar>
    <Grid Background="{StaticResource ApplicationPageBackgroundThemeBrush}">
        <Grid.RowDefinitions>
            <RowDefinition Height="140"/>
            <RowDefinition Height="*"/>
        </Grid.RowDefinitions>
        <Grid>
            <Grid.ColumnDefinitions>
                <ColumnDefinition Width="Auto"/>
                <ColumnDefinition Width="*"/>
            </Grid.ColumnDefinitions>
            <Button
```

```xml
    x:Name="backButton"
    Command="{Binding BackCommand, Mode=OneWay}"
    Style="{StaticResource BackButtonStyle}"/>
            <TextBlock x:Name="pageTitle"
    Text="Bill Reminder"
    Style="{StaticResource PageHeaderTextStyle}"
    Grid.Column="1"/>
        </Grid>
    <!--Controls for inputting Bill details-->
        <StackPanel Grid.Row="1">
            <StackPanel>
                <TextBlock
    Text="{Binding Title}"/>
            </StackPanel>
            <StackPanel Orientation="Horizontal">
                <TextBlock
    Text="Bill Name"/>
                <TextBox
    Text="{Binding Name, Mode=TwoWay}"/>
            </StackPanel>
            <StackPanel Orientation="Horizontal">">
                <TextBlock Text="Category"/>
                <ComboBox
    ItemsSource="{Binding Categories}"
    DisplayMemberPath="Name"
    SelectedItem="{Binding SelectedCategory, Mode=TwoWay}"/>
            </StackPanel>
            <StackPanel Orientation="Horizontal">
                <TextBlock
    Text="Due Date"/>
                    <TextBox
                        Text="{Binding DueDate, Converter={StaticResource
                        DateTimeToStringConverter}, Mode=TwoWay}"/>
            </StackPanel>
            <StackPanel Orientation="Horizontal">
                <TextBlock
    Text="Amount"/>
                    <TextBox
                        Text="{Binding Amount, Converter={StaticResource DecimalToStringConverter},
    Mode=TwoWay}"/>
            </StackPanel>
            <StackPanel Orientation="Horizontal">
                <TextBlock
    Text="Recurring?"/>
                <CheckBox
    IsChecked="{Binding IsRecurring, Mode=TwoWay}"/>
            </StackPanel>
        </StackPanel>
    </Grid>
</Page>
```

Now with all the codes in place, when we run the Bill Reminder app the user will be able to create bills and also mark a recent bill paid, as the one shown in Figure 6-9.

Ideas for Improvement

The Bill Reminder app can be worked on and improved to make it a fully functional financial management app. The following are some of the features that can be added.

- Extend the app by adding support for registering income and expenses to make it a full-fledged personal finance app.

- Localize the app by supporting different languages, currencies, and formats.

- Incude spending analysis tools with dynamic graphs and reports.

- Support live tiles and bill reminder notifications.

Conclusion

This chapter introduced you to SQLite, SQLite wrapper sqlite-net, and MVVM Light and discussed how this framework is used in building a real-world Windows 8 app. Specifically, it discussed integrating SQLite into a Windows 8 app and using it as a local database to store data, building an app that is based on the MVVM pattern.

With this chapter we conclude Part 2 of this book, which explained the various Windows 8 app local storage options. In the next section we look at various remote data access options, including Windows Azure Mobile Services.

CHAPTER 7

■ ■ ■

ASP.NET Web API

In the last three chapters, we saw some of the local storage options that can be used to store data locally and have also built apps that are best suited for storing data locally. Storing data locally will not be a best option in many cases especially when we build line of business (LOB) applications. There are times when our app needs to interact with a very large quantity of data stored in the database servers like SQL Server, Oracle, and so on. As of now we don't have the necessary APIs similar to ADO.NET in WinRT to communicate directly with the database, so we need to build a server-side async/services infrastructure that exposes the data by connecting to the database, which can then be consumed by the Windows 8 app.

In the next three chapters we learn about a few such service infrastructures that can be used to store or retrieve data within Windows 8 apps. To start with, in this chapter we learn to set up a CRUD ASP.NET Web API Rest service and consume this service from a Windows Store JavaScript app by building a Party Planner app.

Introduction to ASP.NET Web API

ASP.NET Web API introduced with ASP.NET MVC 4.0 and .NET 4.5 is a new addition to the ASP.NET stack that allows you to create RESTful and AJAX APIs that lets you build web or HTTP-based client or server endpoints.

Why Should We Use Web API?

ASP.NET Web API is Microsoft's answer to a modern programming landscape for building a service layer that can be easily consumed by most clients. Web API is an ideal platform for building pure HTTP-based services that can be useful while building a multiplatform applications like apps for desktop applications, HTML5, iOS, Android, Windows 8, and Windows Phone, as all these clients can make GET, PUT, POST, and DELETE requests and get the Web API response.

Building the Party Planner Windows 8 App

Organizing a party is a tedious job that involves lot of planning, like creating a guest list, making a shopping list, and so on. With our Party Planner Windows 8 app we no longer have to write these lists on a scrap of paper. This app will help to manage and track various parties by maintaining guest lists and records of party supplies. We create this app using HTML5 and JavaScript with SQL Server as the database. We also build a service layer for data interaction between the HTML client and SQL Server using ASP.NET Web API. EntityFramework Code First will be used as data access layer.

Getting Started

To start with, let's create a new Windows Store Blank App (JavaScript) project and name the project `PartyPlanner.App` and the solution `PartyPlanner`. We add two new pages to the project: `home.html` and `manageparty.html`. Next we add a new Visual C# ASP.NET MVC 4 Web Application to the solution (see Figure 7-1) and name it `PartyPlanner.Web`.

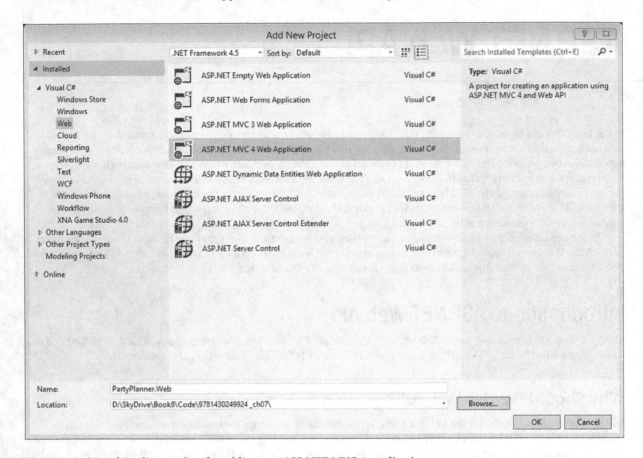

Figure 7-1. *Visual Studio template for adding new ASP.NET MVC 4 application*

In the New ASP.NET MVC 4 Project dialog box (see Figure 7-2), select Web API and click OK to add the PartyPlanner.Web project to the solution.

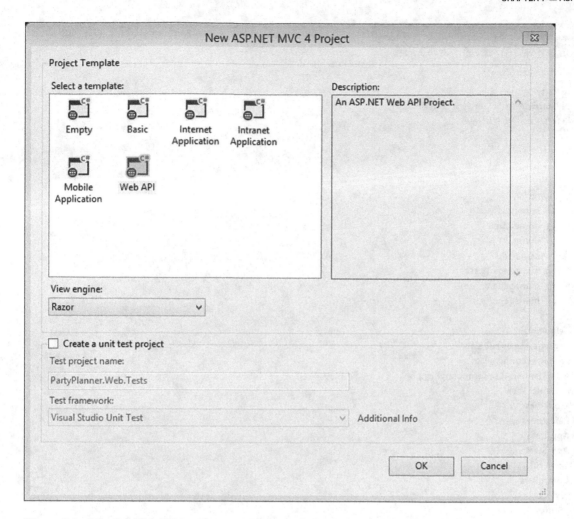

Figure 7-2. *Selecting WebAPI template as project template*

This adds the necessary files and DLL references to the PartyPlanner.Web project. With this addition the PartyPlanner solution will look like the one shown in Figure 7-3.

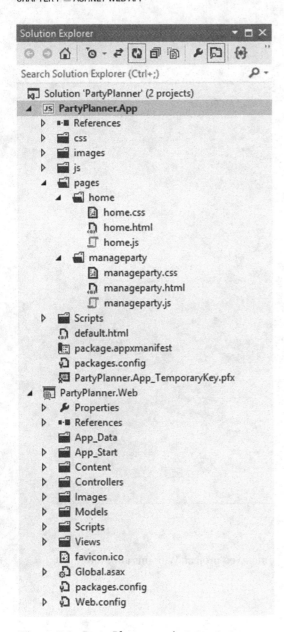

Figure 7-3. Party Planner project structure

Creating Database Tables

The main functionality of the Party Planner app is to help keep track of the shopping lists and guest lists for parties. For this purpose, we create three SQL Server databases with tables using the EntityFramework Code First approach.

- **Party:** Stores the party details.

- **Guest:** Stores the guest list for the party.

- **ShoppingItem:** Stores the list of items that has to be purchased for the party.

EntityFramework Code First

EntityFramework Code First is introduced with EntityFramework. This enables a code-centric approach in building the model instead of working with the designer or XML mapping file. The following are some of the advantages of using Code First.

- It defines an object model using the POCO (plain old CLR object) class with no base class or attributes, so there is no more autogenerated code to work with.

- It supports data persistence without complex configuration.

- It's simple, as there is no edmx model to update or maintain.

- Code-First handles creation and modification of the database schema such that a database is just storage with no logic.

To enable EntityFramework we reference the library in the project using the NuGet package as shown in Figure 7-4 along with JSON.NET.

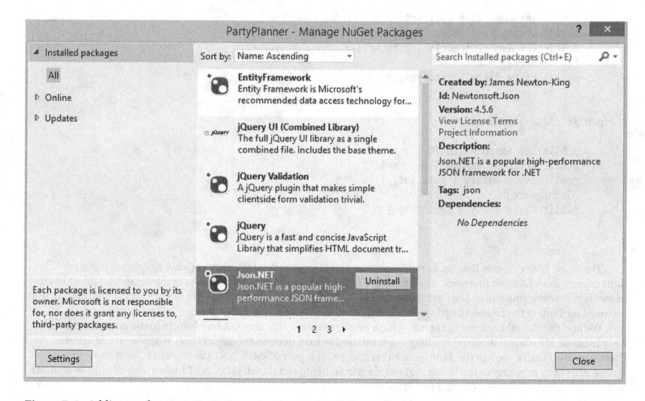

Figure 7-4. *Adding a reference to EntityFramework using the NuGet package*

Next we add the file PartyPlanner.cs to the Models folder in the PartyPlanner.Web project. This file holds three POCO classes that represent the three database tables, Party, Guest, and ShoppingItem, as shown in Listing 7-1.

Listing 7-1. The PartyPlanner EntityFrame Classes

```
namespace PartyPlanner.Models
{

    public class Party
    {
        public int PartyID { get; set; }
        public string PartyName { get; set; }
        public string DateTime { get; set; }
        public bool Completed { get; set; }
        public virtual ICollection<Guest> Guests { get; set; }
        public virtual ICollection<ShoppingItem> ShoppingList { get; set; }
    }

    public class Guest
    {
        public int GuestID { get; set; }
        public string FamilyName { get; set; }
        public int NumberOfPeople { get; set; }
        [JsonIgnore]
        public Party Party { get; set; }
    }

    public class ShoppingItem
    {
        public int ShoppingItemID { get; set; }
        public string ItemName { get; set; }
        public int Quantity { get; set; }
        [JsonIgnore]
        public Party Party { get; set; }
    }
}
```

These are Entity classes that act as model objects that represent the data; they are very simple and have no dependency from EntityFramework. The properties of these classes represent columns of the database table and are of two types: scalar properties like PartyName, ItemName, and navigation properties like Guests and ShoppingList that are used for finding the relationship between the classes.

We add the virtual keyword to the navigation properties to enable lazy loading feature of the entity framework. Lazy loading, also called deferred loading, is a term used to load dependent objects only when we try to access that property. Finally, we use the JsonIgnoreAttribute that is part of JSON.NET (Newtonsoft.Json namespace) to ignore the Party property in the ShoppingItem class from being serialized. JSON.NET has a range of built-in options to fine-tune what gets written from a serialized object.

■ **Note**   JSON.NET is a popular high-performance JSON framework for the .NET Framework that has a range of built-in options to fine-tune what gets written from a serialized object. Please visit www.json.net to learn more about JSON.NET

Web API Controller

With the models in place, next we add an ASP.NET Web API Controller, PartyPlannerController to the project. This controller handles HTTP requests from the client. To add a controller, right-click the Controllers folder in Solution Explorer and then select Add context menu and the Controller to open the Add Controller Wizard. Set the options as shown in Figure 7-5.

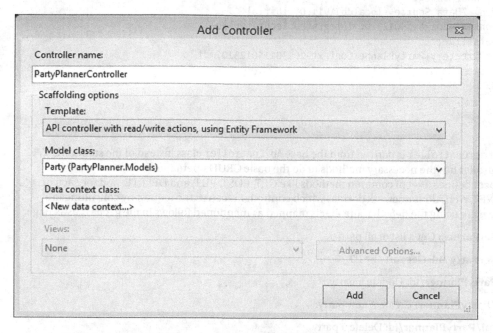

Figure 7-5. Controller template for creating a WebAPI controller from the model

---

■ **Note** Build the project before adding a controller so that the PartyPlanner Models show up in the Add Controller Wizard.

After you click Add, you are prompted to enter the name of the new data context, as shown in Figure 7-6. Once the name is entered, the Visual Studio controller template creates two classes, PartyPlannerController and PartyPlannerContext.

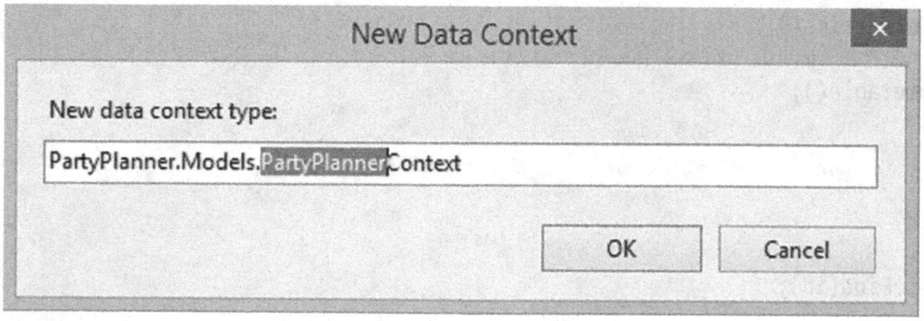

Figure 7-6. Input window for entering the data context class name

The controller template will also update the Web.config (see Listing 7-2) by adding a connectionString that points the PartyPlannerContext to a LocalDB database called PartyPlannerContext.

Listing 7-2. Updated Web.config File with the Connection String

```
<connectionStrings>
  <add name="PartyPlannerContext"
      connectionString="Data Source=(localdb)\v11.0; Initial
Catalog=PartyPlannerContext-20130115012310; Integrated Security=True;
MultipleActiveResultSets=True;
AttachDbFilename=|DataDirectory|PartyPlannerContext-20130115012310.mdf"
      providerName="System.Data.SqlClient" />
</connectionStrings>
```

Add Controller

The generated PartyPlannerController is derived from the base ApiController class instead of the standard MVC controller base. This controller has the necessary methods to do the basic CRUD operations.

The HTTP/1.1 protocol defines a set of common methods like GET, POST, PUT, and DELETE, and for each of these methods, the ASP.NET Web API framework decides which controller receives the request by consulting the route table. In our case, we are using the default route that is mapped as mentioned follows in the global.asax page.

- **GET /api/GetParties:** Get a list of all parties.
- **GET /api/GetParty /id:** Get party by ID.
- **PUT /api/PartyPlanner/id:** Update a party.
- **POST /api/PartyPlanner:** Create a new party.
- **DELETE /api/PartyPlanner/id:** Delete a party.

As this code is good enough only to store and retrieve information from the Party table, we will be including additional methods in this controller to store and retrieve Guest and ShoppingList information along with the party information in the later part of this chapter. As of now, though, Listing 7-3 shows the code generated by the template.

Listing 7-3. PartyPlannerController Code Generated by the Controller Template

```
public class PartyPlannerController : ApiController
{
    private PartyPlannerContext db = new PartyPlannerContext();

    // GET api/PartyPlanner
    public IEnumerable<Party> GetParties()
    {
        return db.Parties.AsEnumerable();
    }

    // GET api/PartyPlanner/5
    public Party GetParty(int id)
    {
        Party party = db.Parties.Find(id);
        if (party == null)
```

```
        {
            throw new HttpResponseException(Request.CreateResponse(HttpStatusCode.NotFound));
        }

        return party;
}

// PUT api/PartyPlanner/5
public HttpResponseMessage PutParty(int id, Party party)
{
    if (ModelState.IsValid && id == party.PartyID)
    {
        db.Entry(party).State = EntityState.Modified;

        try
        {
            db.SaveChanges();
        }
        catch (DbUpdateConcurrencyException)
        {
            return Request.CreateResponse(HttpStatusCode.NotFound);
        }

        return Request.CreateResponse(HttpStatusCode.OK);
    }
    else
    {
        return Request.CreateResponse(HttpStatusCode.BadRequest);
    }
}

// POST api/PartyPlanner
public HttpResponseMessage PostParty(Party party)
{
    if (ModelState.IsValid)
    {
        db.Parties.Add(party);
        db.SaveChanges();

        HttpResponseMessage response = Request.CreateResponse(HttpStatusCode.Created, party);
        response.Headers.Location = new Uri(Url.Link("DefaultApi", new { id = party.PartyID }));
        return response;
    }
    else
    {
        return Request.CreateResponse(HttpStatusCode.BadRequest);
    }
}
```

```
    // DELETE api/PartyPlanner/5
    public HttpResponseMessage DeleteParty(int id)
    {
        Party party = db.Parties.Find(id);
        if (party == null)
        {
            return Request.CreateResponse(HttpStatusCode.NotFound);
        }

        db.Parties.Remove(party);

        try
        {
            db.SaveChanges();
        }
        catch (DbUpdateConcurrencyException)
        {
            return Request.CreateResponse(HttpStatusCode.NotFound);
        }

        return Request.CreateResponse(HttpStatusCode.OK, party);
    }

    protected override void Dispose(bool disposing)
    {
        db.Dispose();
        base.Dispose(disposing);
    }
}
```

Add DataContext

The template also creates a DataContext PartyPlannerContext, as shown in Listing 7-4, that is derived from the EntityFramework base type DbContext. DbContext automatically generates the database using the Entity Class schema and also represents a session with the database and allows it to query the database. The context contains a property DbSet that represents the POCO type Party from our model.

Listing 7-4. PartyPlannerContext Created by the Controller Template

```
public class PartyPlannerContext : DbContext
{
    public PartyPlannerContext() : base("name=PartyPlannerContext")
    {
    }

    public DbSet<Party> Parties { get; set; }
}
```

With the service layer in place, we can integrate it with the Windows 8 app by building the Party Planner app. As mentioned earlier, the Party Planner app has two pages: home.html and manageparty.html.

Designing the App Start Page

Home.html is the start page of this app. It displays the Parties within a grid layout as shown in Figure 7-7 using the WinJS.UI.ListView element by binding to a collection in Home.js. We also define an item template that contains the markup to display the details of each party. This page also has an app bar button that allows us to create a new party (see Listing 7-5).

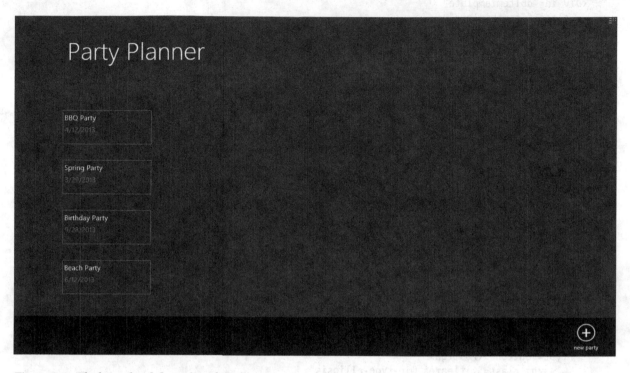

Figure 7-7. The home.html shows list of Parties

■ **Note**   We deleted the default.html page and made home.html the default start page by updating the start page under the Application UI section of the package.appmanifest.

Listing 7-5. home.html with a ListView and App Bar Button

```
<!DOCTYPE html>
<html>
<head>
    <meta charset="utf-8" />
    <title>homePage</title>
    <!-- WinJS references -->
    <link href="//Microsoft.WinJS.1.0/css/ui-dark.css" rel="stylesheet" />
    <script src="//Microsoft.WinJS.1.0/js/base.js"></script>
    <script src="//Microsoft.WinJS.1.0/js/ui.js"></script>
```

```html
        <link href="/css/default.css" rel="stylesheet" />
        <link href="/pages/home/home.css" rel="stylesheet" />
        <script src="/pages/home/home.js"></script>
</head>
<body>
    <!--ListView Item Template-->
     <div id="dbItemtemplate"
        class="itemtemplate"
        data-win-control="WinJS.Binding.Template">
        <div class="item">
            <div class="item-content">
                <h2
                  class="item-title win-type-x-small win-type-ellipsis"
                        data-win-bind="innerHTML: PartyName" />
                <h4
                  class="item-subtitle win-type-x-small win-type-ellipsis"
                  data-win-bind="innerHTML: DateTime"></h4>
            </div>
        </div>
    </div>

    <!-- The content that will be loaded and displayed. -->
    <div class="fragment homepage">
        <header
        aria-label="Header content"
        role="banner">
            <button
        class="win-backbutton"
        aria-label="Back"
        disabled
        type="button"></button>
            <h1 class="titlearea win-type-ellipsis">
                <span class="pagetitle">Party Planner</span>
            </h1>
        </header>
        <section aria-label="Main content" role="main">
            <div id="listView"
        class="resultslist win-selectionstylefilled"
        aria-label="My Party"
                data-win-control="WinJS.UI.ListView"
        data-win-options="{
                itemTemplate: select('#dbItemtemplate'),
                 }">

            }"></div>
        </section>
    </div>
```

```
    <!--App bar-->
<div
    data-win-control="WinJS.UI.AppBar"
    class="appBar"
    id="appBar">
    <button
    data-win-control="WinJS.UI.AppBarCommand"
    data-win-options="{id:'newButton', label:'new party', icon:'add',section:'global'}">
    </button>
</div>
</body>
</html>
```

Home.js

Home.js is the JavaScript file for the home.html page and most of the activities in this file happen in the page ready function. Inside this function we call the PartyPlanner service GetParties using the WinJS.xhr function. WinJS.xhr abstracts all the complexity of the XMLHttpRequest and provides a simple interface that uses Promises to handle the asynchronous responses. GetParties returns an HTTP response in a JSON format that is then parsed to a JSON object. This JSON object is then bound to the ListView. This page also has an itemInvoked function that is attached to the ListView and is called when an item is selected from the ListView. Once called, this function navigates to manageParty.html using the WinJS.Navigation.navigate function. This function takes the detail page location and selected Party object as parameter (see Listing 7-6).

Listing 7-6. Home.js Gets the List of Parties by Calling the ASP.NET Web API Service

```
(function () {
    "use strict";
    var partiesLV;
    WinJS.UI.Pages.define("/pages/home/home.html", {
        ready: function (element, options) {
            partiesLV = document.getElementById('listView').winControl;
            partiesLV.oniteminvoked = this._itemInvoked;
            partiesLV.element.focus();
            document.getElementById("newButton")
                .addEventListener("click", doClickNew, false);
            //update the port of the below URL to the one assigned  by Visual Studio
            var createurl = "http://localhost:21962/api/PartyPlanner/";
            WinJS.xhr({
                type: "GET",
                url: createurl,
                headers: { "Content-type": "application/json; charset=utf-8" }
            }).then(success, error);
```

```
        }, _itemInvoked: function (args) {
            args.detail.itemPromise.done(function itemInvoked(item) {
                //Navigating to the manageparty.html on ListItem click
                WinJS.Navigation.navigate("/pages/manageparty/manageparty.html",
{ partyDetail: item.data });
            });
        }
    });

    function success(arg) {
        //HTTP Response binds to the ListView
        var parties =   [];
        parties = JSON.parse(arg.responseText);
        partiesLV.itemDataSource = new WinJS.Binding.List(parties).dataSource;
    }

    function error(arg) {
        //Display Error
    }

    function doClickNew() {
        //App bar button click
        WinJS.Navigation.navigate("/pages/manageparty/manageparty.html", null);
    }
})();
```

Retrieving the List of Parties

As shown in Listing 7-6, to display the list of parties in the home page, we call the GetParties method that resides in the PartyPlannerController. When this method is called for the first time, the EntityFramework Code First uses a set of conventions to determine the schema and creates the database and necessary tables and referential integrity between the tables. It uses the database connection information from the Web.config file. Once this is created, we will be able to see the database in the VS.NET SQL Server Object Explorer (click Ctrl + \, Ctrl + S), as shown in Figure 7-8.

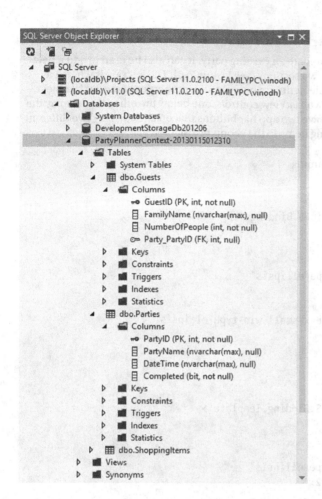

Figure 7-8. *Database created using EntityFramework Code First*

The default code generated for GetParties in PartyPlannerController (see Listing 7-3) will only return the Party entity and will not get the related entities like Guests and ShoppingList for each party. To get that we add three lines of code, as shown in Listing 7-7.

Listing 7-7. GetParties includes Guests and ShoppingList

```
public IEnumerable<Party> GetParties()
{
    db.Configuration.LazyLoadingEnabled = false;
    return db.Parties.Include(g => g.Guests)
                    .Include(s => s.ShoppingList)
                    .AsEnumerable();
}
```

First we disable the lazy loading option and then include those entities that have to be returned along with the Party entity using EntityFramework's Include method.

Designing the Page to Manage a Party

The manageparty.html page helps to create a new party or update an existing party. It can also be used to add a new guest or a shopping item to an existing party. This page has two sections (see Listing 7-8): The left side is where we have HTML elements for creating a party and these HTML elements are bound to the properties of the Party object using WinJS data-win-bind property. On the right we have two ListView controls, one below the other, that display the Guests and Shopping Items. At the bottom of the page, we have two app bar buttons that on click display two different Flyout UIs: one for adding the guests and the other for adding items to the shopping list.

Listing 7-8. The manageparty.html with Left and Right Columns

```
<body>
    <!--Item Templates for ShoppingItem ListView-->
    <div id="shoppingTemplate" data-win-control="WinJS.Binding.Template">
        <div class="item">
            <div class="item-content">
                <h2
        class="item-title win-type-x-small win-type-ellipsis"
        data-win-bind="innerHTML: ItemName"></h2>
                <h4
        class="item-subtitle-shoppingitem win-type-x-small win-type-ellipsis"
        data-win-bind="innerHTML: Quantity"></h4>
            </div>
        </div>
    </div>
    <!--Item Templates for Guest ListView-->
    <div id="guestTemplate" data-win-control="WinJS.Binding.Template">
        <div class="item">
            <div class="item-content">
                <h2
        class="item-title win-type-x-small win-type-ellipsis"
        data-win-bind="innerHTML: FamilyName"></h2>
                <h4
        class="item-subtitle-guests win-type-x-small win-type-ellipsis"
        data-win-bind="innerHTML: NumberOfPeople"></h4>
            </div>
        </div>
    </div>

    <div class="manageparty fragment">
        <header aria-label="Header content" role="banner">
            <button
        class="win-backbutton"
        aria-label="Back"
        disabled
        type="button"></button>
            <h1 class="titlearea win-type-ellipsis">
                <span class="pagetitle">Add/Edit Party Details</span>
            </h1>
        </header>
        <section aria-label="Main content" role="main">
```

```html
    <!—Leftside - Party HTML Elements-->
    <div id="divDetail" class="leftColumn">
        <label for="partyName">Party Name</label>
        <input
            type="text"
    id="partyName"
    name="partyName"
    data-win-bind="value: PartyName Binding.Mode.twoway">
<br />
        <label for="datetime">Date Time:</label>
        <input
        type="text"
                id="datetime"
                name="datetime"
                data-win-bind="value: DateTime Binding.Mode.twoway">
 <br />

        <label for="completed">IsCompleted?</label>
        <input
type="checkbox"
id="completed"
name="completed"
class="boxes"
data-win-bind="checked: Completed Binding.Mode.twoway" />
<br />

        <input
        type="button"
        name="saveParty"
        id="saveParty"
        value="Save Party Details" />
    </div>
    <!--Right Side-->
    <div class="rightColumn">
        <h2>Guest List</h2>
        <div class="item">
        <label  class="labelMessage"  id="lblGuestMessage"/> </div>
        <div
        id="guestListView"
        data-win-control="WinJS.UI.ListView"
        data-win-options="{itemTemplate:select('#guestTemplate')}">
        </div>
        <br />

        <h2>Shopping List</h2>
        <div class="item"> <label class="labelMessage" id="lblItemMessage"/></div>
        <div
        id="shoppingListView"
        data-win-control="WinJS.UI.ListView"
        data-win-options="{itemTemplate:select('#shoppingTemplate')}">
        </div>
    </div>
```

```html
            <!--Shopping Flyout UI-->
            <div id="shoppingItemFlyout" data-win-control="WinJS.UI.Flyout">
                <p>
                    <label for="Item">
                        Name
                        <br />
                    </label>
                    <input type="text" id="shopppingItem" />
                </p>
                <p>
                    <label for="Item">
                        Quantity
                        <br />
                    </label>

                    <input type="text" id="quantity" />
                </p>
                <button id="addToShoppingList">
                    Add</button>
            </div>
            <!--Guest Flyout UI-->
            <div id="guestFlyout" data-win-control="WinJS.UI.Flyout">
                <p>
                    <label for="guestName">
                        Family Name
                        <br />
                    </label>
                    <input type="text" id="guestName" />
                </p>
                <p>
                    <label for="Item">
                        No of Guest
                        <br />
                    </label>
                    <input type="text" id="noofguest" />
                </p>
                <button id="addToGuestList">
                    Add</button>
            </div>
        </section>
    </div>

    <!--App bar-->
    <div data-win-control="WinJS.UI.AppBar" class="appBar" id="appBar">
        <button
        data-win-control="WinJS.UI.AppBarCommand"
        data-win-options="{id:'showGuest', label:'Add Guest', icon:'add',section:'global'}">
        </button>
```

```
    <button
    data-win-control="WinJS.UI.AppBarCommand"
    data-win-options="{id:'showShopping', label:'Add Item', icon:'add',section:'global'}">
    </button>
    </div>
</body>
```

manageparty.js

The manageParty.js is the JavaScript page for manageparty.html. This page's ready function has the event handler for all the buttons in manageparty.html. This function also handles the Party object passed from home.html by assigning the Party object to a local variable and calling the function UpdateUI. UpdateUI binds the Guests and ShoppingItems properties of the Party object to the corresponding ListView controls (see Listing 7-9).

Listing 7-9. Page Ready Sets the Event Handler for the Buttons and Binds the Party Object to the HTML Elements

```
WinJS.UI.Pages.define("/pages/manageparty/manageparty.html", {
    ready: function (element, options) {
        //Hide right column on page ready
        $('.rightColumn').hide();
        //assign the event handler for the buttons
        document.getElementById("saveParty").addEventListener("click", onSaveParty, false);
        document.getElementById("showShopping").addEventListener("click", onShowShopping, false);
        document.getElementById("showGuest").addEventListener("click", onShowGuest, false);
        document.getElementById("addToShoppingList").addEventListener("click", onAddToShoppingList, false);
        document.getElementById("addToGuestList").addEventListener("click", onAddToGuestList, false);

        //ListView control to local variable
        shoppingLV = document.getElementById('shoppingListView').winControl;
        guestLV = document.getElementById('guestListView').winControl;

        //Get the Party object as parameter and update the listview
        if (options != null && options.partyDetail != null) {
            party = options.partyDetail;
            UpdateUI();
        }
        else {
            party = { PartyID: 0, PartyName: "", DateTime: "", Completed: "false" };
        }
        var src = WinJS.Binding.as(party);
        var form = document.getElementById("divDetail");
        WinJS.Binding.processAll(form, src);
    },
});

function UpdateUI() {
    //Check to see if Party is already created
    if (party.PartyID > 0) {
        $('.rightColumn').show();
        if (party.Guests == null) {
            $("#lblGuestMessage").text('No guest is invited to this party!')
```

```
    } else {
        $("#lblGuestMessage").text('');
    }
    if (party.ShoppingList == null) {
        $("#lblItemMessage").text('No item to the shoppinglist is added.')
    } else {
        $("#lblItemMessage").text('');
    }
}
//binding Guests and ShoppingItem to ListViews
shoppingLV.itemDataSource = new WinJS.Binding.List(party.ShoppingList).dataSource;
guestLV.itemDataSource = new WinJS.Binding.List(party.Guests).dataSource;
}
```

Creating a New Party

To create a party, party information is entered as shown in Figure 7-7. one the information is entered and you click Save Party Details, we invoke the onSaveParty function in the manageparty.js, which in turn calls another function sendPartyToService, which posts the Party JavaScript object to the PartyPlanner Web API service using the WinJS.xhr function (see Listing 7-10), which is then handled by the PartyPlannerController's PostParty method.

Listing 7-10. onSaveParty Creates or Updates a Party

```
function onSaveParty() {
    sendPartyToService("POST")
}

function sendPartyToService(method) {
    var createurl = "http://localhost:21962/api/PartyPlanner/" + party.PartyID;
    WinJS.xhr({
        type: method,
        url: createurl,
        headers: { "Content-type": "application/json; charset=utf-8" },
        data: JSON.stringify(party)
    }).then(success, error);
}

function success(arg) {
    party = JSON.parse(arg.responseText);
    UpdateUI();
}

function error(arg) {
    //Display error
}
```

The PostParty method (see Listing 7-11) is used to add or update party details. In this method we first check to see if the PartyID is zero; if so, we insert the Party object into the data context by calling the Add method; otherwise we update the entity state to Modified. Once done, we call the data context SaveChanges method to permanently save the party information in to the database. Once saved, we then return the Party object as an HTTP response.

Listing 7-11. PostParty Sets the Entity State before Saving the Changes

```
public HttpResponseMessage PostParty(Party party)
{
    if (ModelState.IsValid)
    {
        if (party.PartyID == 0)
            db.Parties.Add(party);
        else
        {
            db.Entry(party).State = EntityState.Modified;
        }
        db.SaveChanges();
        HttpResponseMessage response = Request.CreateResponse(HttpStatusCode.Created, party);
        response.Headers.Location = new Uri(Url.Link("DefaultApi", new { id = party.PartyID }));
        return response;
    }
    else
    {
        return Request.CreateResponse(HttpStatusCode.BadRequest);
    }
}
```

Add Guest or Shopping Item

A Guest or a ShoppingItem is added when the user clicks Add in the Flyout UI as shown in Figure 7-9. The information entered by the user is used to construct a Guest or ShoppingItem array and is added to the Party object's Guests or ShoppingItems collection (see Listing 7-12). The Party JavaScript object is then PUT to the PartyPlanner Web API service, PutParty.

Figure 7-9. Party details with Flyout UI for adding new Guest to the Party

Listing 7-12. Add Guest and ShoppingItem to the Database

```
function onAddToShoppingList() {
    if (party.ShoppingList == null) {
        party.ShoppingList = [];
    }
    party.ShoppingList.push(
        {ShoppingItemID:"0", ItemName: $("#shopppingItem").val() , Quantity:    $("#quantity").val()}
    );
    sendPartyToService("PUT");
    document.getElementById("shoppingItemFlyout").winControl.hide();
}

function onAddToGuestList() {
    if (party.Guests == null) {
        party.Guests = [];
    }
    party.Guests.push(
        {GuestID:"0", FamilyName: $("#guestName").val() , NumberOfPeople:    $("#noofguest").val()}
    );
    sendPartyToService("PUT");
    document.getElementById("guestFlyout").winControl.hide();
}
```

The PutParty method resides in the PartyPlannerController and loops through the items in the Guests and ShoppingList collections to update the Entity State before calling the SaveChanges context method to permanently update the changes in the database (see Listing 7-13).

Listing 7-13. Updating the Entity State before Saving to Database

```
public HttpResponseMessage PutParty(int id, Party party)
{
    if (ModelState.IsValid )
    {
        db.Entry(party).State = EntityState.Modified;

        if (party.ShoppingList != null)
        {
            foreach (var item in party.ShoppingList)
            {
                if (item.ShoppingItemID == 0)
                {
                    item.Party = party;
                    db.Entry(item).State = EntityState.Added;
                }
                else
                {
                    db.Entry(item).State = EntityState.Modified;
                }
            }
        }

        if (party.Guests != null)
        {
            foreach (var item in party.Guests)
            {
                if (item.GuestID == 0)
                {
                    item.Party = party;
                    db.Entry(item).State = EntityState.Added;
                }
                else
                {
                    db.Entry(item).State = EntityState.Modified;
                }
            }
        }
        try
        {
            db.SaveChanges();
        }
        catch (DbUpdateConcurrencyException)
        {
            return Request.CreateResponse(HttpStatusCode.NotFound);
        }
```

```
            HttpResponseMessage response = Request.CreateResponse(HttpStatusCode.Created, party);
            response.Headers.Location = new Uri(Url.Link("DefaultApi", new { id = party.PartyID }));
            return response;
        }
        else
        {
            return Request.CreateResponse(HttpStatusCode.BadRequest);
        }
    }
}
```

Now with all the codes in place, when we run the Party Planner app the user will be able to create a party and also will be able to add guests and items to the shopping list as the one shown in Figure 7-9.

Ideas for Improvement

The Party Planner app can be worked on and improved to make it a feature-rich app. The following are some of the features that can be added.

- Importing the guest list from the People app using the Contact Picker contract.

- Integrating with social network options to add the party as a Facebook event and import guests from Facebook.

- Supporting live tiles and sending party reminder notifications.

Conclusion

In this chapter we learned to use SQL Server as the database for storing and retrieving data from a Windows 8 app by building a Service layer using ASP.NET Web API. ASP.NET Web API is a flexible, extendable, and straightforward way to build an HTTP endpoint that can be consumed within Windows 8 app. Also in this chapter we learned to use the EntityFramework Code First approach as our data access framework.

In the next chapter we learn to use WCF services with Windows 8 apps by building yet another app. Also in the next chapter we learn to use Prism for Windows Runtime.

CHAPTER 8

■ ■ ■

WCF Services

In Chapter 7 we learned to build a service infrastructure using ASP.NET Web API to connect to the SQL Server using Entity Framework Code First. Continuing, in this chapter we learn to build the service infrastructure using Windows Communication Framework (WCF).

This chapter begins by briefly looking into building Business Apps for WinRT and then provides introduction to Prism for Windows Runtime, which is used to implement the Model-View-ViewModel (MVVM) pattern with navigation through a loosely coupled communication mechanism called PubSub events and app lifecycle management. We learn these concepts by developing a Bill of Material (BOM) Windows 8 app using XAML/C#, Prism, and Entity Framework Code First with WCF as the Service layer.

Business Apps for WinRT

Business Apps for WinRT can be broadly categorized into two different types of application: business to consumer (B2C) and the line of business (LOB) application. B2C applications are the kind of application that allows people outside the company, mostly consumers, to access the product and services of the company like a reservation system, utility app, and so on, that lets us manage and pay our bills. LOB applications generally facilitate a precise customer transaction or business need, and they could be consumer service apps, Enterprise CRM, invoicing systems, or inventory systems.

Prism Overview

Prism for Windows Runtime is a set of guidance principles for building business applications on WinRT using XAML and C#. Prism is based on various architectural goals like loose coupling, separation of concerns, maintainability, testability, and leveraging WinRT platform features with MVVM. Prism for WinRT provides a couple of downloadable, reusable infrastructure class libraries.

■ **Note** The Prism for Windows 8 app can be downloaded from `http://prismwindowsruntime.codeplex.com/`.

The first library that we briefly see is `Microsoft.Practices.Prism.StoreApps`. This library provides the following features:

- MVVM support by including base classes for Views and ViewModel.

- Navigation.

- Application state management.

- Command support as part of MVVM pattern.

- Validation.

- Support for WinRT platform features like the Search/Setting charm and flyouts.

Next we'll see `Microsoft.Practices.Prism.PubSubEvents`, a library that encapsulates PubSub functionality. The `Pubsub` event in Prism is based on the `EventAggregator` pattern, which helps in achieving loosely coupled communications between ViewModels and Client Services. The general idea of this pattern is that when the components within the system want to communicate between each other, instead of coupling them by type or lifetime, they will be loosely coupled. This is achieved by placing a middle man (i.e., `EventAggregator`) in between the Publisher and Subscriber; instead of directly depending on each other, they will be dependent on the middle man. The `EventAggregator` is a container for event objects and these event objects are the ones that do the lion's share of the work. The event objects are subscribed to by the subscribers and published to by the publisher.

Getting Started with Prism

We use Prism for Windows Runtime's guidance from Microsoft Patterns & Practices. Microsoft Patterns & Practices is a group that provides guidance on best practices and design patterns for Microsoft development technologies. Some of their popular offerings are Enterprise Library and Prism 4. These guidelines help us to write business applications that can be easily maintained, extended, and tested.

The Microsoft Patterns & Practices project web site includes numerous projects and sample applications that showcase best practices. You can find it at `http://pnp.azurewebsites.net/en-us/projects.htm`.

Building a Bill of Material Windows 8 App

A bill of material (BOM) is used to list the parts or items needed to build a component, which can be industrial equipment, software, or physical building materials, by associating each individual item with the component. A BOM app helps to maintain a centralized and accurate record of items for manufacturing, production, and a just-in-time environment. Using this kind of app helps to improve material management, control inventory, and reduce manufacturing costs.

We will create the BOM app (see Figure 8-1) using XAML and C# with SQL Server as the database and display the components and its corresponding parts. Using this app, a user can add new component and part and can also associate one or more parts with the component.

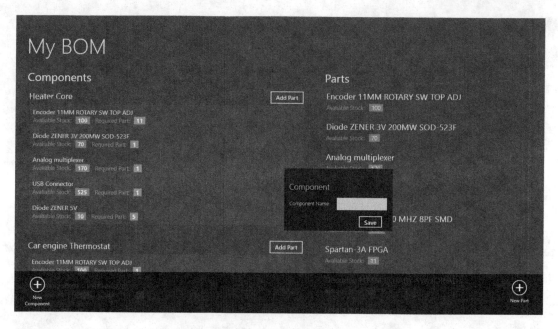

Figure 8-1. Bill of Material app displaying components and parts

We also create a service layer for data interaction between the BOM app and SQL Server using WCF. Just like the Party Planner app in Chapter 6, here also we use Entity Framework Code First as the data access layer.

Getting Started

To start, let's create a new Windows Store Blank App (XAML) project and name it BOM.App. We add the Microsoft.Practices.Prism.StoreApps and Microsoft.Practices.Prism.PubSubEvents projects that are part of the Prism for Windows Runtime download and add them as project references in BOM.App.

Next we add a new WCF Service Application to the solution, as shown in Figure 8-2, and name it BOM.Services.

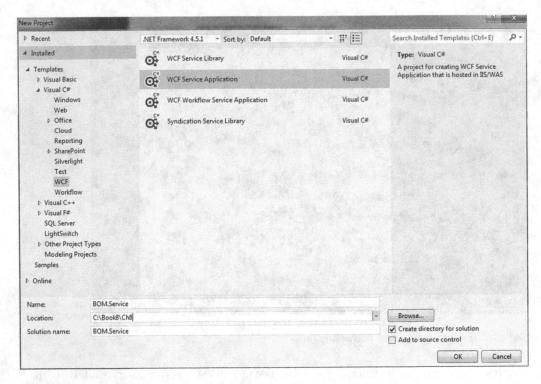

Figure 8-2. *Visual Studio template for adding a new WCF Service Application*

To enable Entity Framework, reference the library in the BOM.Services project using the NuGet package as shown in Figure 8-3.

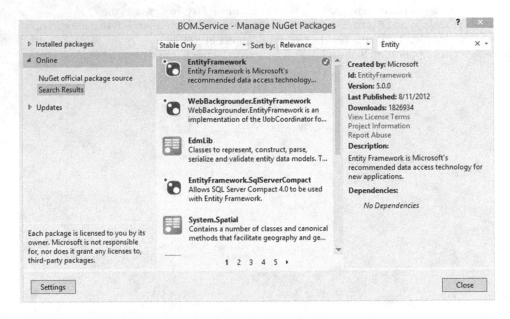

Figure 8-3. *Adding a reference to Entity Framework using NuGet package*

The next step is to create a folder named Models in the BOM.Services project and add a file named BillOfMaterial.cs to it. The BOM Solution project structure will look like the one shown in Figure 8-4.

Figure 8-4. *BOM project structure*

BillOfMaterial.cs holds three POCO classes that represents the three database tables: Component, Part, and BillOfMaterial.

- **Component:** Stores the component details.

- **Part:** Stores the part details.

- **BillOfMaterial:** Stores the BOM information like ComponentID and PartID.

These classes are very simple Entity classes and have no dependency on Entity Framework. The properties of these classes represent columns of the database table. We decorate the classes with the DataContract attribute and properties within the classes with the DataMember (see Listing 8-1) attribute to serialize and transmit data to the WCF Client.

Listing 8-1. BOM Entity Classes

```
using System;
using System.Collections.Generic;
using System.ComponentModel.DataAnnotations;
using System.ComponentModel.DataAnnotations.Schema;
```

```csharp
using System.Linq;
using System.Runtime.Serialization;
using System.Web;

namespace BOM.Service.Models
{
    [DataContract(IsReference = true)]
    public class Part
    {
        [Key]
        [DataMember]
        public int PartID { get; set; }

        [DataMember]
        public string PartName { get; set; }

        [DataMember]
        public int StockCount { get; set; }

        [DataMember]
        public virtual ICollection<BillOfMaterial> BOMParts { get; set; }
    }

    [DataContract(IsReference = true)]
    public class Component
    {

        [Key]
        [DataMember]
        public int ComponentID { get; set; }

        [DataMember]
        public string ComponentName { get; set; }

        [DataMember]
        public virtual ICollection<BillOfMaterial> BOMComponents { get; set; }
    }

    [DataContract(IsReference = true)]
    public class BillOfMaterial
    {
        [Key]
        [DataMember]
        public int BOMID { get; set; }

        [DataMember]
        public int ComponentID { get; set; }

        [DataMember]
        public int PartID { get; set; }
```

```
    [DataMember]
    public int Quantity { get; set; }

    [ForeignKey("PartID"), Column(Order = 0)]

    [DataMember]
    public virtual  Part BOMPart { get; set; }

    [ForeignKey("ComponentID"), Column(Order = 1)]
    [DataMember]
    public virtual Component BOMComponent { get; set; }
    }
}
```

Adding DataContext

We create the tailored database context class BOMDataContext inside the Models folder as shown in Listing 8-2. This class is derived from the Entity Framework base type DbContext. DbContext automatically generates the database using the Entity Class schema and also represents a session with the database and allows it to query the database. The context contains property DbSet, which represents the POCO type classes from our model. We also override the OnModelCreating method to set the required fields and relationship between models.

Listing 8-2. BOMDataContext Class Has Properties That Represent the Model

```
using System;
using System.Collections.Generic;
using System.Configuration;
using System.Data.Entity;
using System.Linq;
using System.Web;

namespace BOM.Service.Models
{
    public class BOMDataContext : DbContext
    {

        public BOMDataContext()
        {
                Configuration.AutoDetectChangesEnabled = true;
                Configuration.LazyLoadingEnabled = true;
                Configuration.ProxyCreationEnabled = true;
                Configuration.ValidateOnSaveEnabled = true;
        }

        protected override void Dispose(bool disposing)
        {
            Configuration.LazyLoadingEnabled = false;
            base.Dispose(disposing);
        }
```

```
public DbSet<Part> Parts { get; set; }
public DbSet<Component> Components { get; set; }
public DbSet<BillOfMaterial> BillOfMaterials { get; set; }

protected override void OnModelCreating(DbModelBuilder modelBuilder)
{
    modelBuilder.Entity<Part>()
        .Property(s => s.PartName)
        .IsRequired();

    modelBuilder.Entity<Component>()
                .Property(s => s.ComponentName)
                .IsRequired();

    modelBuilder.Entity<Part>()
        .HasMany<BillOfMaterial>(e => e.BOMParts);

    modelBuilder.Entity<Component>()
        .HasMany<BillOfMaterial>(e => e.BOMComponents);

    modelBuilder.Entity<BillOfMaterial>()
                .Property(s => s.ComponentID)
                .IsRequired();

    modelBuilder.Entity<BillOfMaterial>()
                .Property(s => s.PartID)
                .IsRequired();
    }
  }
}
```

Adding a Web Service

With the Model and DataContext in place, we now add a WCF Web service BOMServices.svc that handles HTTP requests from the app. This WCF Service has the necessary methods that provide basic CRUD operations as shown in Listing 8-3.

Listing 8-3. The WCF Contract Interface That Defines a Service Contract for the BOM WCF Service

```
using System;
using System.Collections.Generic;
using System.Linq;
using System.Runtime.Serialization;
using System.ServiceModel;
using System.ServiceModel.Web;
using System.Text;
using BOM.Service.Models;
```

```
namespace BOM.Service
{
    [ServiceContract]
    public interface IBOMServices
    {

        [OperationContract]
        IList<Part> GetAllParts();

        [OperationContract]
        IList<Component> GetAllComponents();

        [OperationContract]
        void AddComponent(Component component);

        [OperationContract]
        void DeleteComponent(Component component);

        [OperationContract]
        void AddPart(Part part);

        [OperationContract]
        void DeletePart(Part part);

        [OperationContract]
        void AddBOM(BillOfMaterial bom);

        [OperationContract]
        void RemoveBOM(BillOfMaterial bom);

    }
}
```

To begin with, we define a service contract using an interface marked with the ServiceContractAttribute and the OperationContractAttribute attributes. Let's look at the web methods in detail by implementing the service contract as shown in Listing 8-4.

- **GetAllComponents:** This method retrieves all the components from the Component table along with corresponding navigation properties like Parts and BOM by using the Entity Framework's Include method.

- **GetAllParts:** Retrieves all the parts along with the corresponding BOM.

- **AddComponent:** Adds a row to the Component table.

- **DeleteComponent:** Deletes a component from the table along with all the corresponding rows for that component from the BOM table.

- **AddPart:** Adds a row to the Part table.

- **DeletePart:** Deletes a row from the Part table along with all the corresponding rows for that part from BOM table.

- **AddBOM:** This method first checks to see if there is a matching BOM with a similar ComponentID and PartID. If this exists, it then updates the Quantity for that BOM; otherwise, it will add a new row to the BOM table.

- **RemoveBOM:** Removes a row from the BOM table.

Listing 8-4. Implementing BOMService Methods

```
using System;
using System.Collections.Generic;
using System.Linq;
using System.Runtime.Serialization;
using System.ServiceModel;
using System.ServiceModel.Web;
using System.Text;
using BOM.Service.Models;

namespace BOM.Service
{
    public class BOMServices : IBOMServices
    {
        public IList<Part> GetAllParts()
        {
            using (var ctx = new BOMDataContext())
            {
                ctx.Configuration.ProxyCreationEnabled = false;
                var parts = ctx.Parts
                    .Include("BOMParts")
                    .ToList();
                ctx.Configuration.ProxyCreationEnabled = true;
                return parts;
            }
        }

        public IList<Component> GetAllComponents()
        {
            using (var ctx = new BOMDataContext())
            {
                ctx.Configuration.ProxyCreationEnabled = false;

                var components =  ctx.Components
                    .Include("BOMComponents")
                    .Include("BOMComponents.BOMPart")
                    .ToList();
                ctx.Configuration.ProxyCreationEnabled = true;
                return components;
            }
        }
```

```csharp
public void AddComponent(Component component)
{
    using (var ctx = new BOMDataContext())
    {
        ctx.Components.Add(component);
        ctx.SaveChanges();
    }
}

public void DeleteComponent(Component component)
{
    using (var ctx = new BOMDataContext())
    {
        foreach (var bom in component.BOMComponents)
        {
            ctx.BillOfMaterials.Remove(bom);
        }
        ctx.Components.Remove(component);
        ctx.SaveChanges();
    }
}

public void AddPart(Part part)
{
    using (var ctx = new BOMDataContext())
    {
        ctx.Parts.Add(part);
        ctx.SaveChanges();
    }
}

public void DeletePart(Part part)
{
    using (var ctx = new BOMDataContext())
    {
        foreach (var bom in part.BOMParts)
        {
            ctx.BillOfMaterials.Remove(bom);
        }
        ctx.Parts.Remove(part);
        ctx.SaveChanges();
    }
}

public void AddBOM(BillOfMaterial bom)
{
    using (var ctx = new BOMDataContext())
    {
        var bomv = ctx.BillOfMaterials.Where(b => b.ComponentID ==
bom.ComponentID && b.PartID == bom.PartID);
```

```
                        if (bomv.Any())
                        {
                            var oldBOM = bomv.First();
                            oldBOM.Quantity = oldBOM.Quantity + bom.Quantity;
                        }
                        else
                        {
                            ctx.BillOfMaterials.Add(bom);
                        }
                        ctx.SaveChanges();
                    }
                }

                public void RemoveBOM(BillOfMaterial bom)
                {
                    using (var ctx = new BOMDataContext())
                    {
                        ctx.BillOfMaterials.Remove(bom);
                        ctx.SaveChanges();
                    }
                }
            }
        }
```

When any one of the methods in Listing 8-4 is called for the first time, the Entity Framework Code First uses a set of conventions to determine the schema and creates the database and necessary tables and referential integrity between the tables. It uses the database connection information from the `web.config` file. Once this is created, we are able to see the database in the VS.NET SQL Server Object Explorer (Ctrl + \, Ctrl + S).

Consuming the WCF Service

Consuming the BOM.Services WCF service from the BOM.App is very simple and it's like adding a DLL reference to the project. To consume the service, we first have to add a service reference, which can be done by right-clicking Reference in the the BOM.App project section of the Solution Explorer and selecting Add Service Reference. This displays the Add Service Reference page shown in Figure 8-5. Give the WCF service a logical namespace, BOMWcfServices, and then select OK. This action generates a managed source code file of a client proxy class that we will be using in a client service class `BOMClientServices` (see Listing 8-5).

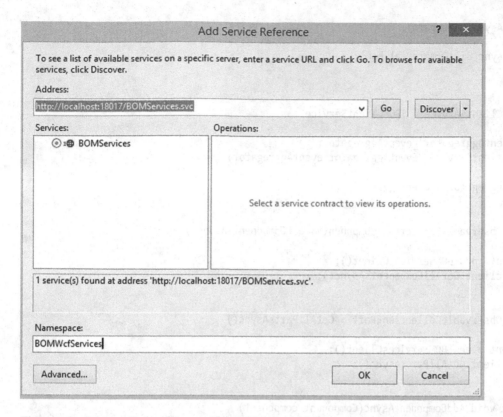

Figure 8-5. *Creating Proxy class using Visual Studio Add Service Reference page*

Listing 8-5. BOMClientService Encapsulates WCF Service Methods

```
using System;
using System.Collections.ObjectModel;
using System.Threading.Tasks;
using BOM.BOMWcfServices;
using Microsoft.Practices.Prism.PubSubEvents;
using BOM.Models;

namespace BOM.Services
{

    public interface IBOMClientService
    {

        Task<ObservableCollection<Component>> GetComponentsAsync();

        Task<ObservableCollection<Part>> GetAllPartsAsync();

        void AddComponentAsync(Component component);
```

```
        void AddPartAsync(Part part);

        void AddBOMAsync(BillOfMaterial bom);

    }

    public class BOMClientService : IBOMClientService
    {
        private IEventAggregator _eventAggregator;
        public BOMClientService(IEventAggregator eventAggregator)
        {
            _eventAggregator = eventAggregator;
        }

        public Task<ObservableCollection<Component>> GetComponentsAsync()
        {
            var client= new BOMServicesClient();
            return  client.GetAllComponentsAsync();
        }

        public Task<ObservableCollection<Part>> GetAllPartsAsync()
        {
            var client = new BOMServicesClient();
            return client.GetAllPartsAsync();
        }

        public async void AddComponentAsync(Component component)
        {
            var client = new BOMServicesClient();
            await client.AddComponentAsync(component);
            _eventAggregator.GetEvent<ComponentSaveEvent>().Publish(null);
        }

        public async void AddPartAsync(Part part)
        {
            var client = new BOMServicesClient();
            await client.AddPartAsync(part);
            _eventAggregator.GetEvent<PartSaveEvent>().Publish(null);
        }

        public async void AddBOMAsync(BillOfMaterial bom)
        {
            var client = new BOMServicesClient();
            await client.AddBOMAsync(bom);
            _eventAggregator.GetEvent<ComponentSaveEvent>().Publish(null);
        }
    }
}
```

BOMClientServices is a client service class that is injected into the ViewModel through dependency injection. This class encapsulates the creation and operations of BOM.Services's WCF Service and uses EventAggregator service to publish the events, which is handled in the ViewModel.

Integrating Prism in the Windows 8 App

The first step in integrating Prism into the BOM.App project is to add references to the libraries Microsoft.Practices.
Prism.StoreApps and Microsoft.Practices.Prism.PubSubEvent. Next, we need to update the App.Xaml App class. The
App class is updated to derive from the MvvmAppBase class from the Microsoft.Practices.Prism.StoreApps library to
get support for MVVM and the core services required by Windows Store apps.

We then override MVVMAppBase's OnLaunchApplication abstract method in the App class and add the start
page navigation code. As the BOM app will have only one page, BillOfMaterialPage.xaml, we add code to navigate
to that page, as shown in Listing 8-6.

Listing 8-6. The App Class with Prism Integration

```
using System;
using System.Globalization;
using BOM.Services;
using Microsoft.Practices.Prism.PubSubEvents;
using Microsoft.Practices.Prism.StoreApps;
using Microsoft.Practices.Prism.StoreApps.Interfaces;
using Microsoft.Practices.Unity;
using Windows.ApplicationModel;
using Windows.ApplicationModel.Activation;
using Windows.ApplicationModel.Resources;
using Windows.UI.Notifications;
using Windows.UI.Xaml;
using Windows.UI.Xaml.Controls;

namespace BOM
{
    sealed partial class App : MvvmAppBase
    {
        // Create the singleton container that will be used for type resolution in the app
        private readonly IUnityContainer _container = new UnityContainer();
        //Bootstrap: App singleton service declarations
        private IEventAggregator _eventAggregator;
        public App()
        {
            InitializeComponent();
            Suspending += OnSuspending;
        }

        protected override void OnLaunchApplication(LaunchActivatedEventArgs args)
        {
            NavigationService.Navigate("BillOfMaterial", null);
        }

        protected override void OnInitialize(IActivatedEventArgs args)
        {
            _eventAggregator = new EventAggregator();

            _container.RegisterInstance(NavigationService);
            _container.RegisterInstance(_eventAggregator);
            _container.RegisterType<IBOMClientService, BOMClientService>(new
ContainerControlledLifetimeManager());
```

```
        ViewModelLocator.SetDefaultViewTypeToViewModelTypeResolver((viewType) =>
        {
            var viewModelTypeName = string.Format(CultureInfo.InvariantCulture
                        , "BOM.ViewModels.{0}ViewModel"
                        , viewType.Name);
            var viewModelType = Type.GetType(viewModelTypeName);
            return viewModelType;
        });
    }

    private void OnSuspending(object sender, SuspendingEventArgs e)
    {
        SuspendingDeferral deferral = e.SuspendingOperation.GetDeferral();
        deferral.Complete();
    }

    protected override object Resolve(Type type)
    {
        return _container.Resolve(type);
    }
    }
}
```

Next we add a reference to the Unity library to the project using the NuGet packages as shown in Figure 8-6. Unity Application Block (Unity) is a lightweight extensible dependency injection container with support for constructor, property, and method call injection. Using Unity helps us make code more maintainable, expandable, and testable.

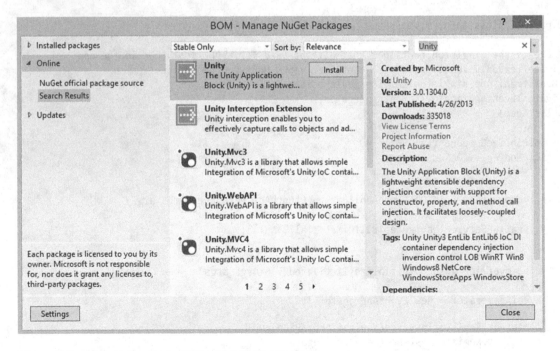

Figure 8-6. *Adding reference to Unity using NuGet package*

Now, with the Unity library in place, we create an instance of the UnityContainer class in the App class (see Listing 8-5), and use the Unity dependency injection container to register and resolve types and instances.

Finally, we override the OnInitialize method in the App class and register types for the Unity container. Here we register the following types.

- **NavigationService:** Helps to navigate between the Views by replacing one view with another within the applications.

- **IEventAggregator:** The EventAggregator class is offered as a service in the container and can be retrieved through the IEventAggregator interface. The event aggregator is responsible for locating or building events and for keeping a collection of the events in the system.

- **BOMClientService:** As mentioned before, the BOMClientService class (see Listing 8-5) is a client service within the container that can be retrieved through IBOMService. This service exposes some of the BOM.Services WCF methods to the app by communicating with the BOM WCF service using the proxy class that we generate by adding Service References to the WCF Service as shown in Figure 8-5.

Designing the BOM App User Interface

The BOM app is a single-page (BillOfMaterialPage.xaml) UI that is divided in to two sections. The left side of the app will list all the components and their corresponding parts as shown in Figure 8-1. This section hosts a ListView control that is bound to a ComponentViewModel collection. The right section lists all the parts for lookup. Apart from these two sections, we also have an app bar at the bottom that holds two buttons for adding new components and parts. BillOfMaterialPage.xaml also has three pop-up controls that hold the interface for adding a Component, Part, and BOM (see Listing 8-7).

Listing 8-7. BillOfMaterialPage.xaml with ListViews, Popup Controls, and App Bar Buttons

```
<Infrastructure:VisualStateAwarePage
x:Name="pageRoot"
x:Class="BOM.Views.BillOfMaterialPage"
DataContext="{Binding DefaultViewModel, RelativeSource={RelativeSource Self}}"
xmlns="http:    //schemas.microsoft.com/winfx/2006/xaml/presentation"
xmlns:x="http: //schemas.microsoft.com/winfx/2006/xaml"
xmlns:local="using:BOM.Views"
xmlns:Infrastructure="using:Microsoft.Practices.Prism.StoreApps"
xmlns:d="http: //schemas.microsoft.com/expression/blend/2008"
xmlns:mc="http://schemas.openxmlformats.org/markup-compatibility/2006"
Infrastructure:ViewModelLocator.AutoWireViewModel="true"
mc:Ignorable="d">
<Page.Resources>
        <x:String x:Key="AppName">Bill of Material</x:String>
<!--Bill of Material Data Template-->
<DataTemplate x:Key="BOMDataTemplate">
        <StackPanel>
                <TextBlock
                        Text="{Binding BOMPart.PartName}"/>
                <StackPanel
                Orientation="Horizontal">
                        <TextBlock
                                Text="Avaliable Stock: "/>
```

```
                            <Border>
                                    <TextBlock
                                            Text="{Binding BOMPart.StockCount}"/>
                            </Border>
                            <TextBlock
                                    Text=" Required Part: "/>
                            <Border>
                                    <TextBlock
                                            Text="{Binding Quantity}"/>
                            </Border>
                    </StackPanel>
            </StackPanel>
    </DataTemplate>
    <!--Component Data Template-->
    <DataTemplate x:Key="ComponentDataTemplate">
            <StackPanel>
            <Grid>
                    <Grid.ColumnDefinitions>
                            <ColumnDefinition/>
                            <ColumnDefinition/>
                    </Grid.ColumnDefinitions>
                    <StackPanel
                            Orientation="Horizontal">
                            <TextBlock
                                    Text="{Binding ComponentName}"/>
                    </StackPanel>
                    <StackPanel
                            Grid.Column="1"
                            Orientation="Horizontal">
                        <Button
                        Content="Add Part"
                        Command="{Binding AddPartsCommand, Mode=OneWay}"/>
                    </StackPanel>
            </Grid>
            <!--ListBox to display Parts of the Componenent-->
            <ListBox
            ItemsSource="{Binding BOMComponents}"
            ItemTemplate="{StaticResource BOMDataTemplate}"/>
            </StackPanel>
    </DataTemplate>
    <!--Part Data Template-->
    <DataTemplate x:Key="PartDataTemplate">
            <StackPanel>
                    <TextBlock
                            Text="{Binding PartName}"/>
                    <StackPanel
                            Orientation="Horizontal">
                            <TextBlock
                                    Text="Avaliable Stock: "/>
```

```
                        <Border>
                                <TextBlock
                                        Text="{Binding StockCount}"/>
                        </Border>
                </StackPanel>
        </StackPanel>
</DataTemplate>
</Page.Resources>
<Infrastructure:VisualStateAwarePage.BottomAppBar>
        <AppBar>
                <Grid>
                <Grid.ColumnDefinitions>
                        <ColumnDefinition/>
                        <ColumnDefinition/>
                </Grid.ColumnDefinitions>
                <StackPanel Orientation="Horizontal">
                        <!-- Button to add component-->
                  <Button x:Name="AddComponent"
                          Command="{Binding OpenComponentCommand, Mode=OneWay}"
                          Style="{StaticResource AddComponentAppBarButtonStyle}"/>
                </StackPanel>
                <StackPanel Grid.Column="1">
                        <!-- Button to add part-->
                <Button x:Name="AddPart"
                        Command="{Binding OpenPartCommand, Mode=OneWay}"
                        Style="{StaticResource AddPartAppBarButtonStyle}"/>
                </StackPanel>
                </Grid>
        </AppBar>
</Infrastructure:VisualStateAwarePage.BottomAppBar>

<Grid
        Style="{StaticResource LayoutRootStyle}">
        <Grid.ColumnDefinitions>
                <ColumnDefinition Width="769*"/>
                <ColumnDefinition Width="597*"/>
        </Grid.ColumnDefinitions>
        <Grid.RowDefinitions>
                <RowDefinition Height="140"/>
                <RowDefinition Height="12*"/>
                <RowDefinition Height="145*"/>
        </Grid.RowDefinitions>
<!-- Popup control to get Component information to add -->
<Popup x:Name="AddComponentPopup"
  x:Uid="AddComponentPopup"
  AutomationProperties.AutomationId="AddComponentPopup"
  IsLightDismissEnabled="True"
  IsOpen="{Binding IsAddComponentPopupOpened, Mode=TwoWay}"
  Grid.RowSpan="3"
  Grid.ColumnSpan="2">
```

```xml
        <Border>
                <Grid>
                        <Grid.RowDefinitions>
                                <RowDefinition Height="Auto" />
                                <RowDefinition Height="Auto" />
                                <RowDefinition Height="38"/>
                        </Grid.RowDefinitions>
                        <Grid.ColumnDefinitions>
                                <ColumnDefinition Width="Auto" />
                                <ColumnDefinition Width="*" />
                        </Grid.ColumnDefinitions>
                        <TextBlock Grid.Column="0"
                                Grid.Row="0"
                                Text="Component"
                                Grid.ColumnSpan="2"
                                Style="{StaticResource HeaderTextStyle}"/>
                        <TextBlock
                                Grid.Column="0"
                                Grid.Row="1"
                                Text="Component Name"
                                Style="{StaticResource ResourceKey=SubheaderTextStyle}" />
                        <TextBox
                                Grid.Column="1"
                                Grid.Row="1" x:Name="txtComponentName"
                                Text="{Binding ComponentName, Mode=TwoWay}"/>
                        <Button
                                Command="{Binding AddComponentCommand, Mode=OneWay}"
                                Content="Save"
                                Grid.Row="2"
                                Grid.Column="1"/>
                </Grid>
        </Border>
</Popup>
<!-- Popup control to get Part information to add -->
<Popup x:Name="AddPartPopup"
x:Uid="AddPartPopup"
AutomationProperties.AutomationId="AddPartPopup"
IsLightDismissEnabled="True"
IsOpen="{Binding IsAddPartPopupOpened, Mode=TwoWay}" Grid.RowSpan="3" Grid.ColumnSpan="2">
<Border>
        <Grid x:Name="addPart">
                <Grid.RowDefinitions>
                        <RowDefinition Height="Auto" />
                        <RowDefinition Height="Auto" />
                        <RowDefinition Height="Auto" />
                        <RowDefinition Height="38"/>
                </Grid.RowDefinitions>
                <Grid.ColumnDefinitions>
                        <ColumnDefinition Width="Auto" />
                        <ColumnDefinition Width="*" />
                </Grid.ColumnDefinitions>
```

```xml
        <TextBlock
                Grid.Column="0"
                Grid.Row="0"
                Text="Part"
                Grid.ColumnSpan="2"
                Style="{StaticResource HeaderTextStyle}" />
        <TextBlock
                Grid.Column="0"
                Grid.Row="1"
                Text="Part Name"
                Style="{StaticResource ResourceKey=SubheaderTextStyle}" />
        <TextBox
                Grid.Column="1"
                Grid.Row="1"
                Text="{Binding PartName, Mode=TwoWay}"/>
        <TextBlock
                Grid.Column="0"
                Grid.Row="2"
                Text="Quantity"
                Style="{StaticResource ResourceKey=SubheaderTextStyle}"/>
        <TextBox
                Grid.Column="1"
                Grid.Row="2"
                Text="{Binding StockCount, Mode=TwoWay}"/>
        <Button
                Command="{Binding AddPartCommand, Mode=OneWay}"
                Content="Save"
                Grid.Row="3"
                Grid.Column="1"/>
    </Grid>
</Border>
</Popup>
<!-- Popup control to select a Part to add it to Component as BOM -->
<Popup x:Name="AddBOMPopup"
        x:Uid="AddBOMPopup"
        AutomationProperties.AutomationId="AddBOMPopup"
        IsLightDismissEnabled="True"
        IsOpen="{Binding IsShowBOMPopupOpened, Mode=TwoWay}"
        Grid.RowSpan="3"
        Grid.ColumnSpan="2">
<Border>
    <Grid>
            <Grid.RowDefinitions>
                    <RowDefinition Height="Auto" />
                    <RowDefinition Height="Auto" />
                    <RowDefinition Height="Auto" />
                    <RowDefinition Height="38"/>
            </Grid.RowDefinitions>
            <Grid.ColumnDefinitions>
                    <ColumnDefinition Width="Auto" />
                    <ColumnDefinition Width="*" />
            </Grid.ColumnDefinitions>
```

```xml
            <TextBlock
                    Grid.Column="0"
                    Grid.Row="0"
                    Text="Add to BOM"
                    Grid.ColumnSpan="2"
                    Style="{StaticResource HeaderTextStyle}" />
            <ListView
                    Grid.Row="1"
                    ItemsSource="{Binding Parts}"
                    SelectedItem="{Binding SelectedPart, Mode=TwoWay}"
                    ItemTemplate="{StaticResource PartDataTemplate}"
                    Grid.Column="0"
                    Grid.ColumnSpan="2">
            <TextBlock
                    Grid.Column="0"
                    Grid.Row="2"
                    Text="Quantity"
                    Style="{StaticResource ResourceKey=SubheaderTextStyle}"/>
            <TextBox
                    Grid.Column="1"
                    Grid.Row="2"
                    Text="{Binding BOMQuantity, Mode=TwoWay}"/>
            <Button
                    Command="{Binding AddBOMCommand, Mode=OneWay}"
                    Content="Save"
                    Grid.Row="3"
                    Grid.Column="1"/>
        </Grid>
</Border>
</Popup>

<Grid Grid.ColumnSpan="2">
        <Grid.ColumnDefinitions>
                <ColumnDefinition Width="Auto"/>
                <ColumnDefinition Width="*"/>
        </Grid.ColumnDefinitions>
        <TextBlock
                Grid.Column="1"
                Text="{Binding HeaderLabel}"
                Style="{StaticResource PageHeaderTextStyle}"/>
</Grid>
<!--ListView Control to disply the Components-->
<ListView
        Grid.Row="2"
        ItemsSource="{Binding Components}"
        ItemTemplate="{StaticResource ComponentDataTemplate}"/>
<TextBlock
        Grid.Row="1"
        Text="Components" />
```

```
<TextBlock
        Grid.Row="1"
        Text="Parts"
        Grid.Column="1"/>
<!--ListView Control to disply the Parts-->
<ListView
        Grid.Row="2"
        ItemsSource="{Binding Parts}"
        ItemTemplate="{StaticResource PartDataTemplate}"
        Grid.Column="1"/>
</Grid>
</Infrastructure:VisualStateAwarePage>
```

■ **Note**   We intentionally left out most of the XAML code related to styling and positioning of the controls in this chapter to simplify the explanations and promote readability. The source code that you can download from the APress web site has the complete implementation.

ViewModel

The BOM.App has two ViewModels: BillOfMaterialPageViewModel and ComponentViewModel, which resides inside the ViewModel folder. The BillOfMaterialPageViewModel is bound to BillOfMaterialPage.xaml using the AutoWireViewModel attached property as shown in Listing 8-7. The AutoWireViewModel attached property tells Prism's ViewModelLocator object to create an instance of the view model that corresponds to this view and set it into the view's DataContext property. The ViewModelLocator object uses a default convention where it looks in the ViewModels namespace for a type with a name that starts with the name of the view and ends with "ViewModel".

BillOfMaterialPageViewModel

BillOfMaterialPageViewModel (see Listing 8-8) is derived from the ViewModel class of the Microsoft.Practices.Prism.StoreApps library to get support for MVVM. In this ViewModel NavigationService, EventAggregator, and BOMService are inserted through the constructor. Also in the constructor we add code to subscribe to the EventAggregator events. Apart from this, the ViewModel exposes methods and commands to accomplish various functionality like displaying components and parts, adding new components and parts to the database, and associating a part with a component.

Listing 8-8. The BillOfMaterialPageViewModel Class

```
using System;
using System.Collections.Generic;
using System.Collections.ObjectModel;
using System.Linq;
using System.Text;
using System.Threading.Tasks;
```

```
using System.Windows.Input;
using BOM.BOMWcfServices;
using BOM.Services;
using Microsoft.Practices.Prism.StoreApps;
using Microsoft.Practices.Prism.StoreApps.Interfaces;
using Microsoft.Practices.Prism.PubSubEvents;
using BOM.Models;

namespace BOM.ViewModels
{
    public class BillOfMaterialPageViewModel : ViewModel
    {
        private readonly INavigationService _navigationService;
        private readonly IBOMService _bomservice;
                private IEventAggregator _eventAggregator;

        private string _headerLabel;

        private bool _isAddComponentPopupOpened;
        private bool _isAddPartPopupOpened;
        private bool _isShowBOMPopupOpened;

        private int _selectedComponentID;
        private Part _selectedPart;
        private string _componentName;
        private string _partName;
        private int _stockCount = 0;
        private int _bomQuantity = 0;

        private ObservableCollection<ComponentViewModel> _components;
        private ReadOnlyCollection<Part> _parts;

        public ICommand OpenComponentCommand { get; private set; }
        public ICommand OpenPartCommand { get; private set; }
        public ICommand AddComponentCommand { get; private set; }
        public ICommand AddPartCommand { get; private set; }
        public ICommand AddBOMCommand { get; private set; }

        public BillOfMaterialPageViewModel(INavigationService navigationService
            ,IEventAggregator eventAggregator
            , IBOMService bomservice)
        {
            _navigationService = navigationService;
            _eventAggregator = eventAggregator;
            _bomservice = bomservice;
            OpenComponentCommand = new DelegateCommand(OpenComponentFlyout);
            OpenPartCommand = new DelegateCommand(OpenPartFlyout);
            AddComponentCommand = new DelegateCommand(AddComponentAsync);
            AddPartCommand = new DelegateCommand(AddPartAsync);
            AddBOMCommand = new DelegateCommand(AddBOMAsync);
```

```
        if (eventAggregator != null)
        {
            eventAggregator.GetEvent<ComponentSaveEvent>().Subscribe(RefreshComponentListAsync);
            eventAggregator.GetEvent<PartSaveEvent>().Subscribe(RefreshPartListAsync);
            eventAggregator.GetEvent<AddBOMEvent>().Subscribe(OpenBOMFlyout);
        }
    }


    //Methods that display the pop-up
    private void OpenComponentFlyout()
    {
        ComponentName = string.Empty;
        IsAddComponentPopupOpened = true;
    }

    private void OpenPartFlyout()
    {
        PartName = string.Empty;
        StockCount = 0;
        IsAddPartPopupOpened = true;
    }

    public async void OpenBOMFlyout(object componentID)
    {
        _selectedComponentID=(int) componentID;
        IsShowBOMPopupOpened = true;
    }
        //Properties that are bound to the Popup IsOpen property
    public bool IsAddComponentPopupOpened
    {
        get { return _isAddComponentPopupOpened; }
        set { SetProperty(ref _isAddComponentPopupOpened, value); }
    }

    public bool IsAddPartPopupOpened
    {
        get { return _isAddPartPopupOpened; }
        set { SetProperty(ref _isAddPartPopupOpened, value); }
    }

    public bool IsShowBOMPopupOpened
    {
        get { return _isShowBOMPopupOpened; }
        set { SetProperty(ref _isShowBOMPopupOpened, value); }
    }

        //App Header
    public string HeaderLabel
    {
        get { return _headerLabel; }
        private set { SetProperty(ref _headerLabel, value); }
    }
```

```csharp
        //Properties bound to the Popup controls for capturing user input
public string ComponentName
{
    get { return _componentName; }
    set { SetProperty(ref _componentName, value); }
}

public string PartName
{
    get { return _partName; }
    set { SetProperty(ref _partName, value); }
}

public int StockCount
{
    get { return _stockCount; }
    set { SetProperty(ref _stockCount, value); }
}

public int BOMQuantity
{
    get { return _bomQuantity; }
    set { SetProperty(ref _bomQuantity, value); }
}

public int SelectedComponentID
{
    get { return _selectedComponentID; }
    set { SetProperty(ref _selectedComponentID, value); }
}

public Part SelectedPart
{
    get { return _selectedPart; }
    set { SetProperty(ref _selectedPart, value); }
}

        //Properties that are bound to the ListViews
public ObservableCollection<ComponentViewModel> Components
{
    get { return _components; }
    private set { SetProperty(ref _components, value); }
}

public ReadOnlyCollection<Part> Parts
{
    get { return _parts; }
    private set { SetProperty(ref _parts, value); }
}
```

```csharp
        //Fires on ViewLoad
public override async void OnNavigatedTo(object navigationParameter,
                        Windows.UI.Xaml.Navigation.NavigationMode navigationMode,
                        System.Collections.Generic.Dictionary<string, object> viewModelState)
{
    HeaderLabel = "My BOM";
    GetComponentsAsync();
    GetPartsAsync();
}

private async void GetComponentsAsync()
{
    var components = await _bomservice.GetComponentsAsync();
    var vmComponents = new ObservableCollection<ComponentViewModel>();
    foreach (Component item in  new ObservableCollection<Component>(components.ToList()))
    {
        ComponentViewModel cvm = new ComponentViewModel(_eventAggregator);
        cvm.ComponentID = item.ComponentID;
        cvm.ComponentName = item.ComponentName;
        cvm.BOMComponents = item.BOMComponents;
        vmComponents.Add(cvm);

    }
    Components = vmComponents;
}

private async void GetPartsAsync()
{
    var items = await _bomservice.GetAllPartsAsync();
    Parts = new ReadOnlyCollection<Part>(items.ToList());
}

private async void AddComponentAsync()
{
    _bomservice.AddComponentAsync(new Component { ComponentName = _componentName });
    IsAddComponentPopupOpened = false;
}

private async void AddPartAsync()
{
    _bomservice.AddPartAsync(new Part { PartName = _partName, StockCount = _stockCount });
    IsAddPartPopupOpened = false;
}

private async void AddBOMAsync()
{
    _bomservice.AddBOMAsync(new BillOfMaterial { ComponentID = _selectedComponentID
                , PartID = _selectedPart.PartID
                , Quantity = _bomQuantity });
    IsShowBOMPopupOpened = false;
}
```

173

```
public async void RefreshComponentListAsync(object notUsed)
{
    GetComponentsAsync();
}

public async void RefreshPartListAsync(object notUsed)
{
    GetPartsAsync();
}

    }
}
```

BillOfMaterialPageViewModel Commands

In BillOfMaterialPageViewModel we add commands that will be bound to the elements of the UI in BillOfMaterialPage.xaml. These commands will be associated with methods that are called when the command is invoked.

BillOfMaterialPageViewModel Properties

We add various properties to the BillOfMaterialPageViewModel and these properties are responsible for holding the components, parts, selected components and parts to add to BOM and properties to set the open status of the pop-ups in the UI. Listing 8-7 lists all the properties in BillOfMaterialPageViewModel with comments above each that detail the purpose of that property.

BillOfMaterialPageViewModel Events

As mentioned earlier, this ViewModel subscribes to three events (see Listing 8-9).

- **ComponentSaveEvent:** When fired, this event calls the RefreshComponentListAsync method, which in turn calls GetComponentsAsync to refresh the Component list.

- **PartSaveEvent:** This event is called when a new part is added. This event calls the RefreshPartListAsync method, which in turn calls the GetPartsAsync method to refresh the Parts list.

- **AddBOMEvent:** This event is fired from the ComponentViewModel and upon receipt is handled by the OpenBOMFlyout method, which sets the IsShowBOMPopupOpened property to true to display the Pop-up to pick a part for a component.

Listing 8-9. The BillOfMaterialPageViewModel Events

```
using Microsoft.Practices.Prism.PubSubEvents;
using System;
using System.Collections.Generic;
using System.Linq;
using System.Text;
using System.Threading.Tasks;
```

```
namespace BOM.Models
{

    public class ComponentSaveEvent : PubSubEvent<object>
    {
    }

    public class PartSaveEvent : PubSubEvent<object>
    {
    }

    public class AddBOMEvent : PubSubEvent<object>
    {
    }

}
```

BillOfMaterialPageViewModel Methods

We have already discussed the properties, events, and commands of the `BillOfMaterialPageViewModel`, so that leaves us with methods. Let's look at some of the important methods in the ViewModel.

- **GetComponentsAsync:** This method calls the `GetComponentsAsync` method from BOMService for retrieving all the Components from the database. Using this, it builds an `ObservableCollection` based on ComponentViewModel (see Listing 8-8) and assigns the collection to the `Components` property.

- **GetPartsAsync:** This method calls the `GetAllPartsAsync` method from BOMService for retrieving all the parts from the database and assigns that to the `Parts` property.

- **AddComponentAsync:** This method builds a component object and passes it as a parameter to the BOMService's `AddComponentAsync` method to add a component to the database table. This method also sets the `IsAddComponentPopupOpened` property to false to hide the pop-up used to add the component.

- **AddPartAsync:** This method creates a Part object and passes it as a parameter to the BOMService's `AddPartAsync` method to add a row to the Part table. This method also sets the `IsAddPartPopupOpenedproperty` to false to hide the pop-up control used to add the part.

- **AddBOMAsync:** Similar to `AddComponentAsync` and `AddBOMAsync`, this method creates a BOM object and passes it as a parameter to the BOMService's `AddBOMAsync` method to add a row to the BOM table. To hide the pop-up, this method sets the `IsShowBOMPopupOpened` property to false.

Apart from these methods, we also override the `OnNavigatedTo` method of the ViewModel. This method will be fired when the View loads and in this method we set the Header of the app and then call the methods `GetComponentsAsync` and `GetPartsAsync`. As mentioned earlier, these methods, when called, set the `Components`, `Parts` properties, which in turn bind to the ListView controls in the View to display the Components and Parts information as shown in Figure 8-1.

ComponentViewModel

This ViewModel is also derived from the ViewModel class. It has three properties: ComponentID, ComponentName, and BOMComponents. It also has a DelegateCommand AddPartsCommand as shown in Listing 8-10.

Listing 8-10. The ComponentViewModel Class

```
using System;
using System.Collections.Generic;
using System.Collections.ObjectModel;
using System.Linq;
using System.Text;
using System.Threading.Tasks;
using System.Windows.Input;

namespace BOM.ViewModels
{
    public class ComponentViewModel : ViewModel
    {
        private int _componentID;
        private string _ComponentName;
        private ObservableCollection<BillOfMaterial> _bOMComponents;

        public ICommand AddPartsCommand { get; private set; }
        private IEventAggregator _eventAggregator;

        public ComponentViewModel(IEventAggregator eventAggregator)
        {
            _eventAggregator = eventAggregator;
            AddPartsCommand = new DelegateCommand(RaiseAddBOM);
        }

        public int ComponentID
        {
            get { return _componentID; }
            set { SetProperty(ref _componentID, value); }
        }

        public string ComponentName
        {
            get { return _ComponentName; }
            set { SetProperty(ref _ComponentName, value); }
        }

        public ObservableCollection<BillOfMaterial>  BOMComponents
        {
            get { return _bOMComponents; }
            set { SetProperty(ref _bOMComponents, value); }
        }
```

```
        private void RaiseAddBOM()
        {
            _eventAggregator.GetEvent<AddBOMEvent>().Publish(ComponentID);
        }
    }
}
```

When bound to the ListBox in BillOfMaterialPage.xaml, this command publishes an AddBOM Event that is subscribed in the BillOfMaterialPageViewModel that sets a flag IsShowBOMPopupOpened to true, which is bound to the pop-up control's IsOpen property. Setting this property opens the pop-up control to display the list of parts to pick as a BOM to the component as shown in Figure 8-7.

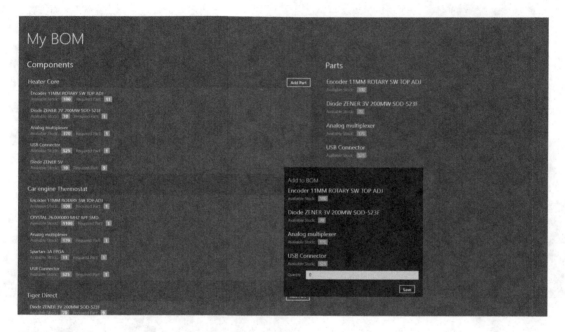

Figure 8-7. *The Parts list to be picked to add it to BOM*

Conclusion

In this chapter we learned to use SQL Server as the database for storing and retrieving data from a Windows 8 app by building a service layer using WCF Services. WCF Services is widely used and makes it easier to expose and consume WCF services. Also in this chapter we learned to use Prism, as it helps to easily design and build rich, flexible, and easy to maintain Windows 8 apps.

In the next chapter we will learn to use SQL Azure as a data storage option with Windows Azure Mobile Services as the service layer by building an Instagram-inspired Windows 8 app.

CHAPTER 9

■■■

Windows Azure Mobile Services

In the last two chapters, we have seen two different approaches to consuming data from SQL Server, one using ASP.NET Web API and the other using WCF. In this chapter we learn to use Windows Azure Mobile Services to leverage data in a Windows 8 app. Windows Azure Mobile Services allows us to quickly connect any mobile client like Windows 8, Windows Phone, iOS, Android, or HTML5 apps to a cloud-based back end hosted on Windows Azure.

This chapter begins by helping us get started with Windows Azure Mobile Services using the Windows Azure Mobile Service setup. We learn to integrate Live SDK for user authentication, storing data in Windows Azure storage. We learn these steps by developing an Instagram-inspired app called Instashots that allows users to edit and add filters to the photos in a way similar to Instagram by using the Aviary SDK and storing data in Windows Azure storage.

Introduction to Windows Azure Mobile Services

Windows Azure Mobile Services is a new addition to Windows Azure. The idea behind it is to allow developers to build a scalable services for multiple mobile platforms. Windows Azure Mobile Services currently provides support through the client libraries that are available for Windows 8, Windows Phone, iOS, Android, and HTML5 apps. This service provides the necessary infrastructure to quickly create back-end services by enabling some common scenarios like storing data, authentication, app notification, monitoring and logging for services.

- **Data:** With Windows Azure, we are able to store data in the Windows Azure SQL database as tables. One of the best features of Windows Azure Mobile Services is the ability to work with a dynamic schema to automatically insert new columns for fields that it has never received before.

- **Authentication:** Windows Azure Mobile Services has built-in support for various third-party identity providers like Microsoft Account, Facebook Login, Twitter Login, and Google Login.

- **Notification:** Windows Azure Mobile Services supports push notification and can be integrated with the notification services of iOS, Android, Windows 8, and Windows Phones to deliver push notifications.

- **Monitoring and logging:** Windows Azure Mobile Services provides a dashboard that displays a usage timeline, usage overview, and logging information (see Figure 9-1).

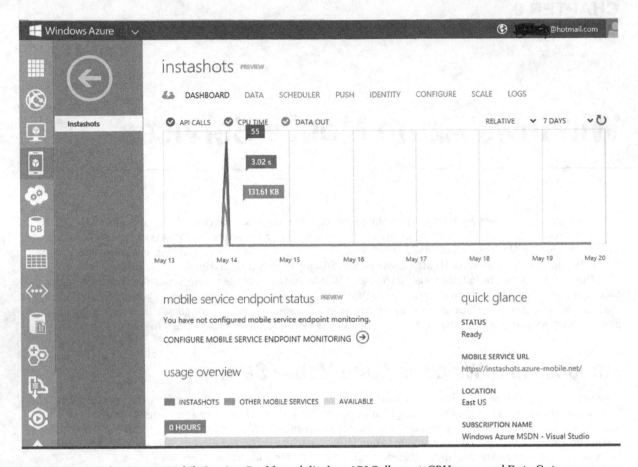

Figure 9-1. Windows Azure Mobile Services Dashboard displays API Call count, CPU usage and Data Out

---

■ **Note** Similar to Windows Azure Mobile Services, Amazon also provides a cloud-based solution called Amazon Web Services (AWS) for storing structured information in the cloud. AWS has a .NET SDK that has support for both Windows 8 and Windows Phone 8 app development. You can download the SDK at http://aws.amazon.com/sdkfornet/.

Creating the Instashots App

The Instashots app is an Instagram-inspired online photo sharing service that enables its users to add filters to photos and post them online. By building this service we learn how to do the following.

- Create and manage Windows Azure Mobile Services.
- Store data in a Windows Azure SQL database.
- Store images in the Windows Azure storage.
- Integrate Live SDK and use it to authenticate users.
- Integrate Aviary SDK for photo editing.

Creating Windows Azure Mobile Services in the Management Portal

To enable Windows Azure Mobile Services in our app we need to sign up for the Windows Azure services. Microsoft provides a trial version for people who like to experiment with it beforehand. Once registered, log in to the Windows Azure Management Portal (*http://manage.windowsazure.com*) and click the +New button at the bottom left of the page to create a new Mobile Service named Instashots, as shown in Figure 9-2.

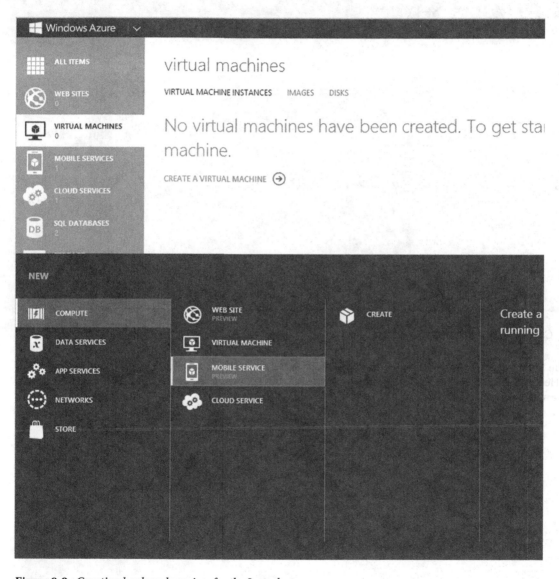

Figure 9-2. *Creating back end services for the Instashots app*

On the Create a Mobile Service page shown in Figure 9-3, type **Instashots** as the subdomain name . The URL for our Windows Azure Mobile Services will be `http://instashots.azure-mobile.net/`.

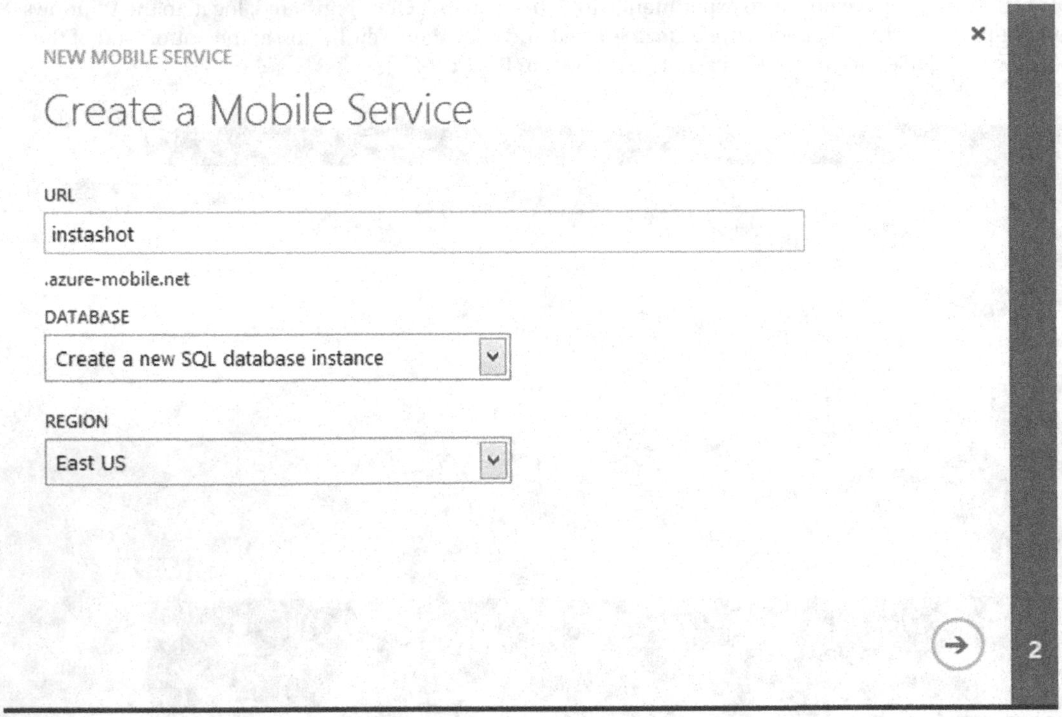

NEW MOBILE SERVICE

Create a Mobile Service

URL

instashot

.azure-mobile.net

DATABASE

Create a new SQL database instance

REGION

East US

Figure 9-3. Creating the Mobile Services for Instashots app

With the Mobile Service created, next the wizard takes us to the Specify Database Settings page shown in Figure 9-4. Here we create a new database and name it **instashot_db**. Figure 9-5 shows the Instashots mobile service ready for the app to use.

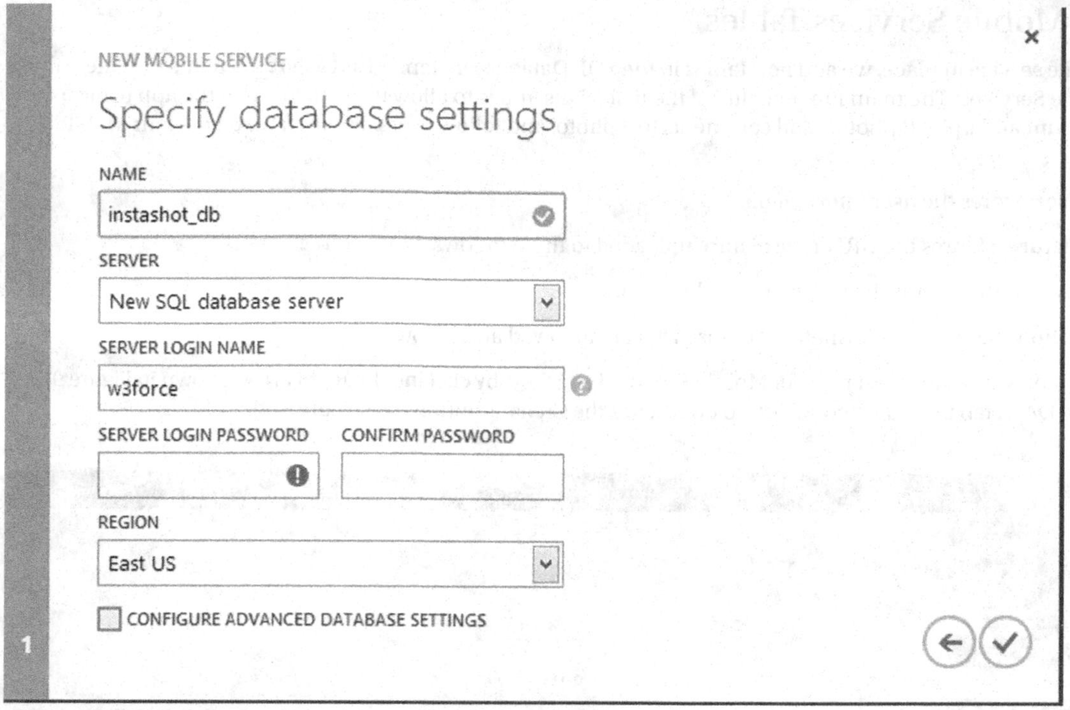

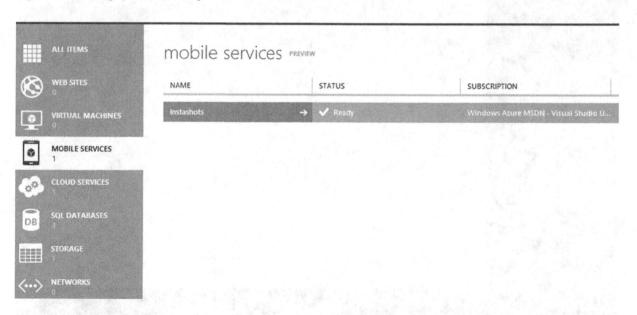

Figure 9-4. *Setting up the database for the Instashots Mobile Service*

Figure 9-5. *Instashots mobile service is ready for the Windows 8 app to use*

Creating Mobile Services Tables

With the mobile service in place, we add new tables in the SQL Database instance instashot_db that we created along with the Mobile Services. The main functionality of the Instashots app is to allow users to log in to the app using a Microsoft account and upload photos, add comments to a photo, and follow users. For that, we create four Mobile Services tables.

- **User:** Stores the user information.

- **Pictures:** Stores the URI of the picture uploaded to the Windows Azure storage.

- **Comments:** Stores the comments of the pictures.

- **Follow:** Stores the information of those who are followed and followers.

To create tables, go to the Start page for Mobile Services Instashots by clicking the Right arrow shown in Figure 9-5. Navigate to the DATA tab to create new tables. To do so, click the Create + button (see Figure 9-6).

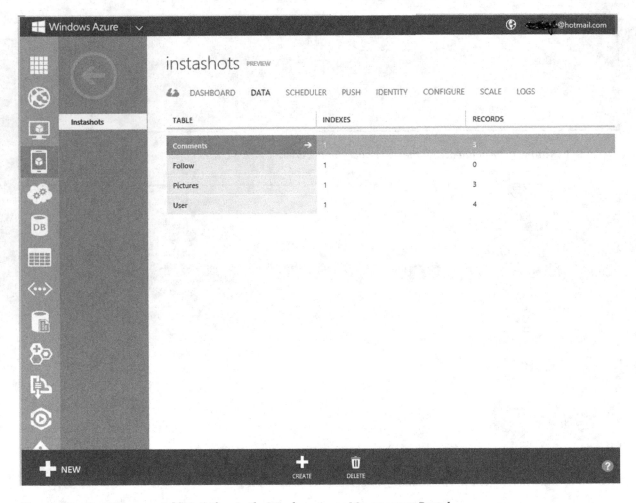

Figure 9-6. *Creating a new table interface in the Windows Azure Management Portal*

The Pictures table is essential, as it stores photo data to the mobile services. When the Instashots app tries to perform any of the CURD operations like inserting, updating, deleting, or reading, we can specify what permission the user needs to perform this operation. In our case we will allow only authenticated users to perform insert, update, and delete operations, but everyone can read the data (see Figure 9-7). Now the table is locked and it will not be possible for anyone to insert, update, or delete without proper authorization. Similar to the Pictures table, we also create tables to store user data, comments, and follower information. Once created, the DATA tab will look like the one shown in Figure 9-6.

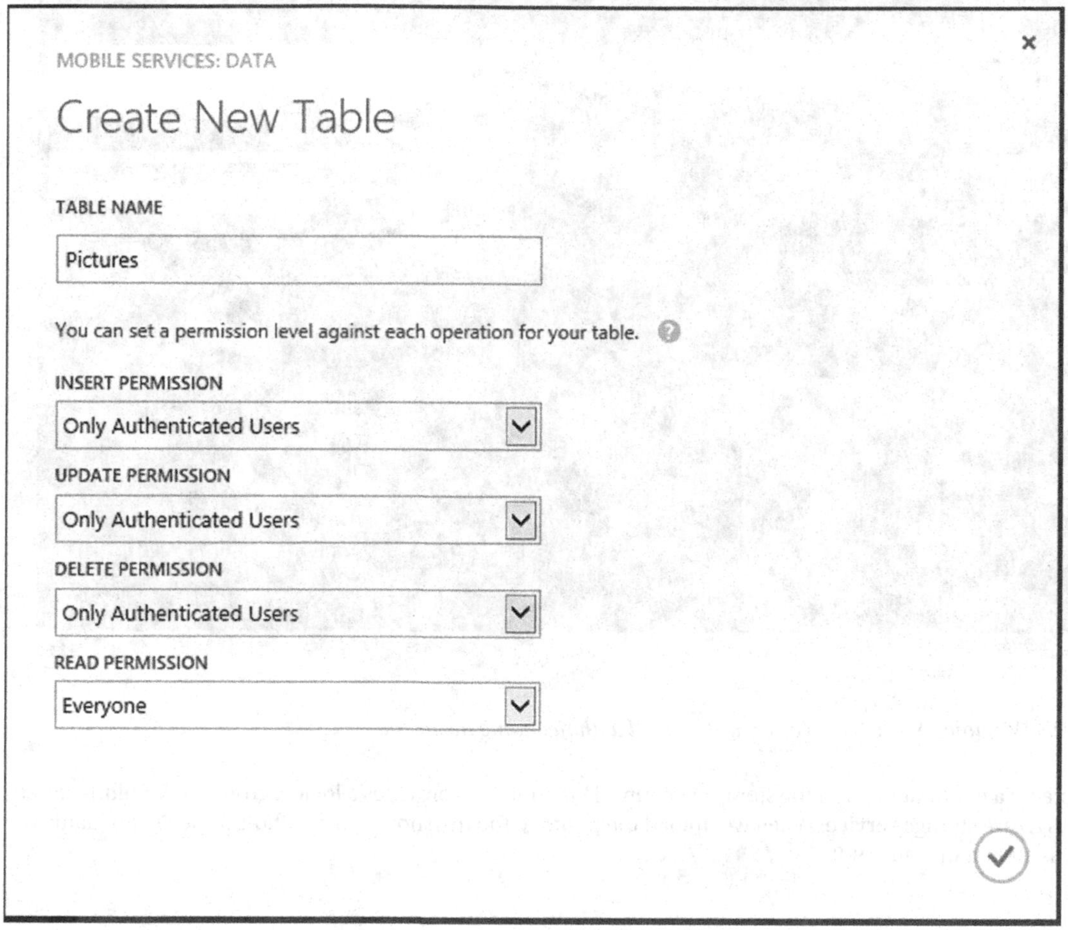

Figure 9-7. Creating a new storage table Pictures for storing photo data

Creating Windows Azure Storage

Even though a photo's information, like title and uploaded date, are stored in the Picture table, the image files will be stored in the Windows Azure Storage. For this we need to create a Windows Azure storage (see Figure 9-8) and a container within that storage to store the pictures that we upload from the Instashots app.

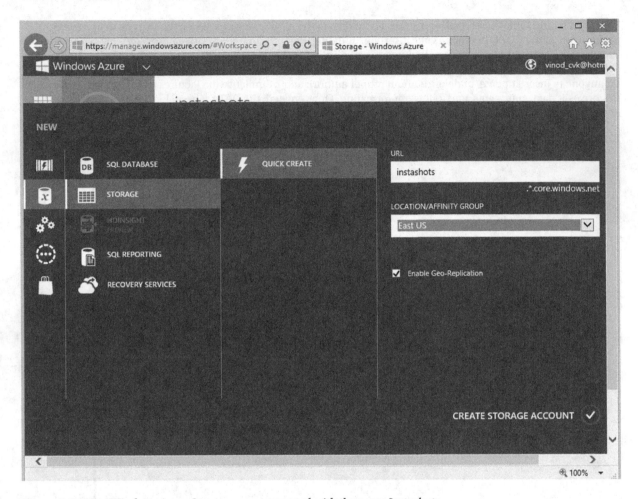

Figure 9-8. *New Windows Azure Storage account created with the name Instashots*

Next we create a container within the storage account. This container provides a logical grouping for blobs stored in the Windows Azure storage service. When we upload the photo to the Instshots app, we should specify the name of the container, as shown in Figure 9-9.

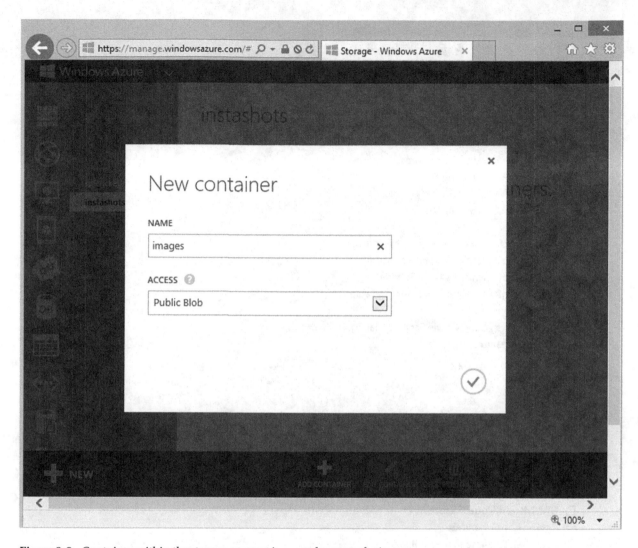

Figure 9-9. *Container within the storage account is created to store the images*

Setting Up the Development Environment

The mobile service Start screen generates a Windows 8 app that can be downloaded. This app is preconfigured to access the Instashots back end and is ready to run. WinJS (HTML5/JavaScript) or C# (.NET/XAML) can be chosen for download. We'll choose C# here and include the following reference from the NuGet packages.

- MVVM Light
- Windows Azure Mobile Services
- Windows Azure storage

We also add references to the Live SDK and the Aviary Photo Editing SDK as shown in Figure 9-10. The Aviary Photo Editing SDK provides us with an intuitive photo editing tool for everything from quick fixes and one-tap autoenhance to stylistic effects, cropping, red eye removal, and adding filters, frames, and stickers to the photos.

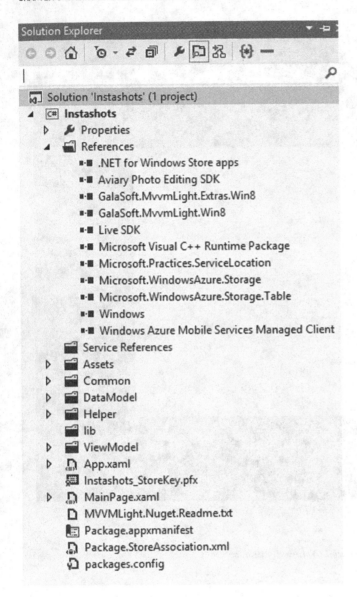

Figure 9-10. Instashots Windows 8 App project structure

■ **Note** Aviary SDK for Windows 8 can be downloaded from http://www.aviary.com/w8. As of now this SDK is compatible only with C++/XAML and C#/XAML.

Drilling into the Solution Explorer we notice two files, App.xaml and MainPage.xaml, and a little bit of stub code that is already added to App.xaml as shown in Listing 9-1. This helps the Client component of the app to talk to the mobile services.

Listing 9-1. *A Simpler Key URL That Will Map to the Instashots Mobile Services, Which Helps the App Talk to the Mobile Services*

```
// This MobileServiceClient has been configured to communicate with Mobile Service's url
      // and application key. You're all set to start working with your Mobile Service!

        public static MobileServiceClient MobileService = new MobileServiceClient(
            "https://instashots.azure-mobile.net/",
            "TVqTZaDDCuvOKGPMmKwrJhdAFCTECy75"
        );
```

We create four classes: User, Comment, Picture, and Follow (see Listing 9-2) that models the entities that we created in Windows Azure table storage using the Management console. We add the DataTable attributes to all these classes to specify that this class represent Mobile Services tables.

Listing 9-2. Table Classes That Model the Entities of the Windows Azure Table Storage

```
using Microsoft.WindowsAzure.MobileServices;
using System;
using System.Runtime.Serialization;

[DataTable(Name = "User")]
public class User
{
    public int Id { get; set; }

    [DataMember(Name = "username")]
    public string UserName { get; set; }

    [DataMember(Name = "userid")]
    public string UserID { get; set; }

    [DataMember(Name = "lastaccessed")]
    public DateTime? LastAccessed { get; set; }
}

  [DataTable(Name = "Pictures")]
    public class Picture
    {
        public int Id { get; set; }

        [DataMember(Name = "name")]
        public string Name { get; set; }

        [DataMember(Name = "title")]
        public string Title { get; set; }

        [DataMember(Name = "userid")]
        public string UserId { get; set; }

        [DataMember(Name = "imageurl")]
        public string Imageurl { get; set; }
```

```csharp
        [DataMember(Name = "sasQueryString")]
        public string sasQueryString { get; set; }

        [DataMember(Name = "likes")]
        public int Likes { get; set; }

        [IgnoreDataMember]
        public List<Comment> Comments { get; set; }

    }

[DataTable(Name = "Comments")]
    public class Comment
    {
        public int Id { get; set; }

        [DataMember(Name = "text")]
        public string CommentText { get; set; }

        [DataMember(Name = "userid")]
        public int UserId { get; set; }

        [DataMember(Name = "pictureid")]
        public int PictureId { get; set; }

        [DataMember(Name = "createdDate")]
        public DateTime? CreatedDate { get; set; }

        [IgnoreDataMember]
        public User CommentedBy { get; set; }
    }

    [DataTable(Name = "Follow")]
    public class Follow
    {
        public int Id { get; set; }

        [DataMember(Name = "followeruserid")]
        public int FollowerUserId { get; set; }

        [DataMember(Name = "followinguserid")]
        public int FollowingUserId { get; set; }

        [DataMember(Name = "lastUpdated")]
        public DateTime? LastUpdatedDate { get; set; }
    }
```

Designing Instashots User Interface

The Instashots app is a single-page UI (MainPage.xaml) as shown in Listing 9-3, which is divided into four sections via Header section, which contains the App name and a sign-out button. The Feed section is at the left and will display photos posted by the logged-in user and all of the users that the logged-in user is following. The next section is above the Feed section and displays the selected photo from the feed list. From this section users are able to link the picture, view comments, and add comments to the picture. On the right side we can display the Instashots users who are following and whom the user follows, but considering the length of this chapter, we do not discussing this implementation. Readers are encouraged to explore this as a further exercise.

Listing 9-3. MainPage.xaml View Defined in the XAML

```xml
<Grid Background="White">
<Grid Margin="50,50,10,10">
<Grid.ColumnDefinitions>
<ColumnDefinition Width="653*" />
<ColumnDefinition Width="427*" />
<ColumnDefinition Width="226*"/>
</Grid.ColumnDefinitions>
<Grid.RowDefinitions>
<RowDefinition Height="Auto" />
<RowDefinition Height="*" />
</Grid.RowDefinitions>
<!--Header Section-->
<Grid Grid.Row="0"
Grid.ColumnSpan="2"
Margin="0,0,0,20">
<StackPanel>
<TextBlock>
                <Run Text="Instashots"/>
        </TextBlock>
</StackPanel>
</Grid>
<StackPanel Grid.Row="1">
<StackPanel>
<local:QuickStartTask
        Number="1"
        Title="Photo Feed"
        Description="Photos posted by you and your followers" />
        <!--Selected Photo Section-->
        <StackPanel
                Margin="10,20,0,20"
                Visibility="{Binding ShowSelectedPhoto}">
        <StackPanel
                Margin="2,0,0,0"
                Orientation="Horizontal">
                <TextBlock
                        Text="{Binding SelectedTitle}"/>
                <TextBlock
                        Text="{Binding SelectedLikeCount}"
                        VerticalAlignment="Center"
```

```xml
                        Foreground="{StaticResource
                                SliderTrackDecreasePressedBackgroundThemeBrush}"
                        />
            <Button
                    Command="{Binding LikeCommand, Mode=OneWay}"
                    Content="Like"
                    />
        </StackPanel>
        <Border>
                <Image
                        Source="{Binding SelectedPicture,
                                Converter={StaticResource UrlToBitmapImageConverter}}"
                        Stretch="UniformToFill"/>
        </Border>
        <StackPanel
                Margin="22,10,0,0"
                Orientation="Vertical">
                <StackPanel Orientation="Horizontal">
                        <TextBlock/>
                        <Button
                                Command="{Binding ShowCommentCommand, Mode=OneWay}"
                                Content="Add Comment"/>
                </StackPanel>
                <!--ListView the loads the comment of the selected picture-->
                <ListView
                        ItemsSource="{Binding PictureComments}"
                        SelectionMode="None"
                        IsSwipeEnabled="false"
                        IsItemClickEnabled="True"
                        ItemTemplate="{StaticResource CommentTemplate}" />
        </StackPanel>
</StackPanel>
<!--Feed List-->
<StackPanel
        Orientation="Horizontal"
        Margin="10,0,0,0">
        <ListView
                ItemsSource="{Binding MyPictures}"
                SelectedItem="{Binding SelectedItem, Mode=TwoWay}"

                IsSwipeEnabled="false"
                IsItemClickEnabled="True"
                ItemTemplate="{StaticResource 80PxTemplate}"
                SelectionMode="Single">
                <ListView.ItemsPanel>
                        <ItemsPanelTemplate>
                                <WrapGrid Orientation="Horizontal" />
                        </ItemsPanelTemplate>
                </ListView.ItemsPanel>
        </ListView>
</StackPanel>
```

```xml
        </StackPanel>
    </StackPanel>

    <Grid Grid.Row="1" Grid.Column="1" Grid.ColumnSpan="2">
    <Grid.RowDefinitions>
    <RowDefinition Height="Auto" />
    <RowDefinition />
    </Grid.RowDefinitions>
    <!-- Users list to follow-->
    <StackPanel>
    <local:QuickStartTask
            Number="2"
            Title="Instashots Users"
            Description="Follow or unfollow a user from the list" />
    </StackPanel>

    <ListView
    x:Name="ListItems"
    Margin="62,10,0,0" Grid.Row="1">
    <ListView.ItemTemplate>
            <DataTemplate>
                    <StackPanel Orientation="Horizontal">
                            <CheckBox
                                    x:Name="CheckBoxComplete"
                                    IsChecked="{Binding Complete, Mode=TwoWay}"
                                    Content="{Binding Text}" Margin="10,5"
                                    VerticalAlignment="Center"/>
                    </StackPanel>
            </DataTemplate>
    </ListView.ItemTemplate>
    </ListView>
    </Grid>
    <StackPanel Margin="0,0,0,20" Grid.Column="2">
    <TextBlock
    x:Name="txtWelcome"/>
    <Button Margin="72,0,0,0"
    x:Name="btnSignOut"
    Command="{Binding SignoutCommand}"
    Content="Sign Out"/>
    </StackPanel>
    </Grid>
```

MainViewModel

We add a ViewModel class *MainViewModel*. MVVM Light's *ViewModelBase* class is used as the base class for this ViewModel and this ViewModel exposes methods and commands to accomplish various functionalities, like authenticating users against a Microsoft Account, uploading photos to the Windows Azure storage services, and getting the photos and user details from Windows Azure Mobile Services.

MainViewModel Commands

In *MainViewModel* (see Listing 9-4) we add commands that will be bound to the elements of the user interfaces in *MainPage.xaml*. These commands will be associated with methods that are called when the command is invoked.

Listing 9-4. Commands to Bind User Interface with Logic

```
public RelayCommand SignoutCommand { get; private set; }
public RelayCommand EditPhotoCommand { get; private set; }
public RelayCommand UploadPhotoCommand { get; private set; }
public RelayCommand AddCommentCommand { get; private set; }
public RelayCommand ShowCommentCommand { get; private set; }
public RelayCommand LikeCommand { get; private set; }

public MainViewModel()
    {
        if (!IsInDesignMode)
        {
            this.SignoutCommand = new RelayCommand(this.SignOutAction, CanSignOut);
            this.UploadPhotoCommand = new RelayCommand(this.UploadAction, CanUpload);
            this.EditPhotoCommand = new RelayCommand(this.EditPhotoAction , CanEditPhoto);
            this.AddCommentCommand = new RelayCommand(this.AddCommentAction);
            this.ShowCommentCommand = new RelayCommand(this.ShowCommentAction);
            this.LikeCommand = new RelayCommand(this.LikeAction);
            Authenticate();
        }
    }
```

MainViewModel Properties

We will add various properties to the *MainViewModel* and these properties are responsible for holding the photo feeds, changing the visible state of the controls, and editing the photo details. Listing 9-5 shows all the properties in *MainViewModel* with comments above each that detail the purpose of that property.

Listing 9-5. MainViewModel Properties That Hold the Information

```
//User welcome text
public string WelcomeTitle
{
    get
    {
        return welcomeTitle;
    }
    set
    {
        welcomeTitle = value;
        RaisePropertyChanged("WelcomeTitle");
    }
}string welcomeTitle;
```

```csharp
//Uploading Photo Title
public string PhotoTitle
{
    get
    {
        return photoTitle;
    }
    set
    {
        photoTitle = value;
        RaisePropertyChanged("PhotoTitle");
    }
}string photoTitle;

//Photo Like count
public string SelectedLikeCount
{
    get
    {
        return selectedLikeCount;
    }
    set
    {
        selectedLikeCount = value;
        RaisePropertyChanged("SelectedLikeCount");
    }
}string selectedLikeCount;

//Show popup UI to entry title and upload
public bool ShowUploadPopup
{
    get
    {
        return showUploadPopup;
    }
    set
    {
        showUploadPopup = value;
        RaisePropertyChanged("ShowUploadPopup");
    }
}bool showUploadPopup;

//Show popup UI to add comment
public bool ShowCommentPopup
{
    get
    {
        return showCommentPopup;
    }
```

```csharp
        set
        {
            showCommentPopup = value;
            RaisePropertyChanged("ShowCommentPopup");
        }
}bool showCommentPopup;

//Selected Photo from the Feed
public Picture SelectedItem
{
    get
    {
        return selectedItem;
    }
    set
    {

        selectedItem = value;
        SelectedTitle = selectedItem.Title;
        SelectedPhoto = SelectedItem.Imageurl ;
        ShowSelectedPhoto = Visibility.Visible;
        SelectedLikeCount = string.Format("{0} {1}"
            , SelectedItem.Likes, SelectedItem.Likes > 1 ? "Likes" : "Like");
        RaisePropertyChanged("SelectedItem");
        LoadComment();
    }
}Picture selectedItem;

//Set visibility of the Selected Photo section
public Visibility ShowSelectedPhoto
{
    get
    {
        return showSelectedPhoto;
    }
    set
    {
        showSelectedPhoto = value;
        RaisePropertyChanged("ShowSelectedPhoto");
    }
}Visibility showSelectedPhoto = Visibility.Collapsed;

//Selected Photo title from the feed
public string SelectedTitle
{
    get
    {
        return selectedTitle;
    }
```

```
        set
        {
            selectedTitle = value;
            RaisePropertyChanged("SelectedTitle");
        }
}string selectedTitle;

//Comment to be added to the selected photo
public string CommentText
{
    get
    {
        return commentText;
    }
    set
    {
        commentText = value;
        RaisePropertyChanged("CommentText");
    }
}string commentText;

//Azure storage URL of the selected photo from the feed
public string SelectedPhoto
{
    get
    {
        return selectedPhoto;
    }
    set
    {
        selectedPhoto = value;
        RaisePropertyChanged("SelectedPhoto");
    }
}string selectedPhoto;

//WritableBitmap of the edited photo from Aviary UI
public WriteableBitmap EditedImage
{
    get
    {
        return editedImage;
    }
    set
    {
        editedImage = value;
        RaisePropertyChanged("EditedImage");
    }
}WriteableBitmap editedImage;
```

Authentication with Live SDK

Windows Azure Mobile Services has bulit-in functionality to authenticate and authorize users by using a variety of identity providers, like Microsoft Accounts, Facebook, Twitter, and Google.

To configure Instashots to use the Microsoft account for authentication, we have to update the settings on the Mobile Services IDENTITY tab in the Windows Azure Management Portal. On this tab we can configure for Microsoft Account, Facebook, Twitter, and Google; for the Instashots app, though, we configure only the Microsoft account. Navigate to the Live Portal (`http://manage.dev.live.com`) and register the application as shown in Figure 9-11. Get the Client ID and Client Secret key and update them in the Microsoft Account settings as shown in Figure 9-12. Finally, set the redirect domain in Live Connect, which is essentially our Windows Azure Mobile Service URL, `https://instashots.azure-mobile.net/`.

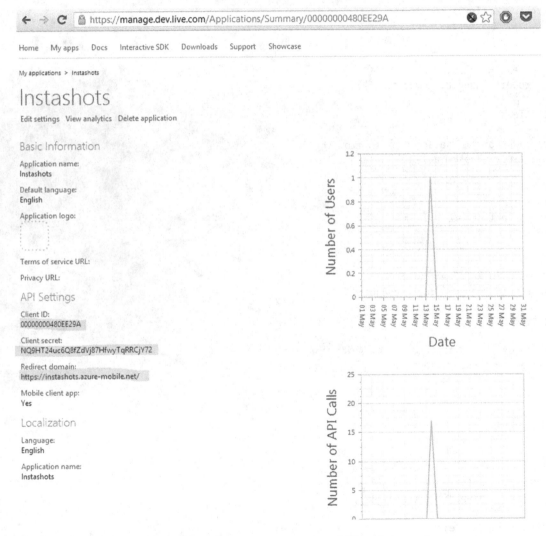

Figure 9-11. *Live developer portal to register an app to support Microsoft Account*

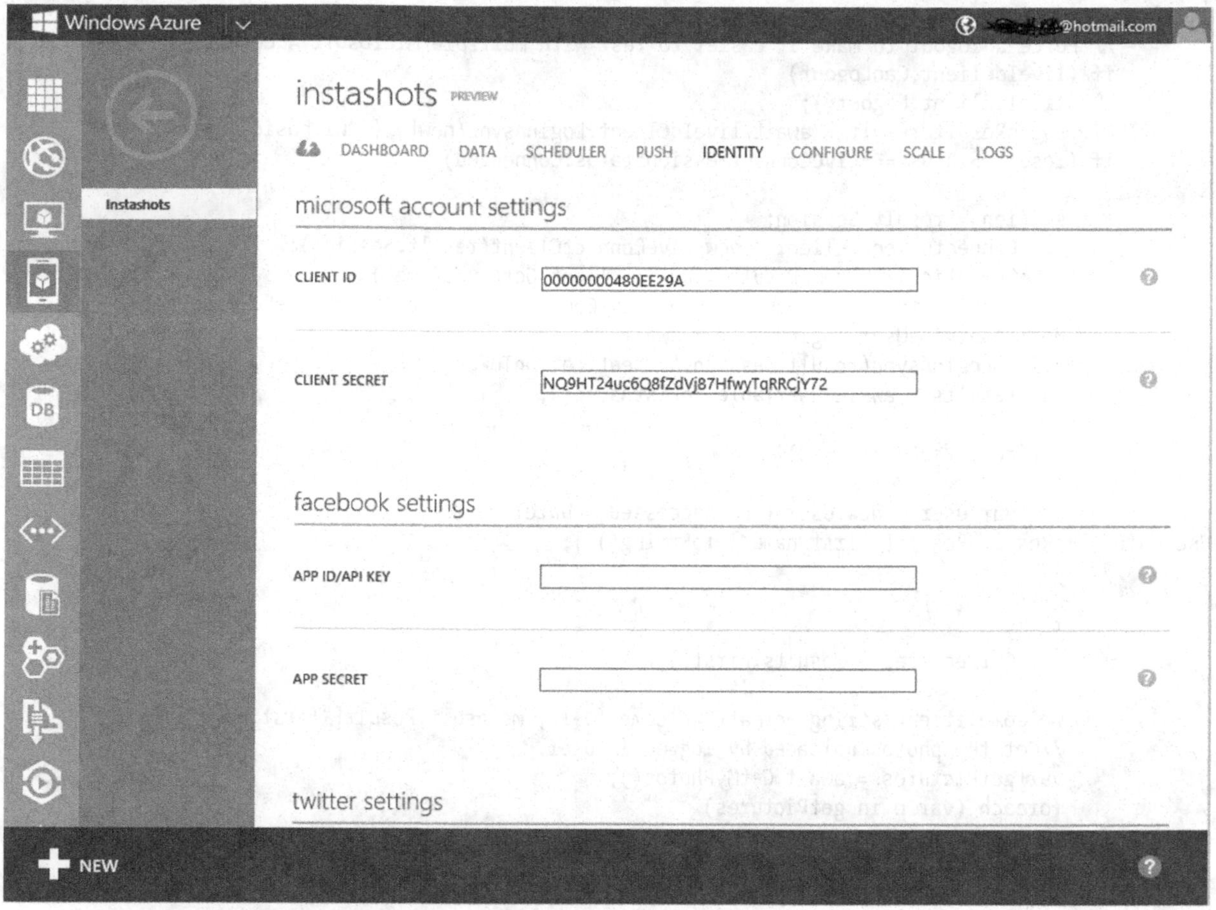

Figure 9-12. *Setting up Microsoft Account for authentication*

As of now, the Mobile Services API only provides very basic information about logged in users, like username, but we would like to get some more information, like the logged-in user's first name, so that we can provide a customized greeting for the user when he or she logs into the app. To achieve that, instead of using the Mobile Services API for authenticating a user, we use Live SDK APIs to authenticate and then assign the token to the Mobile Services User object as shown in Listing 9-6. We will have all this logic in an asyn method, `Authenticate`. This method resides inside the `MainViewModel` and will be invoked when the user launches the app. This method authenticates the user, and once authenticated it will check to see if the user is an existing user. If so, it then gets the User object for that user; otherwise, it creates a new User object and saves the information to the Mobile Services storage table.

Listing 9-6. Authenticating the User Using Live SDK

```
LiveAuthClient liveIdClient = new LiveAuthClient("https://instashots.azure-mobile.net/");
private LiveConnectSession session;

private async System.Threading.Tasks.Task Authenticate()
{
    while (session == null)
```

```
        {
            // Force a logout to make it easier to test with multiple Microsoft Accounts
            if (liveIdClient.CanLogout)
                liveIdClient.Logout();
            LiveLoginResult result = await liveIdClient.LoginAsync(new[] { "wl.basic" });
            if (result.Status == LiveConnectSessionStatus.Connected)
            {
                session = result.Session;
                LiveConnectClient client = new LiveConnectClient(result.Session);
                LiveOperationResult meResult = await client.GetAsync("me");
                //assigning the token generated by LiveConnectClient to the MobileServiceUser
                MobileServiceUser loginResult = await
App.MobileService.LoginAsync(result.Session.AuthenticationToken);
                var results = await userTable.ToListAsync();

                if (results.Count == 0)
                {
                    var user = new User { LastAccessed = DateTime.Now,
UserName = meResult.Result["first_name"].ToString() };
                }
                else
                {
                    CurrentUser = results.First();
                }
                WelcomeTitle = string.Format("Welcome {0}!", meResult.Result["first_name"]);
                //Get the photos uploaded by logged in user.
                var getPictures = await GetMyPhotos();
                foreach (var p in getPictures)
                {
                    myPictures.Add(p);
                }
                RaisePropertyChanged("MyPictures");
            }
            else
            {
                session = null;
                var dialog = new MessageDialog("You must log in.", "Login Required");
                dialog.Commands.Add(new UICommand("OK"));
                await dialog.ShowAsync();
            }
        }
    }
}
```

Windows Azure Mobile Services enables us to define custom business logic that is run on the server. This logic is provided as a JavaScript function that is registered to an insert, read, update, or delete operation on a given table. In our case before inserting a row in the User table, we get the authenticated user ID from the User parameter of the insert script and set it to the User table userid column as shown in Figure 9-13.

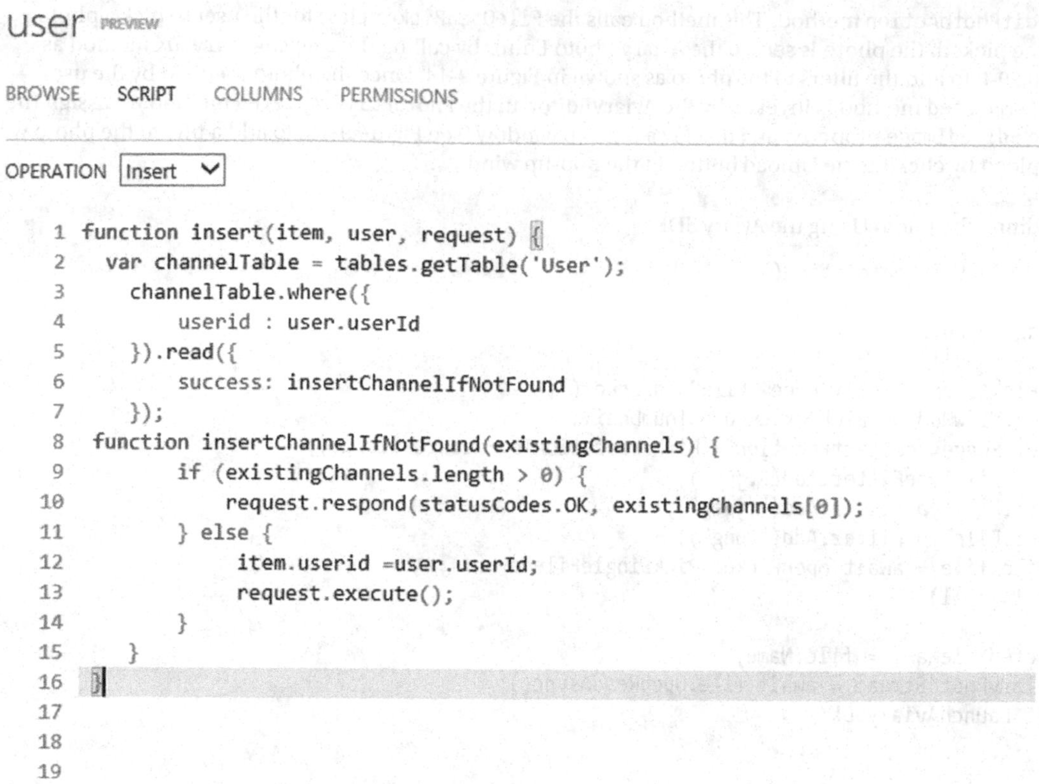

user PREVIEW

BROWSE   SCRIPT   COLUMNS   PERMISSIONS

OPERATION [Insert ▼]

```
1  function insert(item, user, request) {
2    var channelTable = tables.getTable('User');
3    channelTable.where({
4        userid : user.userId
5    }).read({
6        success: insertChannelIfNotFound
7    });
8  function insertChannelIfNotFound(existingChannels) {
9        if (existingChannels.length > 0) {
10           request.respond(statusCodes.OK, existingChannels[0]);
11       } else {
12           item.userid =user.userId;
13           request.execute();
14       }
15    }
16  }
17
18
19
```

Figure 9-13. *Insert script to get the UserID and update the table*

Retrieving the Photo Feed

Once the user is authenticated, the Authenticate method will call the GetMyPhotos (see Listing 9-7) method to get the Pictures and populate them into the MyPictures collection. This collection is bound to the ListView as shown earlier in Listing 9-3.

Listing 9-7. Retrieving the PhotoFeed from the Pictures Table

```
private async Task<List<Picture>> GetMyPhotos()
{
    return await pictureTable.ToListAsync();
}
```

Uploading Photos to Windows Azure Storage

As mentioned before, the Instashots app allows a logged-in user to add filters to a photo and upload it to the Windows Azure Storage and update the Photo table with the photo title and Windows Azure Storage URI. To upload a photo, the user will click the Upload button on the app bar, which invokes the EditPhotoAction command that calls the EditPhotoAction method. This method calls the FileOpenPicker class for the user to pick a photo for editing. Once picked, the photo is sent to the Aviary Photo Editor by calling the LaunchAviarySDK method as shown in Listing 9-8 to add the filters to the photo as shown in Figure 9-14. Once the photo is edited by the user, the PhotoEditCompleted method is invoked by the AviaryEditor. In the PhotoEditCompleted method we assign the edited photo to EditedImage property, and display a pop-up window (see Figure 9-15) to add a title to the photo with an option to upload by clicking the Upload button in the pop-up window.

Listing 9-8. Editing the Photo Using the Aviary SDK

```
public async void EditPhotoAction()
{
    editedImage = null;
    PhotoTitle = null;
    FileOpenPicker openPicker = new FileOpenPicker();
    openPicker.ViewMode = PickerViewMode.Thumbnail;
    openPicker.SuggestedStartLocation = PickerLocationId.PicturesLibrary;
    openPicker.FileTypeFilter.Add(".jpg");
    openPicker.FileTypeFilter.Add(".jpeg");
    openPicker.FileTypeFilter.Add(".png");
    StorageFile file = await openPicker.PickSingleFileAsync();
    if (file != null)
    {
        selectedFileName = file.Name;
        m_aviaryPhotoStream = await file.OpenReadAsync();
        await LaunchAviarySDK();
    }
}

private async System.Threading.Tasks.Task LaunchAviarySDK()
{
    if (m_aviaryPhotoStream == null)
    {
        return;
    }
    //Load editor with IRandomAccessStream from a picture file
    AviaryEditorTask.SetAviaryEditorAccentColor(Windows.UI.Colors.LightGray, true);
    AviaryEditorTask task = await AviaryEditorTask.FromRandomAccessStream(m_aviaryPhotoStream, true);
    task.Completed += PhotoEditCompleted;
    task.Show();
}

private void PhotoEditCompleted(object sender, AviaryTaskCompletedEventArgs e)
{
    //check the Result to see if editing was successfully completed before accessing the Edited
Photo
    if (e.Result == AviaryTaskResult.Completed)
    {
        EditedImage = e.EditedPhoto.Image;
        ShowUploadPopup = true;
    }
}
```

Figure 9-14. Photo edited using the Aviary Editor

Figure 9-15. Adding a title to the photo before uploading

When the user clicks the Upload button, UploadCommand (see Listing 9-9) is invoked. This calls the UploadAction method. The very first thing we do is save the photo temporarily in a local storage location. Next, we insert the photo information in the Pictures table and upload the photo to the Windows Azure storage. For that we create the Picture object and insert it into the table.

Listing 9-9. Uploading Photo to the Windows Azure Storage

```
public async void UploadAction()
{
    string fileName = string.Format("{0}_{1}"
            , Guid.NewGuid()
            , selectedFileName);
    var picture = new Picture { Name = fileName
        , Title= PhotoTitle };
    await App.MobileService.GetTable<Picture>().InsertAsync(picture);
    string container = "instashots";
    string imageUrl = string.Format("http://{0}.blob.core.windows.net/{1}/{2}"
        , "splcricket"
        , container
        , fileName);
    StorageCredentials cred = new StorageCredentials(picture.sasQueryString);
    var imageUri = new Uri(picture.Imageurl);
    // Instantiate a Blob store container based on the info in the returned item.
    CloudBlobContainer cloudcontainer = new CloudBlobContainer(
    new Uri(string.Format("https://{0}/{1}"
        , imageUri.Host
        , container))
        , cred);
    CloudBlockBlob blobFromSASCredential =
    cloudcontainer.GetBlockBlobReference(fileName);

        //Save File to local folder.
    await EditedImage.SaveToFile(
                    ApplicationData.Current.LocalFolder,
                    fileName,
                    CreationCollisionOption.GenerateUniqueName);

    var localFolder = Windows.Storage.ApplicationData.Current.LocalFolder;
    var savedFile = await localFolder.GetFileAsync(fileName);

    using (var fileStream = await savedFile.OpenStreamForReadAsync())
    {
        await blobFromSASCredential.UploadFromStreamAsync(fileStream.AsInputStream());
    }
    MyPictures.Add(picture);
}
```

To upload photo to Windows Azure storage, we need to generate the upload URI with Shared Access Signature (SAS). SAS is a secure URI that we can use to upload file in a Windows Azure storage account without providing the storage credential. The upload URI will be generated within the Photo table Insert script as shown in Figure 9-16. With the SAS URI in place, we instantiate a Blob store container (using the CloudBlockBlob class) based on SAS URI and upload the saved file using the UploadFromStreamAsync method in the CloudBlockBlob class. Finally, we add the photo object to the MyPhotos collection so that the uploaded photo will display in the Feed ListView.

pictures PREVIEW

BROWSE   SCRIPT   COLUMNS   PERMISSIONS

OPERATION Insert ✔

```
3  function insert(item, user, request) {
4      var accountName = 'instashots';
5      var accountKey = 'tPjQ2R9sHzJuLBPxkEUxbGiuOa8BwfRpQCiGGOStkFM5bls7TjPmhjknGNHgxv39xV13h9LpxTwOJV+xVlVyLw▓
6      var host = accountName + '.blob.core.windows.net';
7      var canonicalizedResource = '/instashots/' + item.name;
8      item.userid= user.userId ;
9  // If it does not already exist, create the container
10 // with public read access for blobs.
11 var blobService = azure.createBlobService(accountName, accountKey, host);
12 blobService.createContainerIfNotExists('instashots', {
13     publicAccessLevel: 'blob'
14 }, function(error) {
15     if (!error) {
16         // Provide write access to the container for the next 5 mins.
17         var sharedAccessPolicy = {
18             AccessPolicy: {
19                 Permissions: azure.Constants.BlobConstants.SharedAccessPermissions.WRITE,
20                 Expiry: new Date(new Date().getTime() + 5 * 60 * 1000)
21             }
22         };
23         // Generate the upload URL with SAS for the new image.
24         var sasQueryUrl =
25             blobService.generateSharedAccessSignature('instashots',
26             item.name, sharedAccessPolicy);
27         // Set the query string.
28         item.sasQueryString = qs.stringify(sasQueryUrl.queryString);
29         // Set the full path on the new new item,
30         // which is used for data binding on the client.
31         item.imageurl = sasQueryUrl.baseUrl + sasQueryUrl.path;
32     } else {
33         console.error(error);
34     }
35     request.execute();
36 });
37 }
38
```

Figure 9-16. *Insert script to get the SAS URI and update it to the Picture table*

Implementing Comments and Likes Functionality

Displaying comments, adding comments, and liking a selected photo is a straightforward task, as shown in Listing 9-10. On selecting a photo from the feed, we can display a larger version of the photo along with the list of comments entered for that photo. We also have two buttons: one to add a comment and another to like the photo. When a user clicks the Add Comment button, a pop-up window will display (see Figure 9-17) for entering a comment. On submission, the comment will be saved to the Comment storage table.

Listing 9-10. Implementing Comments and Likes

```
public void ShowCommentAction()
{
    showCommentPopup = true;
    RaisePropertyChanged("ShowCommentPopup");
}

private async void LoadComment()
{
    var comments = await commentTable
        .Where(b => b.PictureId == SelectedItem.Id)
        .OrderByDescending(c => c.CreatedDate)
        .ToListAsync();
    pictureComments.Clear();
    foreach (var c in comments)
    {
        c.CommentedBy = await userTable.LookupAsync(c.UserId);
        pictureComments.Add(c);
    }
    RaisePropertyChanged("PictureComments");
}

public async void AddCommentAction()
{
    var comment = new Comment { CommentText = commentText
        , PictureId = SelectedItem.Id
        ,UserId=CurrentUser.Id
        , CreatedDate= DateTime.Now };
    await App.MobileService.GetTable<Comment>().InsertAsync(comment);
    pictureComments.Add(comment);
}

public async void LikeAction()
{
    await App.MobileService.GetTable<Picture>().UpdateAsync(SelectedItem);
}
```

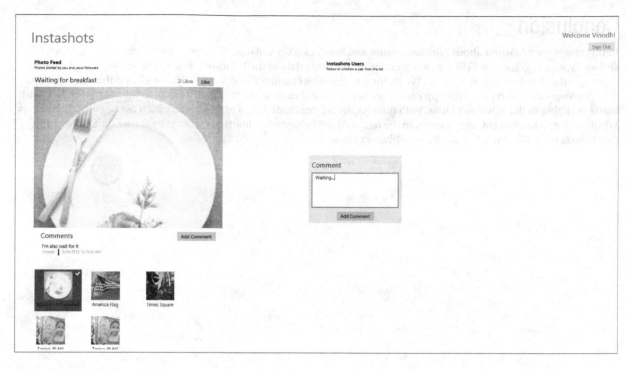

Figure 9-17. *Adding a comment to the Instashots app*

Now with all the codes in place, when we run the Instashots app, the user will be now able to authenticate against the Microsoft Account and will be able to upload photos, add comments, and like photos. The final app will be linked the one shown in Figure 9-17.

Ideas for Improvement

The Instashots app can be worked on and improved to make it a fully functional photo-sharing social app. The following are some of the features that can be added.

- As mentioned before, the user section can be created by displaying the list of users that you are following with an option to unfollow them.

- Add an option to share photos using the Share charm feature of Windows 8.

- Search for new users to follow using the Search charm.

- Enable the Windows 8 PlayTo functionality to stream photos to devices, also providing an option to share it using NFC (Tap and Send).

- Extend the authentication to include Facebook, Google, and Twitter logins as support for this is already in built into Windows Azure Mobile Services.

Conclusion

In this chapter we learned about Windows Azure and how to set up and use Windows Azure Mobile Services as a service layer, integrate Live SDK for user authentication, store data in the Windows Azure SQL database, and upload images to the Windows Azure storage. We learned all these by creating a real-world Windows 8 app that uses some of the Windows Azure services. This app can be further extended to make it more feature rich, as mentioned earlier, and made available in the Windows Store. With this chapter we conclude Part 3 of this book, which overviewed the various Windows 8 app remote storage options. In the next and final chapter we learn to create yet another data-driven app that targets both Windows 8 and Windows Phone platforms.

■ ■ ■

CHAPTER 10

Windows Phone 8 Data Access

We end this book by learning the data access options available for Windows Phone apps. This chapter starts by discussing the code sharing techniques between Windows Phone and Windows 8 apps and then introduces you to the Windows Phone built-in database option, SQL Server Compact for Windows Phone, and walk you through the procedure to get started with the Windows Phone app development. We then port the Bill Reminder Windows 8 app that we built in Chapter 6 to a Windows Phone app using the SQLServer Compact database as data storage. Finally we briefly introduce you to the other data storage options that we learned in this book that can be also used in Windows Phone apps.

Sharing the Code

Windows Phone 8 is a major upgrade to Windows Phone 7.x. It replaces the core with the same core as Windows 8, which means the .NET Compact Framework is replaced with the .NET CLR. Apart from this, the Windows Phone API adds Windows Phone Runtime, which has lot in common with WinRT. With this new Windows Phone API, developers will be able to develop apps in VB/C# and C++. Windows Phone 8 also supports native development using Direct3D, xAudio2 Win32, COM, and MF.

Separate UI from App Logic

The strategy to build a successful app that targets both Windows 8 and Windows Phone 8 is to separate the UI from app logic. Model-View-ViewModel (MVVM), which we used extensively in building the various apps in this book, is the only neat approach to separate the UI from the app logic. Using MVVM we can encapsulate one or more ViewModels and on top of that we can have one or more Views that represent Windows Phone Page or Windows 8 Page.

Sharing Portable .NET Code in Portable Class Library

Portable Class Library is one of the important blocks that we can use to share code between Windows 8 and Windows Phone apps written using XAML/VB/C#, as this shares common .NET libraries. In Visual Studio when we create a Portable Class Library a pop-up, shown in Figure 10-1, allows us to select the targeted framework. The project will have set of libraries that shows .NET is currently portable with the platform that we are targeting. Once compiled, these libraries become compatible with the targeted framework and in our case Windows Phone and Windows 8. Apart from creating our own portable libraries, we can also reference some of the common portable libraries like MVVM Light inside our Portable Library project.

Figure 10-1. *Selecting the targeted frameworks for the Portable Class Library*

Using Common Windows Runtime API (Add as Link)

Windows 8 comes with the Common Windows Runtime API, which gives access to sensors, media, and proximity. Along with that we also get Windows Phone 8 Runtime API, which shares a subset of APIs with Windows 8. Whenever we use this set of APIs, we can write once and use it in both Windows 8 and Windows Phone 8 apps using the Add as link functionality available in Visual Studio as shown in Figure 10-2. By doing this the class file will not be copied to the project, and instead will be copied as a link from the source. If we make any changes to the code, therefore, it will be reflected in all the linked references.

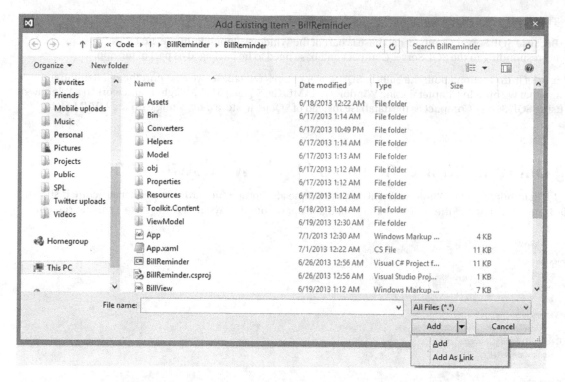

Figure 10-2. *Adding an existing file as a link to the Visual Studio Project*

■ **Note** Windows Runtime API can't be referenced into the portable libraries while creating portal libraries targeting Windows 8 and Windows Phone 8, as the binary compatibility is not supported and the code has to be compiled for each platform separately.

Using the technique just discussed, we are able to create a compiling app that targets both Windows Phone 8 and Windows 8 by sharing a similar code base.

SQL Server Compact for Windows Phone

Unlike Windows 8, Windows Phone provides built-in support for SQL Server Compact as a local database. This database resides in the Isolated Storage of the app and is an in-memory relational database. The following are the some of the features of SQL Server Compact.

- SQL Server Compact database runs within the Windows Phone application's process. Unlike SQL Server, the database doesn't run continuously in the background; instead, an instance is created only when the app is in use.

- As the database is stored in the app's Isolated Storage, this database can only be accessed by that app and can't be shared with any other apps.

- Transaction SQL is not supported. Instead, LINQ to SQL is used as the ORM engine.

- Because SQL Server Compact database is part of the Windows Phone Runtime, no DLLs corresponding to the SQL Server Compact database need to be packaged as part of the app.

With this brief introduction about the built-in SQL Server compact database, we next port the Bill Reminder Windows 8 app that we built in Chapter 6 using Windows 8 XAML/C#, SQLite, MVVM Light Framework to a Windows Phone app using SQL Server Compact as the database instead of SQLite to store data, along with the MVVM Light Framework.

Porting Bill Reminder Windows 8 App to Windows Phone

Porting the Bill Reminder app for Windows Phone is quite simple and straightforward. The project structure is shown in Figure 10-3, and most parts of the code remain unchanged, apart from the layout that adapts to a smaller screen.

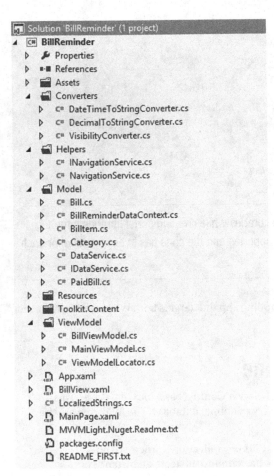

Figure 10-3. *BillReminder Windows Phone app project structure, which looks similar to the BillReminder Windows 8 app*

Setting Up the Windows Phone 8 Development Environment

Windows Phone SDK 8.0 can be downloaded from http://go.microsoft.com/fwlink/?LinkId=259416. This SDK includes all the necessary tools like Visual Studio Express 2012 for Windows Phone, project templates for creating new Windows Phone apps, and the Windows Phone emulator for testing. After installing the SDK, we create a new Windows Phone app as shown in Figure 10-4.

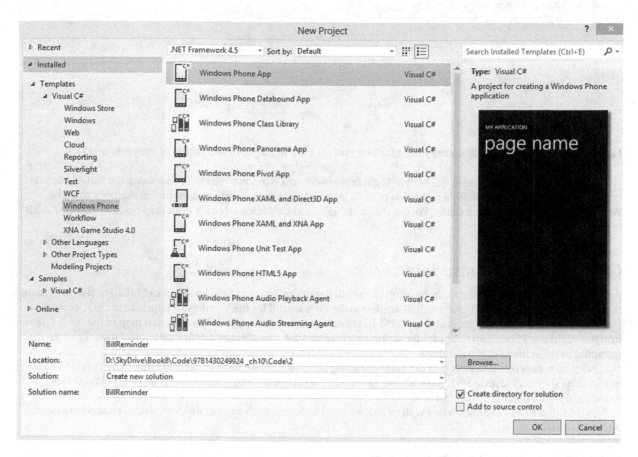

Figure 10-4. *Windows Phone app project template*

After creating the app, we are prompted to select the targeted Windows Phone OS version as shown in Figure 10-5. Select the Windows Phone OS 8.0, but you can always go for Windows Phone OS 7.1 to support both versions, as Windows Phone 8 OS provided backward compatibility of the app developed targeting Windows Phone 7.1.

Figure 10-5. *Selecting the Windows Phone platform that we want to target, in this case Windows Phone OS 8.0*

We add project references to the MVVM Light Framework and Windows Phone Toolkit using the NuGet package. Windows Phone Toolkit provides a collection of controls, animation framework, and extension methods to make Windows Phone development easier. We use the DatePicker and ListPicker controls from the Windows Phone Toolkit in our project.

Creating the Database Table

As mentioned in Chapter 6, the main function of the Bill Reminder app is to help keep track of bills. For this, we create three tables via Category, Bill, and PaidBill, similar to the ones we did for the Windows 8 app. Like the SQLite wrapper sqlite-net, SQL Server Compact is also an ORM-based database, so we copy the class files that map to the three tables into the Windows Phone app Model folder as shown in Figure 10-3. These classes define our object model and its mapping to the schema of the database.

Next, to access the data stored in the database using LINQ to SQL, we have to decorate this class with the [Table] attribute as shown in Listing 10-1. Basically we can use this attribute to designate a class as an entity class that is associated with a database table or view.

In addition to associating classes with tables, we need to denote each field or property that we intend to associate with a database column.

Listing 10-1. Category, Bill, and PaidBill Classes

```
[Table]
public class Category
{
    [Column(IsPrimaryKey = true, IsDbGenerated = true)]
    public int CategoryID { get; internal set; }

    [Column(CanBeNull = false)]
    public string Name { get; internal set; }
}

[Table]
public class Bill
```

```csharp
{
    [Column(IsPrimaryKey = true
        , IsDbGenerated = true
        , DbType = "INT NOT NULL Identity"
        , CanBeNull = false
        , AutoSync = AutoSync.OnInsert)]
    public int BillID { get; internal set; }

    [Column(CanBeNull = false)]
    public string Name { get; internal set; }

    [Column(CanBeNull = false)]
    public DateTime DueDate { get; internal set; }

    [Column(CanBeNull = false)]
    public bool IsRecurring { get; internal set; }

    [Column(CanBeNull = true, UpdateCheck = UpdateCheck.Never)]
    public int CategoryID{get; internal set; }

    private EntityRef<Category> category;

    [Association(Storage = "category"
        , ThisKey = "CategoryID"
        , OtherKey = "CategoryID"
        , IsForeignKey = true)]
    public Category Category
    {
        get { return category.Entity; }
        set
        {
            if (value != null)
            {
                CategoryID = value.CategoryID;
            }
            category.Entity = value;
        }
    }

    [Column(CanBeNull = false)]
    public Decimal Amount { get; internal set; }
}

[Table]
public class PaidBill
{
    [Column(IsPrimaryKey = true, IsDbGenerated = false)]
    public int PaidBillID { get; internal set; }
```

```
[Column(CanBeNull = false, UpdateCheck = UpdateCheck.Never)]
public int BillID { get; internal set; }

private EntityRef<Bill> bill;

[Association(Storage = "bill"
    , ThisKey = "BillID"
    , OtherKey = "BillID"
    , IsForeignKey = true)]
public Bill Bill
{
    get { return bill.Entity; }
    set
    {
        if (value != null)
        {
            BillID = value.BillID;
        }

        bill.Entity = value;

    }
}

[Column(CanBeNull = true)]
public DateTime PaidDate { get; internal set; }

[Column(CanBeNull = true)]
public Decimal Amount { get; internal set; }

}
```

Creating the DataContext Class

The DataContext class inherits from System.Data.Linq.DataContext and is used to expose the database to the rest of the code through properties of type Table<TEntity> as shown in Listing 10-2.

Listing 10-2. BillReminderDataContext Class Exposes the Database

```
using System.Data.Linq;

namespace BillReminder.Model
{
    public class BillReminderDataContext : DataContext
    {
        public BillReminderDataContext(string connectionString)
            : base(connectionString)
        {
        }
```

```
    public Table<Bill> Bills
    {
        get
        {
            return this.GetTable<Bill>();
        }
    }

    public Table<Category> Categories
    {
        get
        {
            return this.GetTable<Category>();
        }
    }

    public Table<PaidBill> PaidBills
    {
        get
        {
            return this.GetTable<PaidBill>();
        }
    }
    }
}
```

Next we create the database using the DataContext object at the App initialization in App.xaml.cs. The DataContext object is initialized by passing the connection string, which basically tells the app how to connect to the database. Once the app is initialized, we check if the database exists; if it doesn't we create the database by calling the CreateDatabase() method of the DataContext. We also add some default value to the Category table by adding the Category object to the data context using the InsertOnSubmit method and calling the data context SubmitChanges method to permanently add the data as a row in the database (see Listing 10-3).

Listing 10-3. Creating the Database in App Initialization Using DataContext

```
public partial class App : Application
{
    public static PhoneApplicationFrame RootFrame { get; private set; }
    public App()
    {
        UnhandledException += Application_UnhandledException;
        InitializeComponent();
        InitializePhoneApplication();
        InitializeLanguage();
        if (Debugger.IsAttached)
        {
            Application.Current.Host.Settings.EnableFrameRateCounter = false;
            PhoneApplicationService.Current.UserIdleDetectionMode = IdleDetectionMode.Disabled;
        }
```

```
    try
    {
        app = this;
        DB = new BillReminderDataContext("isostore:/BillReminder.sdf");
        InitializeDatabase();
    }
    catch(Exception ex)
    {
        Debug.WriteLine(ex.Message);
    }

}

private static App app;
public static App CurrentApp
{
    get { return app; }
}

public BillReminderDataContext DB { get; set; }

private void InitializeDatabase()
{
    if (DB.DatabaseExists()) return;
    DB.CreateDatabase();
    if (!App.CurrentApp.DB.Categories.Any())
    {
        DB.Categories.InsertOnSubmit(new Category()
        {
            Name = "Credit Card"
        });
        DB.Categories.InsertOnSubmit(new Category()
        {
            Name = "Loan"
        });
        DB.Categories.InsertOnSubmit(new Category()
        {
            Name = "Utilities"
        });
        DB.SubmitChanges();
    }
}
```

Updating the Model

Apart from the new DataContext class BillReminderDataContext all of the other classes inside the Model folder will
be carried from the Windows 8 Bill Reminder app with a few minor changes to the DataService class. Here we replace
the code that references the SQLite database to refer to the SQL Server Compact database, but all within the same
methods as shown in Listing 10-4.

Listing 10-4. Methods to Retrieve Bill Details and Add, Update, and Delete Bills

```csharp
using System;
using System.Collections.Generic;
using System.Collections.ObjectModel;
using System.Linq;

namespace BillReminder.Model
{
    public class DataService : IDataService
    {
        public void AddBill(Bill bill)
        {
            App.CurrentApp.DB.Bills.InsertOnSubmit(bill);
            App.CurrentApp.DB.SubmitChanges();
        }

        public Bill GetBillByID(int billId)
        {
            return App.CurrentApp.DB.Bills.First(b => b.BillID == billId);
        }

        public ObservableCollection<BillItem> GetBills(DateTime month)
        {
            var bills = new ObservableCollection<BillItem>();
            var fromDate = new DateTime(month.Year, month.Month, 1); //first day of the month
            var toDate = fromDate.AddMonths(1).AddDays(-1); // last day of the month
            var query = from bill in App.CurrentApp.DB.Bills
                        join cat in App.CurrentApp.DB.Categories on bill.CategoryID equals
                            cat.CategoryID
                        join paid in App.CurrentApp.DB.PaidBills on bill.BillID equals paid.BillID into
                            pp
                        from paid in pp.DefaultIfEmpty()
                        where (bill.IsRecurring || (bill.DueDate >= fromDate && bill.DueDate <= toDate))
                        select new BillItem(this)
                            {
                                BillID = bill.BillID
                                ,
                                Name = bill.Name
                                ,
                                Category = cat.Name
                                ,
                                DueDate = bill.DueDate
                                ,
                                Amount = bill.Amount
                                ,
                                PaidAmount = paid.Amount
                                ,
                                PaidDate = paid.PaidDate
                            };
```

```csharp
        foreach (var item in query)
        {
            item.IsPaid = (item.PaidAmount > 0 && item.PaidDate > DateTime.MinValue);
            bills.Add(item);
        }

        return bills;
    }

    public IList<Category> GetCategories()
    {
        return App.CurrentApp.DB.Categories.ToList();
    }

    public Category GetCategoryByID(int categoryId)
    {
        return App.CurrentApp.DB.Categories.First(c => c.CategoryID == categoryId);
    }

    public void MarkPaid(int billId, decimal amount)
    {
        PaidBill paidBill;
        if (App.CurrentApp.DB.PaidBills.Count() > 0)
        {
            paidBill = App.CurrentApp.DB.PaidBills.First(b => b.BillID == billId);
        }
        else
        {
            paidBill= new PaidBill();
            paidBill.BillID = billId;
            App.CurrentApp.DB.PaidBills.InsertOnSubmit(paidBill);
        }
        paidBill.Amount = amount;
        paidBill.PaidDate = DateTime.Now;
        App.CurrentApp.DB.SubmitChanges();
    }

    public void UpdateBill(Bill bill)
    {
        App.CurrentApp.DB.SubmitChanges();
    }
}
}
```

No Update to the ViewModel

Apart from minor framework-level changes that we have to make for navigating between pages, we have not made any changes to the ViewModel from the one we used with the Windows 8 Bill Reminder app.

Views

Because the Phone form factor is not the same as a tablet devices on which our Windows 8 app runs, we have to make changes to the layout of the Views as shown in Figure 10-6 to suit the smaller devices. Similar to the Windows 8 app, MainPage.xaml (see Listing 10-5) is the starting page of the Bill Reminder Windows Phone app. This view has a LongListSelector control and two app bar buttons for navigating to the Bill.xaml page, again similar to the navigation of the Windows 8 app. The LongListSelector control is similar to Windows 8 GridView Xaml control, which binds to the Bill property in the MainViewModel and displays the recent bills as a list using a DataTemplate. The displayed bill information two modes, depending on the status of the Bill object's IsPaid property. If the IsPaid property is false, then we display a Textbox for entering the bill amount and a Button to mark the bill as paid. This button command is bound to the PaidCommand in the MainViewModel. But if the bill is paid instead, then both these controls' Visibility property is set to Collapsed using a ValueConverter VisibilityConverter.

Figure 10-6. *Bill Reminder app displaying recent bills*

Listing 10-5. MainPage.xaml Includes a LongListSelector with Data Template to Display Recent Bills

```
<phone:PhoneApplicationPage
    x:Class="BillReminder.MainPage"
    xmlns="http://schemas.microsoft.com/winfx/2006/xaml/presentation"
    xmlns:x="http://schemas.microsoft.com/winfx/2006/xaml"
    xmlns:phone="clr-namespace:Microsoft.Phone.Controls;assembly=Microsoft.Phone"
    xmlns:shell="clr-namespace:Microsoft.Phone.Shell;assembly=Microsoft.Phone"
    xmlns:d="http://schemas.microsoft.com/expression/blend/2008"
    xmlns:mc="http://schemas.openxmlformats.org/markup-compatibility/2006"
```

```xml
    mc:Ignorable="d"
   FontFamily="{StaticResource PhoneFontFamilyNormal}"
   FontSize="{StaticResource PhoneFontSizeNormal}"
   Foreground="{StaticResource PhoneForegroundBrush}"
   SupportedOrientations="Portrait" Orientation="Portrait"
   shell:SystemTray.IsVisible="True"
   xmlns:i="clr-namespace:System.Windows.Interactivity;assembly=System.Windows.Interactivity"
   xmlns:ec="clr-namespace:Microsoft.Expression.Interactivity.Core;assembly=Microsoft.Expression.
Interactions"
   xmlns:abu="clr-namespace:AppBarUtils;assembly=AppBarUtils"
  xmlns:converters="clr-namespace:BillReminder.Converters"
   DataContext="{Binding Main, Source={StaticResource Locator}}">
  <phone:PhoneApplicationPage.ApplicationBar>
      <shell:ApplicationBar
          IsVisible="True"
          IsMenuEnabled="True"
          Opacity="0.99">
          <shell:ApplicationBarIconButton
              x:Name="addBill"
              IconUri="/Assets/AppBar/new.png"
              Text="new" />
          <shell:ApplicationBarIconButton
              x:Name="editBill"
              IconUri="/Assets/AppBar/edit.png"
              Text="edit" />
      </shell:ApplicationBar>
  </phone:PhoneApplicationPage.ApplicationBar>
  <i:Interaction.Behaviors>
      <abu:AppBarItemCommand Id="new" Command="{Binding AddCommand, Mode=OneWay}"/>
      <abu:AppBarItemCommand Id="edit" Command="{Binding EditCommand, Mode=OneWay}"/>
  </i:Interaction.Behaviors>

  <!--LayoutRoot is the root grid where all page content is placed-->
  <Grid x:Name="LayoutRoot" Background="Transparent">
      <Grid.RowDefinitions>
          <RowDefinition Height="Auto"/>
          <RowDefinition Height="*"/>
      </Grid.RowDefinitions>
      <StackPanel x:Name="TitlePanel"
                  Grid.Row="0"
                  Margin="12,17,0,28">
          <TextBlock Text="Bill Reminder"
                  Style="{StaticResource PhoneTextNormalStyle}"
                  Margin="12,0"/>
          <TextBlock Text="Recent Bills"
                  Margin="9,-7,0,0"
                  Style="{StaticResource PhoneTextTitle1Style}"/>
      </StackPanel>
```

```
<!--ContentPanel - place additional content here-->
<Grid x:Name="ContentPanel"
      Grid.Row="1" Margin="12,0,12,0">
    <phone:LongListSelector ItemsSource="{Binding Bills}"
                            SelectedItem ="{Binding SelectedBill, Mode=TwoWay}"
                            ItemTemplate="{StaticResource DataTemplate}">
    </phone:LongListSelector>
    </Grid>
  </Grid>
</phone:PhoneApplicationPage>
```

BillView.xaml as shown in Figure 10-7 is used to create and edit a bill. This page has controls like TextBox, ListPicker, DatePicker, and CheckBox that bind to the properties of the BillViewModel. ListPicker and DatePicker are not part of the Windows Phone default control set, but instead they can be included by referencing the Windows Phone toolkit from NuGet packages. Also on the page we have two app bar buttons. The Save button is used to save the Bill object to the database and this button's command property is bound to the BillViewModel's SaveCommand. BackButton is used to navigate back to the MainPage.xaml. The ListPicker control allows the user to pick a bill category. This ListPicker is bound to the Categories property of the ViewModel, and the SelectedItem is bound two-way to the SelectedCategory property (see Listing 10-6).

Figure 10-7. *Bill Detail page for adding and editing a bill*

Listing 10-6. BillView.xaml Has Controls to Input Bill Information

```xml
<phone:PhoneApplicationPage
    xmlns="http://schemas.microsoft.com/winfx/2006/xaml/presentation"
    xmlns:x="http://schemas.microsoft.com/winfx/2006/xaml"
    xmlns:phone="clr-namespace:Microsoft.Phone.Controls;assembly=Microsoft.Phone"
    xmlns:shell="clr-namespace:Microsoft.Phone.Shell;assembly=Microsoft.Phone"
    xmlns:d="http://schemas.microsoft.com/expression/blend/2008"
    xmlns:mc="http://schemas.openxmlformats.org/markup-compatibility/2006"
    xmlns:converters="clr-namespace:BillReminder.Converters"
  xmlns:i="clr-namespace:System.Windows.Interactivity;assembly=System.Windows.Interactivity"
    xmlns:abu="clr-namespace:AppBarUtils;assembly=AppBarUtils"
    xmlns:toolkit="clr-namespace:Microsoft.Phone.Controls;assembly=Microsoft.Phone.Controls.Toolkit"
    x:Class="BillReminder.BillView"
    mc:Ignorable="d"
    SupportedOrientations="Portrait" Orientation="Portrait"
    shell:SystemTray.IsVisible="True"
>
<phone:PhoneApplicationPage.Resources>
      <converters:DateTimeToStringConverter x:Key="DateTimeToStringConverter"/>
    <converters:DecimalToStringConverter x:Key="DecimalToStringConverter"/>
</phone:PhoneApplicationPage.Resources>
<phone:PhoneApplicationPage.FontFamily>
  <StaticResource ResourceKey="PhoneFontFamilyNormal"/>
</phone:PhoneApplicationPage.FontFamily>
<phone:PhoneApplicationPage.FontSize>
  <StaticResource ResourceKey="PhoneFontSizeNormal"/>
</phone:PhoneApplicationPage.FontSize>
<phone:PhoneApplicationPage.Foreground>
  <StaticResource ResourceKey="PhoneForegroundBrush"/>
</phone:PhoneApplicationPage.Foreground>
<phone:PhoneApplicationPage.DataContext>
  <Binding Path="Bill" Source="{StaticResource Locator}"/>
</phone:PhoneApplicationPage.DataContext>
<phone:PhoneApplicationPage.ApplicationBar>
      <shell:ApplicationBar IsVisible="True" IsMenuEnabled="True" Opacity="0.99">
          <shell:ApplicationBarIconButton  x:Name="save"
                                    IconUri="/Assets/AppBar/save.png"
                                    Text="save" />

      </shell:ApplicationBar>
  </phone:PhoneApplicationPage.ApplicationBar>
  <i:Interaction.Behaviors>
      <abu:AppBarItemCommand Id="save"
                          Command="{Binding SaveCommand, Mode=OneWay}"/>
  </i:Interaction.Behaviors>
  <!--LayoutRoot is the root grid where all page content is placed-->
  <Grid x:Name="LayoutRoot" Background="Transparent">
  <Grid.RowDefinitions>
    <RowDefinition Height="Auto"/>
    <RowDefinition Height="*"/>
  </Grid.RowDefinitions>
  <StackPanel x:Name="TitlePanel"
```

```xml
                     Grid.Row="0"
                     Margin="12,17,0,28">
    <TextBlock Text="Bill Reminder"
                     Style="{StaticResource PhoneTextNormalStyle}"
                     Margin="12,0"/>
    <TextBlock Text="{Binding Title}"
                     Margin="9,-7,0,0"
                     Style="{StaticResource PhoneTextTitle1Style}"/>
</StackPanel>

    <!--ContentPanel - place additional content here-->
<Grid x:Name="ContentPanel"
        Grid.Row="1"
        Margin="12,0,12,0">
  <StackPanel    Grid.Row="1">
    <StackPanel HorizontalAlignment="Left"
                        VerticalAlignment="Top"
                        Width="383"
                        Orientation="Horizontal"
                        Margin="5">
      <TextBlock TextWrapping="Wrap"
                        Text="Bill Name"
                        Margin="10,0,30,0"
                        FontSize="16"
                        Width="100"
                        VerticalAlignment="Center"/>
      <TextBox TextWrapping="Wrap"
                        Margin="0,0,0,-2"
                        Width="283"
                        Text="{Binding Name, Mode=TwoWay}"/>
    </StackPanel>
    <StackPanel HorizontalAlignment="Left"
                        VerticalAlignment="Top"
                        Width="383"
                        Orientation="Horizontal"
                        Margin="5">
      <TextBlock TextWrapping="Wrap"
                        Text="Category"
                        Margin="10,0,30,0"
                        FontSize="16"
                        Width="100"
                        VerticalAlignment="Center"/>

      <toolkit:ListPicker Width="229"
                                ItemsSource="{Binding Categories}"
                                DisplayMemberPath="Name"
                                SelectedItem="{Binding SelectedCategory, Mode=TwoWay}"
                                Margin="12,6,6,6"/>

    </StackPanel>
    <StackPanel HorizontalAlignment="Left"
```

```xml
                              VerticalAlignment="Top"
                              Width="383"
                              Orientation="Horizontal"
                              Margin="5">
        <TextBlock TextWrapping="Wrap"
                              Text="Due Date"
                              Margin="10,0,30,0"
                              FontSize="16"
                              Width="100"
                              VerticalAlignment="Center"/>
        <toolkit:DatePicker Value= "{Binding DueDate, Mode=TwoWay}" />
    </StackPanel>
    <StackPanel HorizontalAlignment="Left"
                              VerticalAlignment="Top"
                              Width="383"
                              Orientation="Horizontal"
                              Margin="5">
        <TextBlock TextWrapping="Wrap"
                              Text="Amount"
                              Margin="10,0,30,0"
                              FontSize="16"
                              Width="100" VerticalAlignment="Center"/>
        <TextBox TextWrapping="Wrap"
                              Margin="0,0,0,-2"
                              Width="283"
                              Text="{Binding Amount, Converter={StaticResource
DecimalToStringConverter}, Mode=TwoWay}"/>
    </StackPanel>
    <StackPanel HorizontalAlignment="Left"
                              VerticalAlignment="Top"
                              Width="383"
                              Orientation="Horizontal"
                              Margin="5">
        <TextBlock TextWrapping="Wrap"
                              Text="Recurring?"
                              Margin="10,0,30,0"
                              FontSize="16" Width="100"
                              VerticalAlignment="Center"/>
        <CheckBox  VerticalAlignment="Stretch"
                              IsChecked="{Binding IsRecurring, Mode=TwoWay}"/>
    </StackPanel>
  </StackPanel>
 </Grid>
 </Grid>
</phone:PhoneApplicationPage>
```

Other Data Storage Options

Apart from the SQL Server Compact, we can use many different data storage options as we did for Windows 8 apps. Let's briefly look at some of these options.

File-Based Data Storage

Similar to Windows 8 apps, Windows Phone apps also have app-specific isolated storage. We can use this storage to build a file-based storage solution for Windows Phone apps. Like the WinRT File Based Database we saw in Chapter 5, there are many similar libraries like SterlingDB that we can use for Windows Phone. Sterling can be referred in a project by using NuGet package. Sterling is a lightweight NoSQL object-oriented database that can be used in .NET 4.0, Silverlight, and Windows Phone that works with our existing class structures. Also using Sterling DB we can quickly sterilize objects with support for LINQ to Object.

SQLite

We can also use SQLite as a data storage option for a Windows Phone app and the steps to integrate this are very similar those by which we integrated SQLite in a Windows 8 app, as detailed in Chapter 6.

Windows Azure Mobile Services

Another interesting option that is familiar to readers is Windows Azure Mobile Services, which we saw in detail in Chapter 9. The Windows Azure Mobile Services SDK provides the necessary library to integrate it inside a Windows Phone app; in fact, the Windows Azure Mobile service start screen generates a sample app for Windows Phone (see Figure 10-8) that can be downloaded. This app is preconfigured to access the back end and is ready to run.

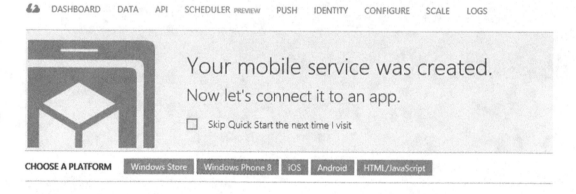

Figure 10-8. *Windows Azure Mobile Services sample Windows Phone 8 project that we can download from the Windows Azure Management portal*

Similarly we can create a service layer using ASP.NET Web API or WCF to access any back end like SQL Server from Windows Phone.

Conclusion

In this chapter we ported the Bill Reminder Windows 8 app to Windows Phone. By doing so we used the Windows Phone built-in data access option SQL Server Compact database as the data strorage. The intention of this chapter is to highlight the options available for you as a developer to build apps that can target both Windows 8 and Windows Phone apps. We did so by detailing various techniques that we can use to share code between the two platforms. Also at the end of the chapter, we briefly looked at the various other data storage options that can be used in developing a Windows Phone app.

With this chapter, we have completed this book and I hope it has helped you learn various data access options for developing Windows 8 apps. This book has provided an overview of the Windows 8 app framework, and you have also learned to use various development tools and libraries that can be incorporated into many Windows 8 apps. In each chapter of this book we built a Windows 8 app using different data access techniques, and we also provided ideas for improving the app. I hope this will be a good starting point for you to add additional features to the apps to make them fully functional. Perhaps you will even submit them to the Windows app stores, so that millions of people can download them and appreciate your efforts. Happy app developing!

Index

■ X, Y, Z